Original

Title	**Taylors Eye Witness**
Date	**Unknown** (possibly 1930-50's from binding)
Source	Private Collection (JC)
Pages	150
Size	250mm x 370 Portrait
Condition	Good. There are a couple of pages missing and a couple that have been cut.
Binding	Post bound individual pages

Contents (approximate number of pages)

45	**Folding knives**
16	**Fixed knives**
43	**Table wear**
26	**Scissors**
6	**Razors**
3	**Tools**
	Medical

Scan

Date	14 July 2022
Scanned by	Grace Horne, Sheffield
Issues and observations	This catalogue was 'post' bound, allowing the pages to be removed. This scan includes sections A, B, D & E - it is unknown what other section existed. Dating is extremely hard as some sections are clearly drawn at different times. This has been reproduced slightly smaller than the original.

TAYLOR'S EYE WITNESS

1st Edition
Copyright©2023 Grace Horne
All rights reserved

Taylor's Witness Table Cutlery

LONDON OFFICE & SHOWROOMS:
BATH HOUSE
57 HOLBORN VIADUCT E.C.1
Telephone: City 7982

SCOTTISH OFFICE & SHOWROOMS:
65 BATH STREET, GLASGOW
Telephone: Douglas 1559

Offices & Showrooms:
DUBLIN   MELBOURNE   SYDNEY
GEORGETOWN   CAPETOWN
JOHANNESBURG   NAIROBI
CALGARY   MONTREAL   PARIS

Is produced under modern conditions and combines best quality materials, highest skilled workmanship, careful inspection, and over a century of practical experience in its manufacture.

The "Eye Witness" trade-mark branded on each knife is the manufacturers guarantee that each article is perfect, and is an assurance of satisfaction to buyers.

Solid construction and superior finish make "Eye Witness" Table Cutlery a profitable and easy selling stock line.

The method of heat treatment of the steel used in the manufacture of "Eye Witness" Stainless Steel Knives ensures the blades retaining a fine cutting edge, and at the same time, enhances their stain-proof qualities.

The illustrations shown in the following pages are actual full size photographs, with the exception of the Bread Knives and Carvers, which owing to the limited size of the page have been reduced approximately by one-third.

To ensure prompt despatch of orders entrusted to us large stocks are held ready for immediate delivery.

For prices of patterns shown see price list

NEEDHAM, VEALL & TYZACK, LTD.

CUTLERS & SILVERSMITHS

Telegrams:
EYEWITNESS
SHEFFIELD

Telephone:
CENTRAL
4428 & 4429

Manufacturers of
TAYLOR'S "EYE WITNESS"
TABLE CUTLERY   POCKET CUTLERY
BUTCHERS' KNIVES AND STEELS
SCISSORS   RAZORS
SILVER AND ELECTRO-PLATED WARE
IN DESIGNS TO SUIT ALL MARKETS

Codes:
A B C 4th 5th & 6th Eds.
MARCONI INTERNATIONAL
WESTERN UNION 5 LETTER
BENTLEY'S
LIEBER'S 1898

EYE WITNESS WORKS, SHEFFIELD, ENG.

SECTION A
PAGE 2

Taylor's Witness Table Knives

STEEL BLADES. UNGRAINED IVORIDE HANDLES

These Illustrations are actual size of article

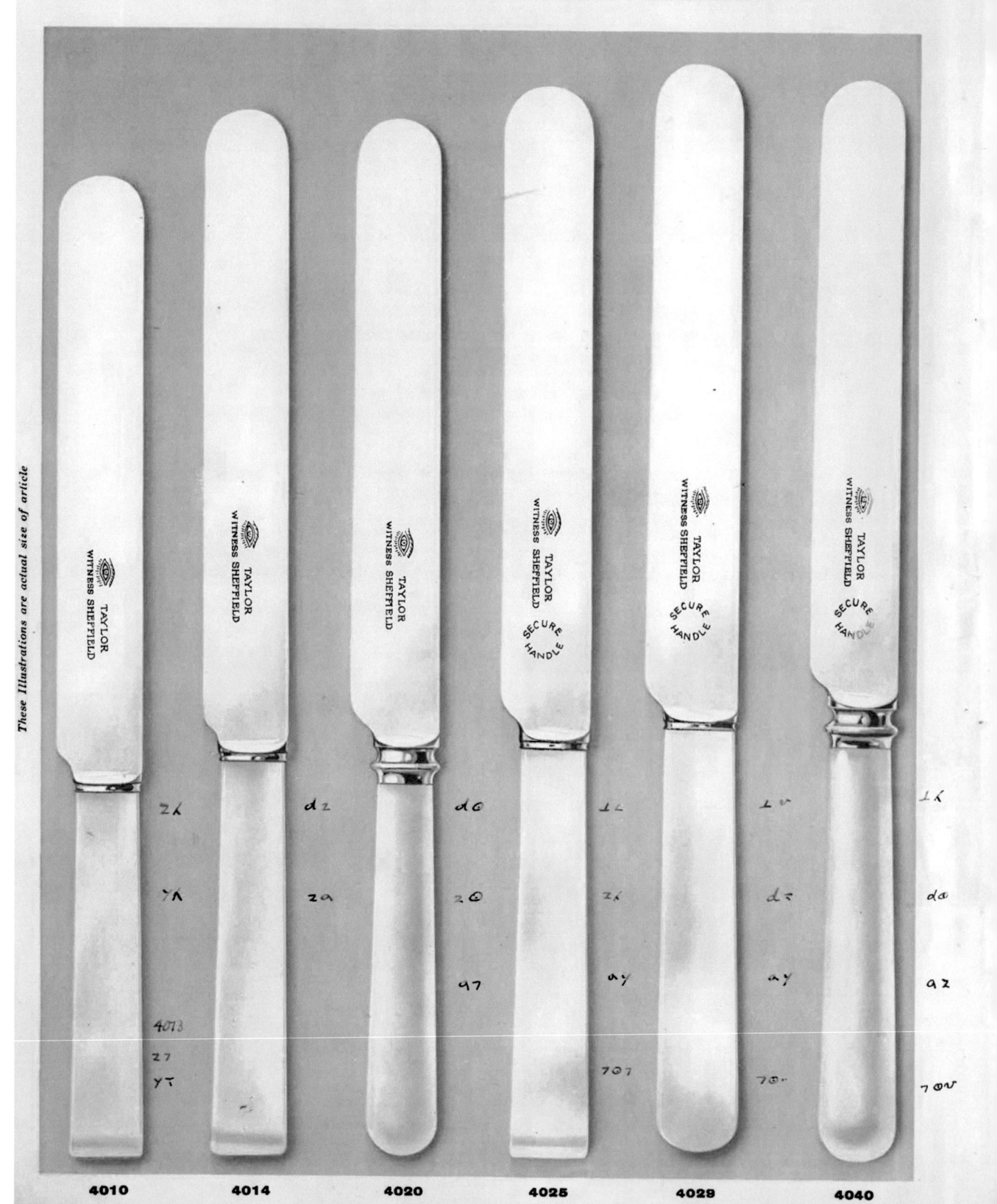

| 4010 | 4014 | 4020 | 4025 | 4029 | 4040 |

Taylor's Witness

Table Knives

STEEL BLADES.   GRAINED IVORIDE HANDLES

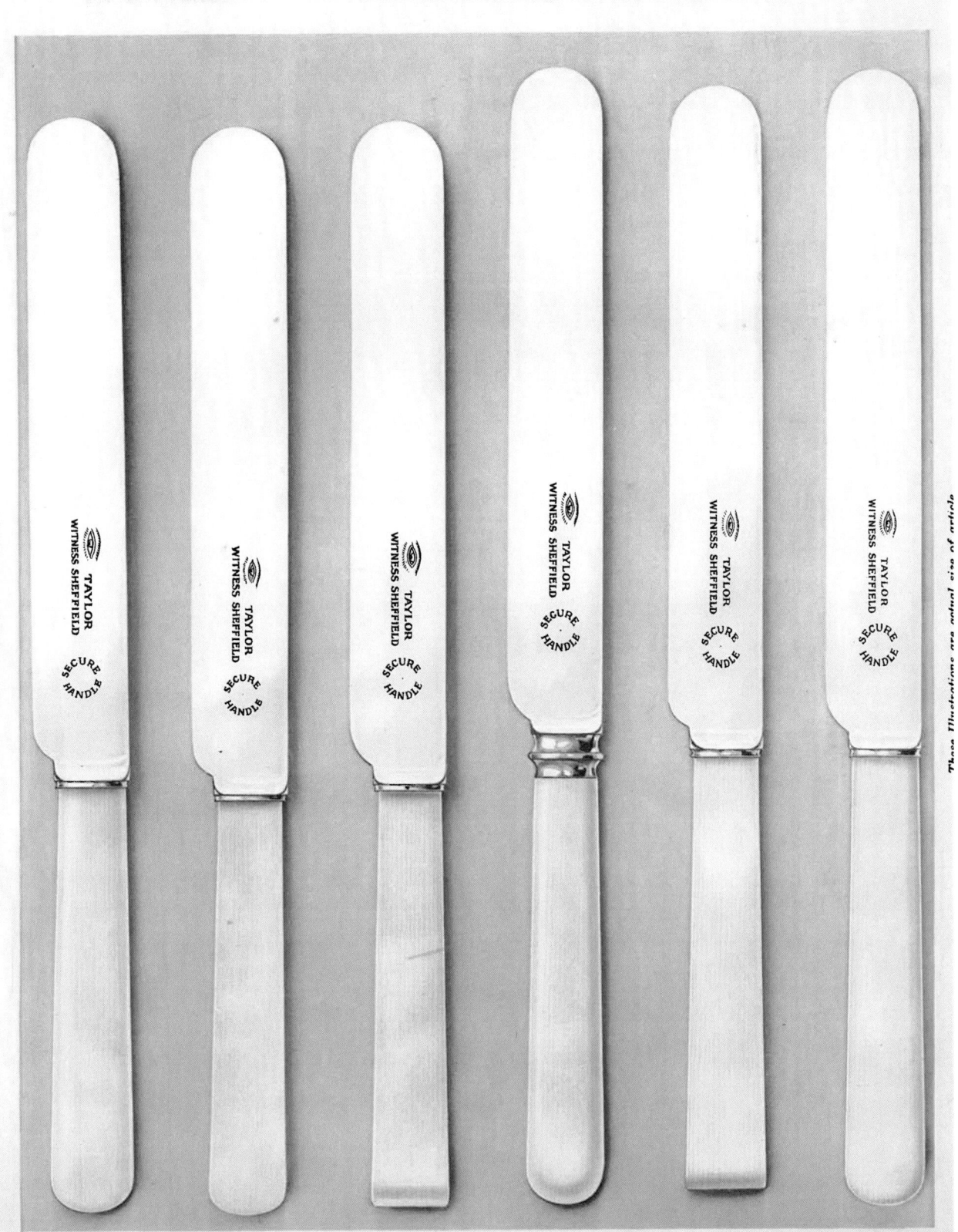

SECTION A
PAGE 3

| 4151 | 4154 | 4155 | 4160 | 4163 | 4167 |

SECTION A
PAGE 4

Taylor's Witness Table Knives

STEEL BLADES.   BEST AFRICAN GRAINED IVORIDE HANDLES

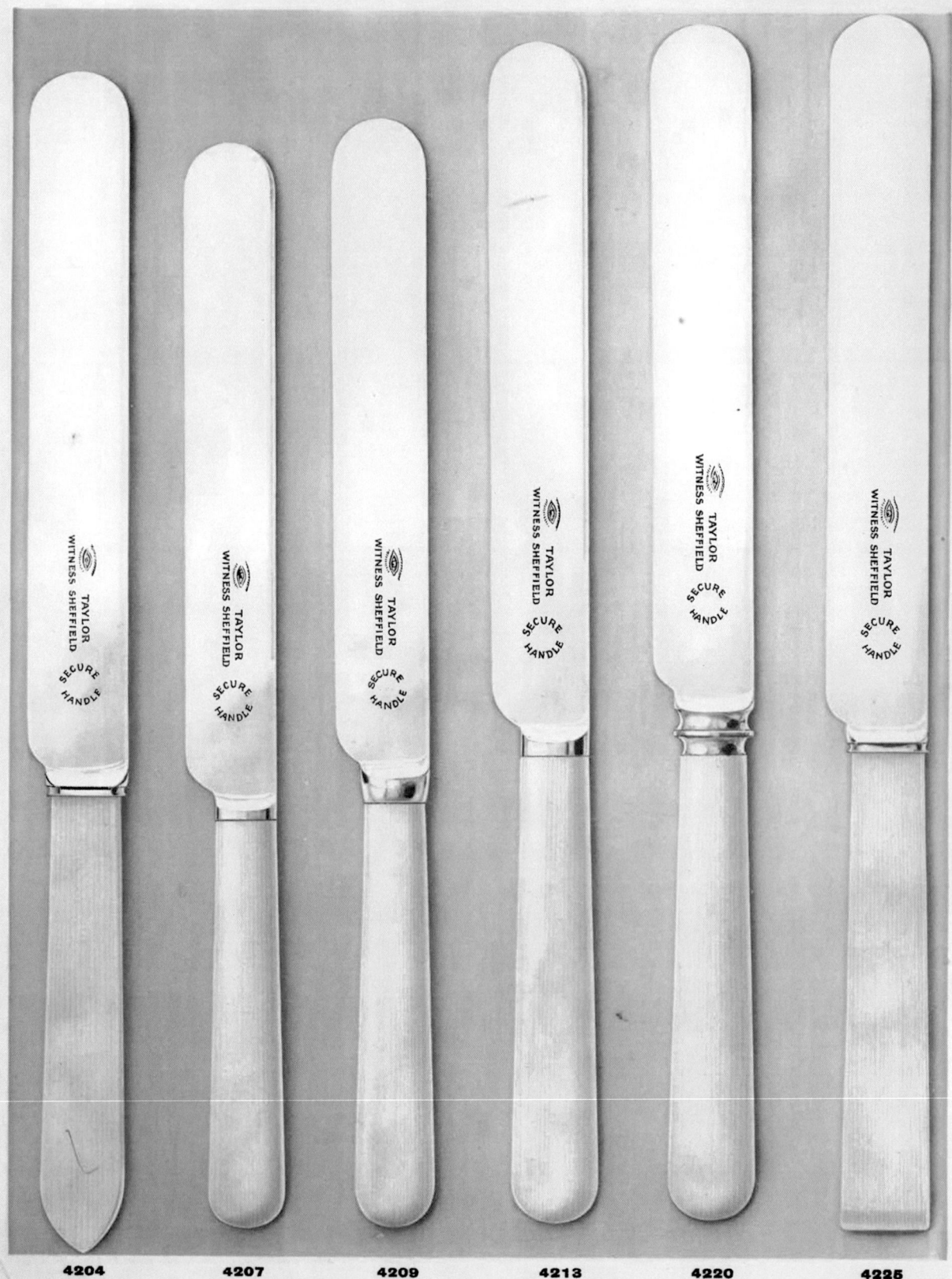

These Illustrations are actual size of article

| 4204 | 4207 | 4209 | 4213 | 4220 | 4225 |

Taylor's Witness

Table Knives

STEEL BLADES, WITH POLISHED BEVELLED BACKS
BEST AFRICAN GRAINED IVORIDE HANDLES

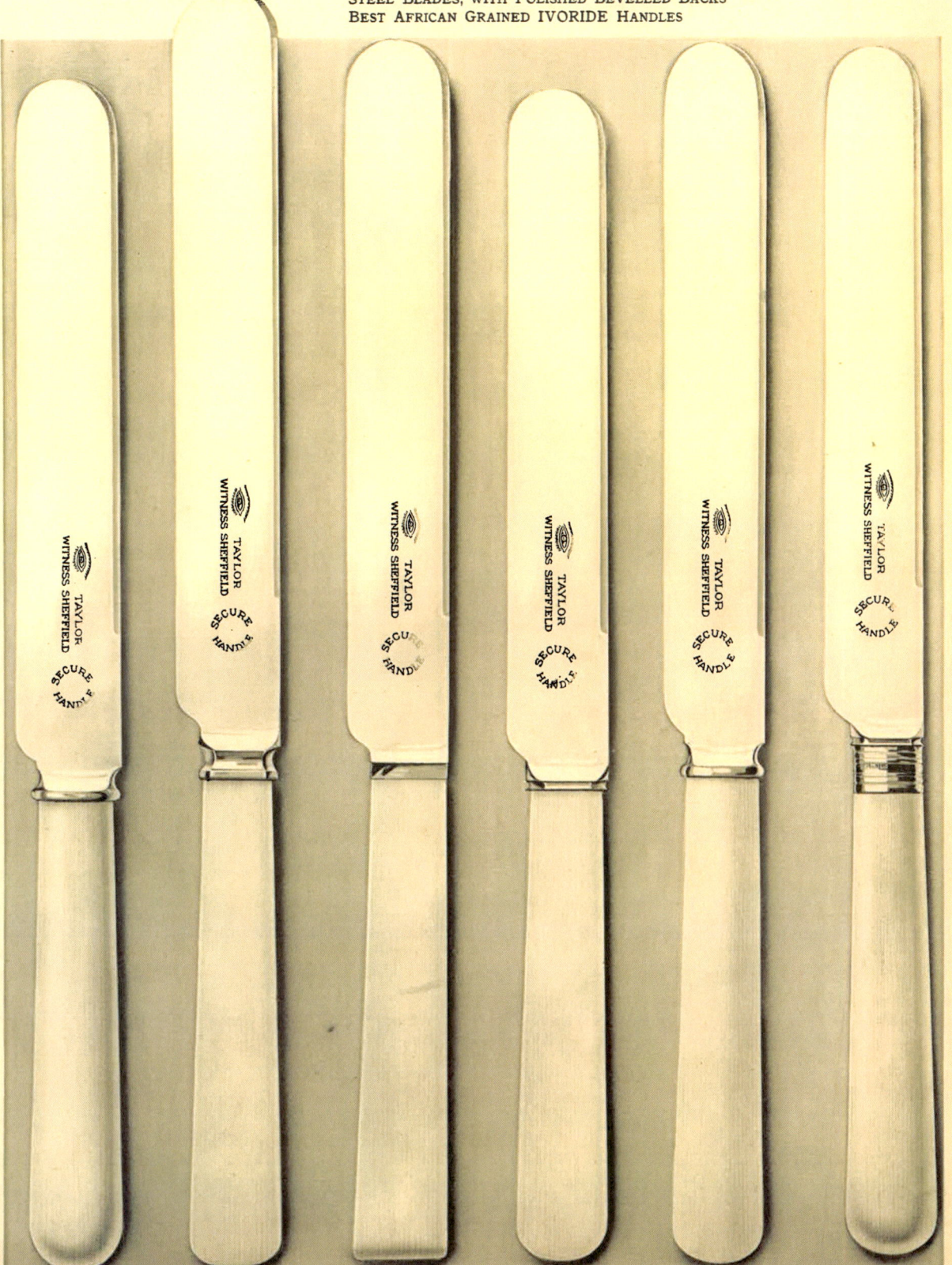

SECTION A
PAGE 5

| 4231 | 4236 | 4241 | 4243 | 4246 | 4250 Silver Ferrule |

Taylor's Witness — Table Knives

Stainless Steel Blades. Ungrained Ivoride Handles

| 5012 | 5020 | 5025 | 5026 | 5028 | 5035 |

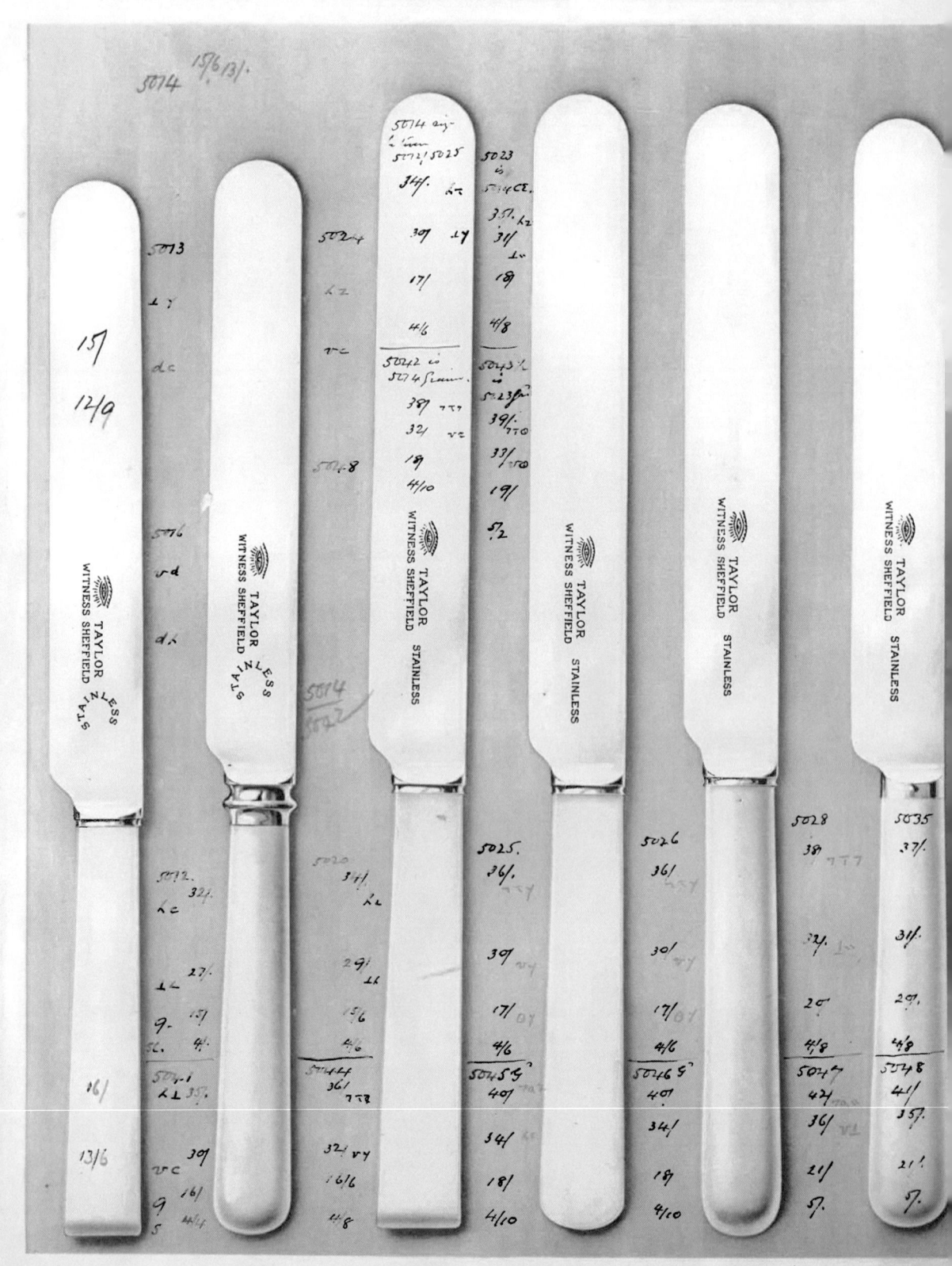

Taylor's Witness Table Knives

Steel Blades, with Polished Bevelled Backs
Best African Grained IVORIDE Handles

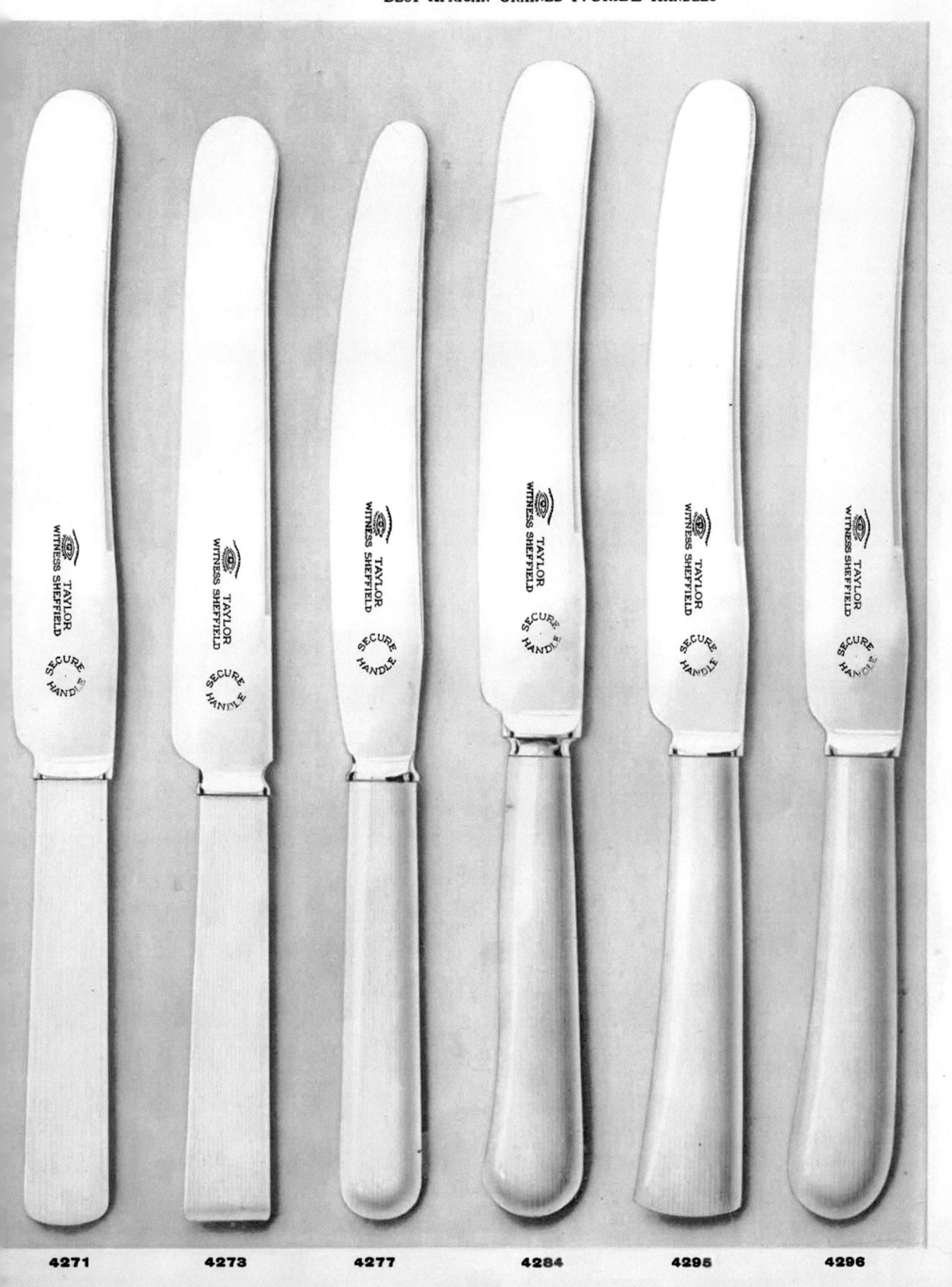

| 4271 | 4273 | 4277 | 4284 | 4295 | 4296 |

SECTION A
PAGE 12

Taylor's Witness Table Knives

Stainless Steel Blades
Best African Grained IVORIDE Handles

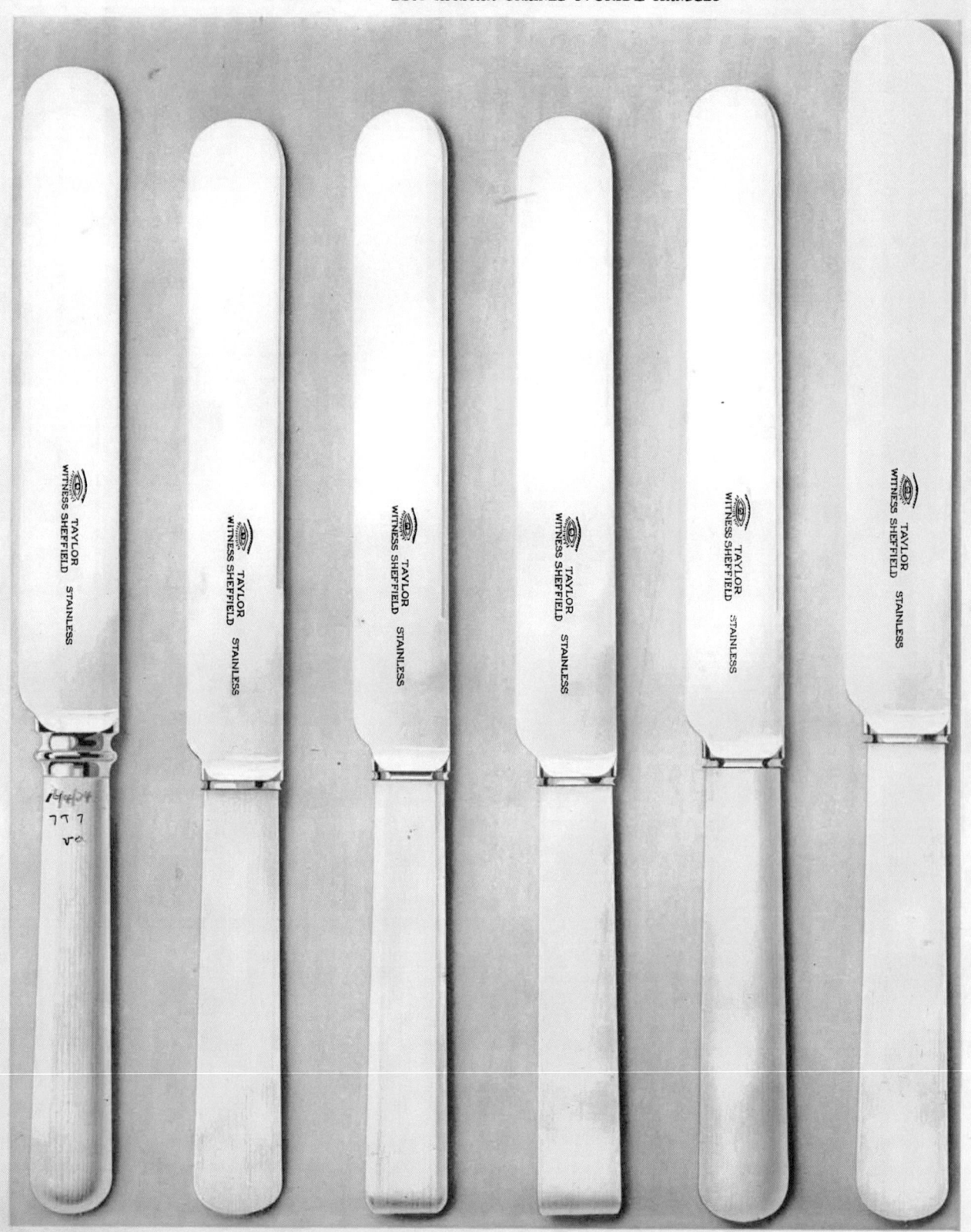

| 5220 | 5227 | 5230 | 5233 | 5243 | 5248 |

Taylor's Witness

Table Knives

STAINLESS STEEL BLADES, WITH POLISHED BEVELLED BACKS
BEST AFRICAN GRAINED IVORIDE HANDLES

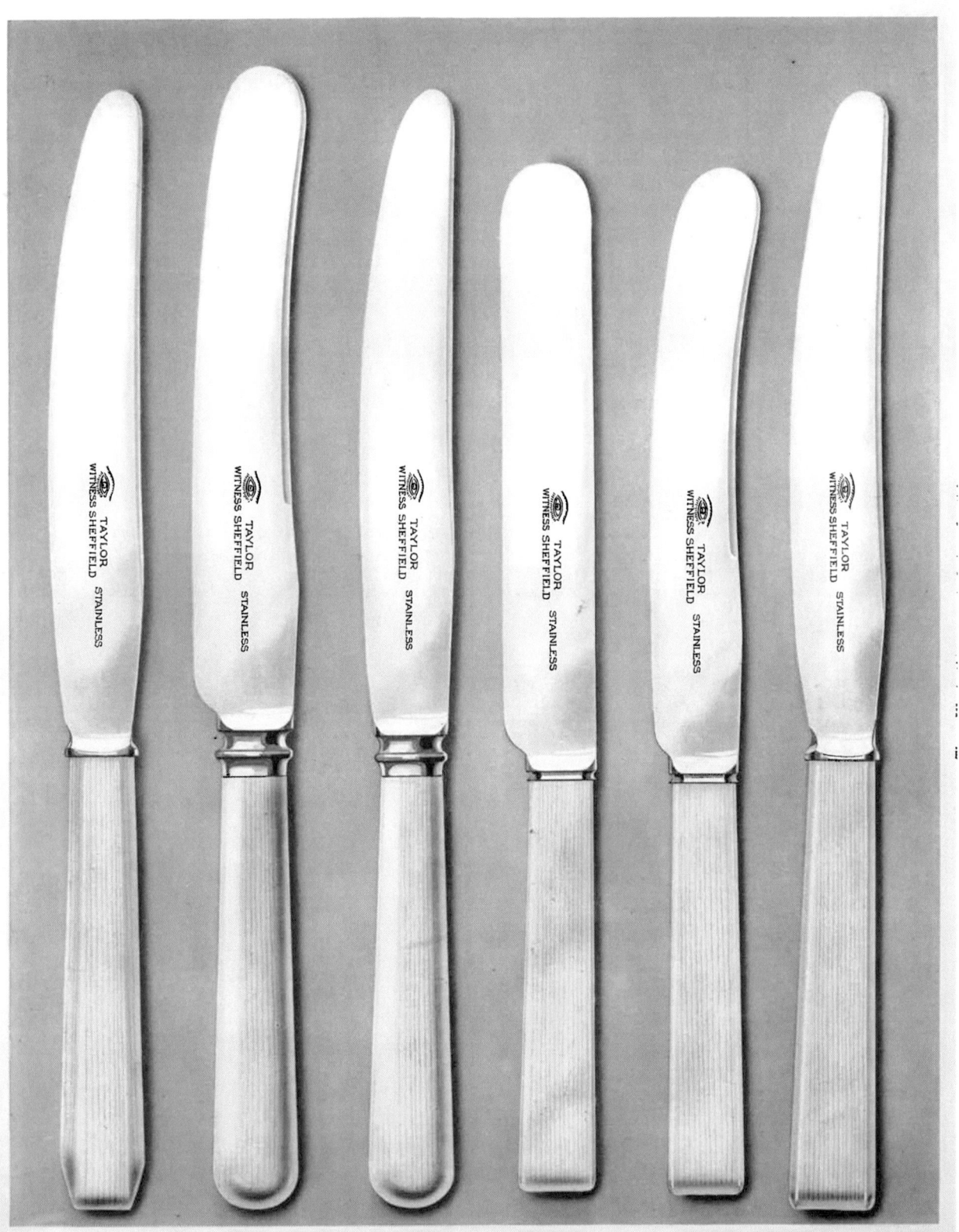

SECTION A
PAGE 13

| 5255 | 5258 | 5260 | 5262 (not bevelled) | 5263 | 5265 |

BREAKFAST KNIVES

SECTION A
PAGE 14

TAYLOR'S WITNESS

Table Knives

STAINLESS STEEL BLADES, WITH POLISHED BEVELLED BACKS
BEST AFRICAN GRAINED IVORIDE HANDLES

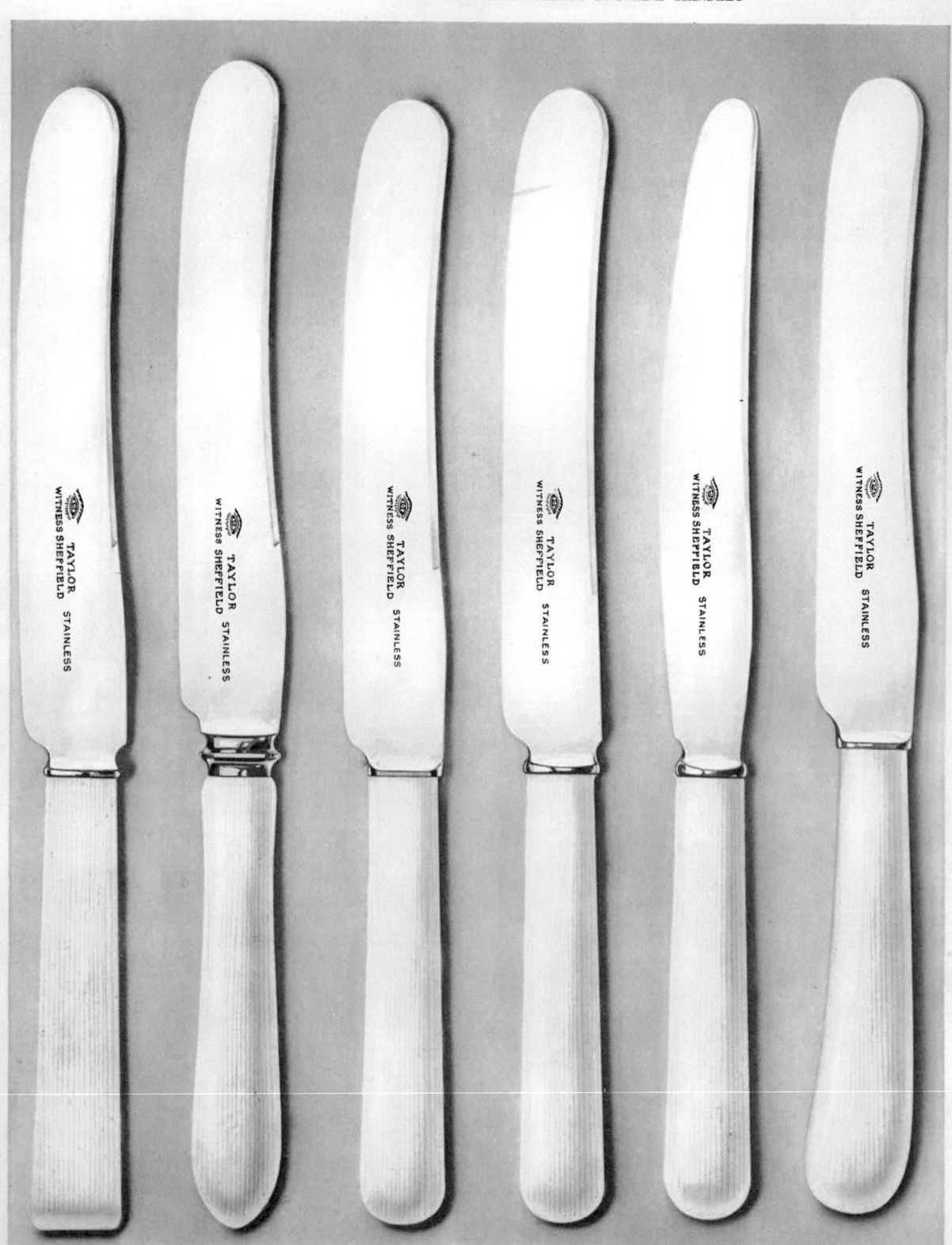

These illustrations are actual size of article

| 5270 | 5272 | 5274 | 5276 | 5277 | 5296 |

Taylor's Witness

Table Knives

SECTION A
PAGE 19

STAINLESS STEEL BLADES
HEAVILY SILVER-PLATED HANDLES, HARD SOLDERED TO BLADES

These Illustrations are actual size of article

| 5602 | 5605 | 5606 | 5610 | 5613 | 5614 |

SECTION A
PAGE 20

TAYLOR'S WITNESS

Table Knives

STAINLESS STEEL BLADES
HEAVILY SILVER-PLATED HANDLES, HARD SOLDERED TO BLADES

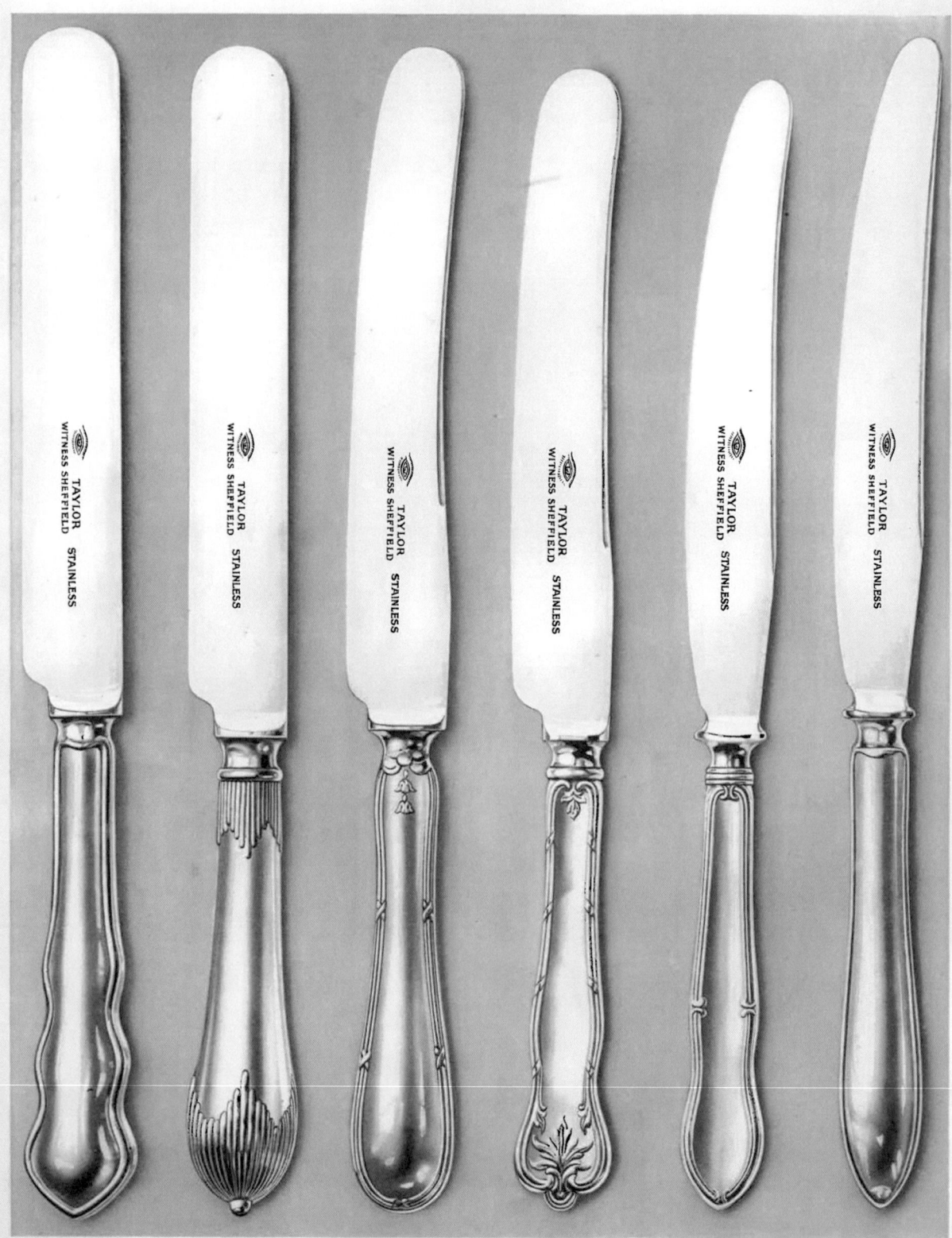

These illustrations are actual size of article

| 5616 | 5618 | 5621 | 5622 | 5624 | 5625 |

Taylor's Witness — Table Knives

SECTION A — PAGE 23

Solid Stainless Steel throughout—Made in one piece. Handles are highly polished.

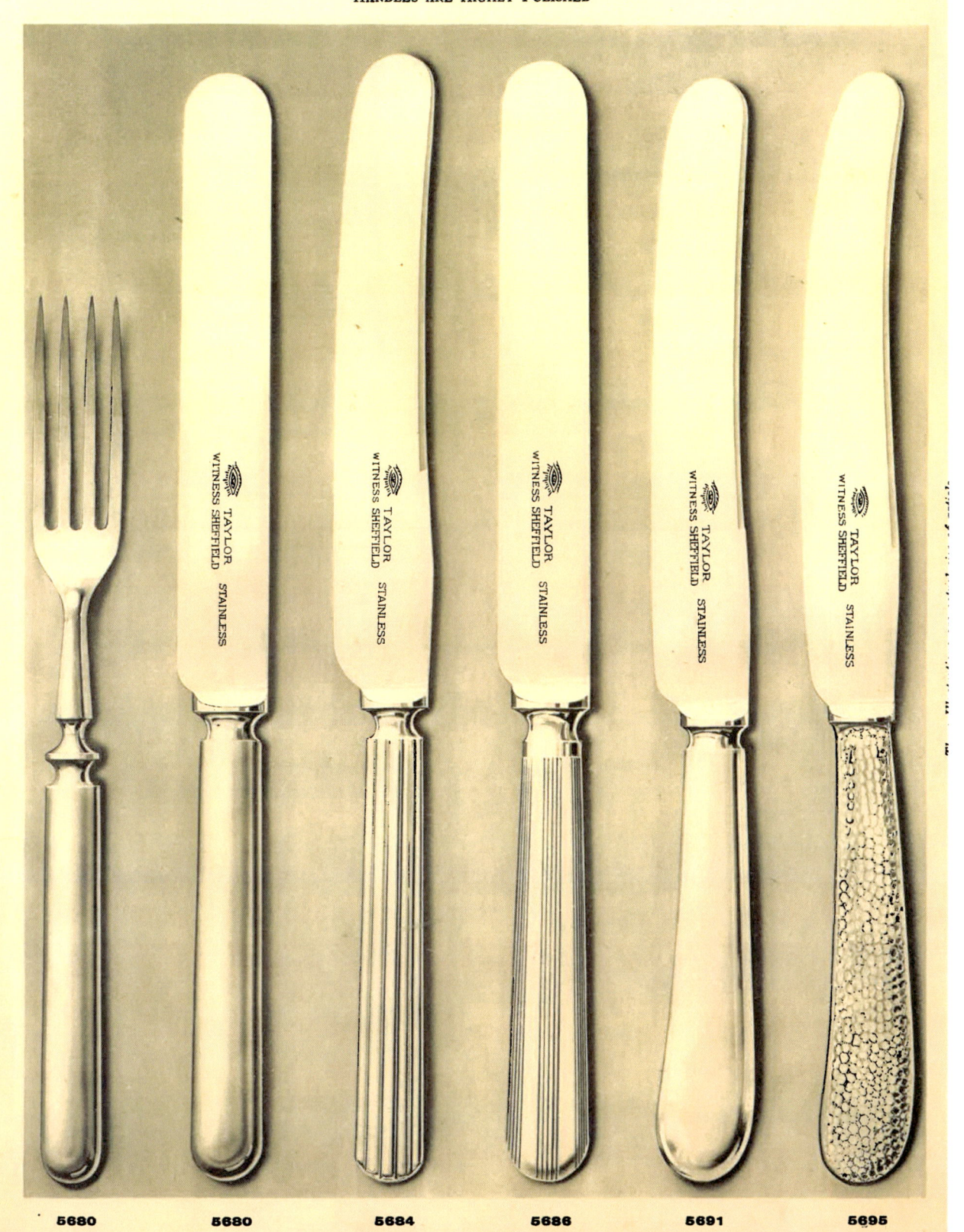

| 5680 | 5680 | 5684 | 5686 | 5691 | 5695 |

STAINLESS STEEL FORKS can also be supplied to match the above Knives

SECTION A
PAGE 24

Taylor's Witness Tea Knives

Stainless Steel Blades. **Ivoride Handles**

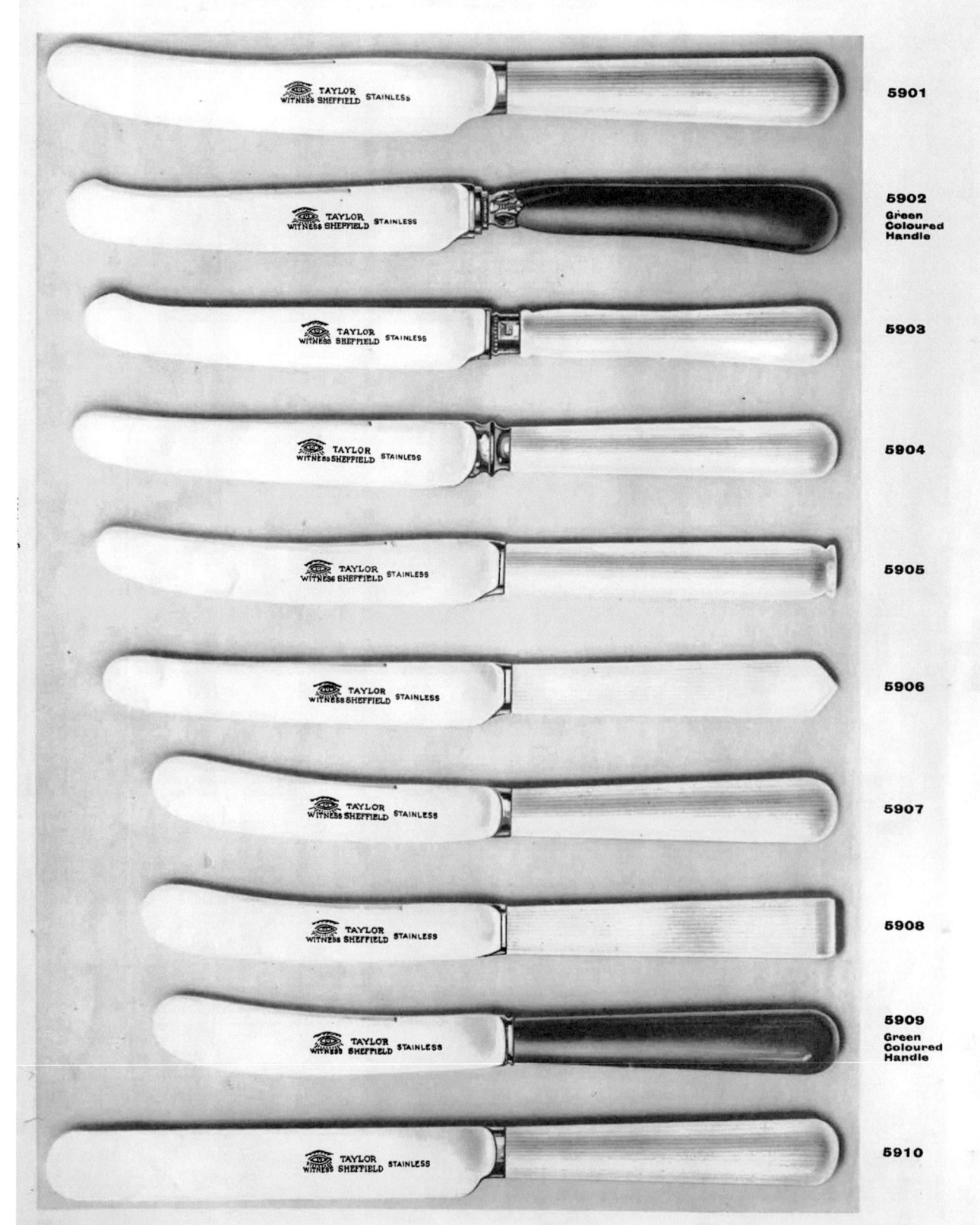

- 5901
- 5902 Green Coloured Handle
- 5903
- 5904
- 5905
- 5906
- 5907
- 5908
- 5909 Green Coloured Handle
- 5910

TAYLOR'S WITNESS

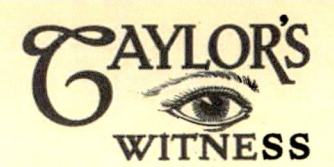

Tea Knives

Stainless Steel Blades.   Silver-Plated Handles

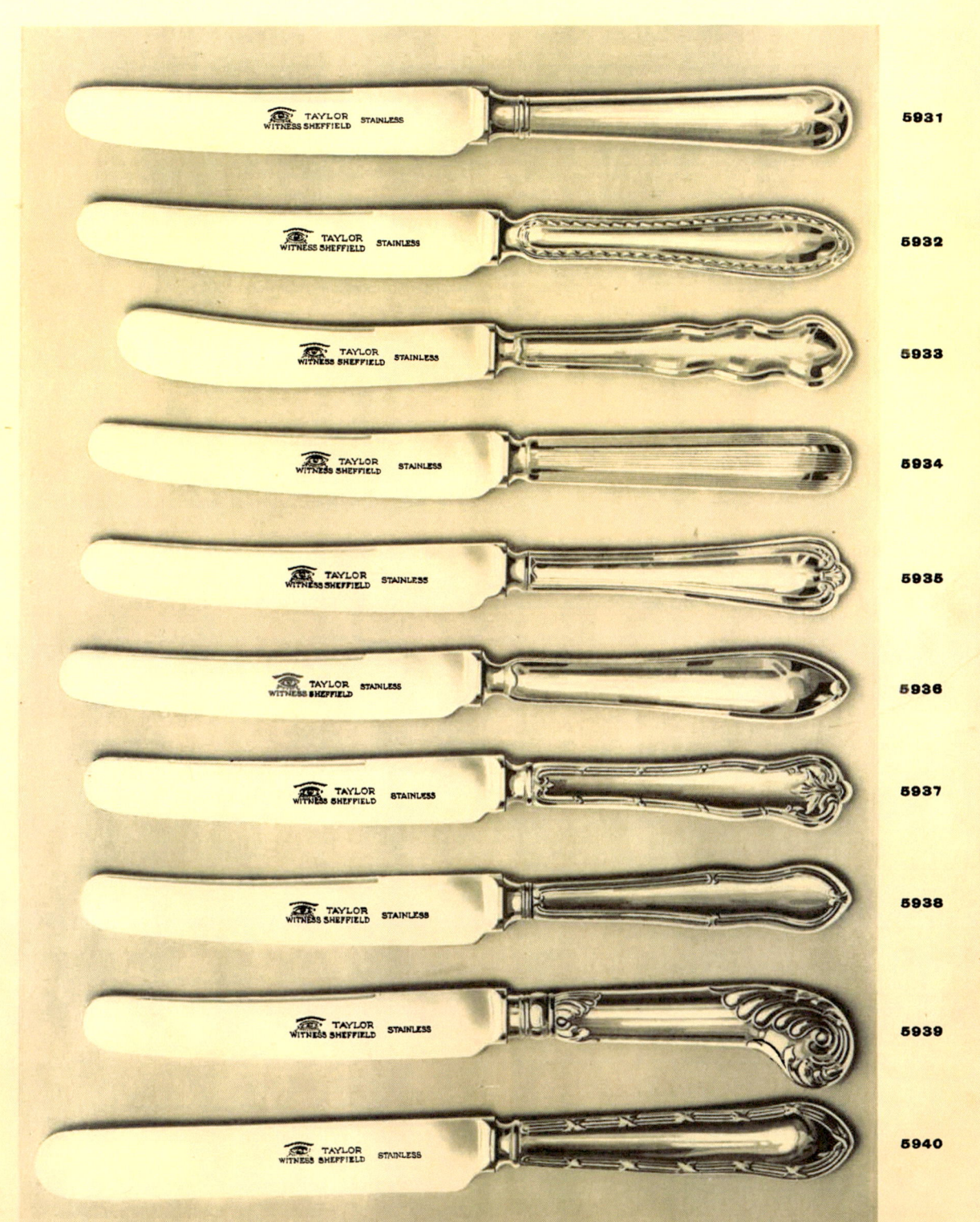

SECTION A
PAGE 25

	5931
	5932
	5933
	5934
	5935
	5936
	5937
	5938
	5939
	5940

These Illustrations are actual size of article

SECTION A
PAGE 26

Taylor's Witness Bread Knives

STEEL BLADES.   HAND-CARVED BOXWOOD HANDLES

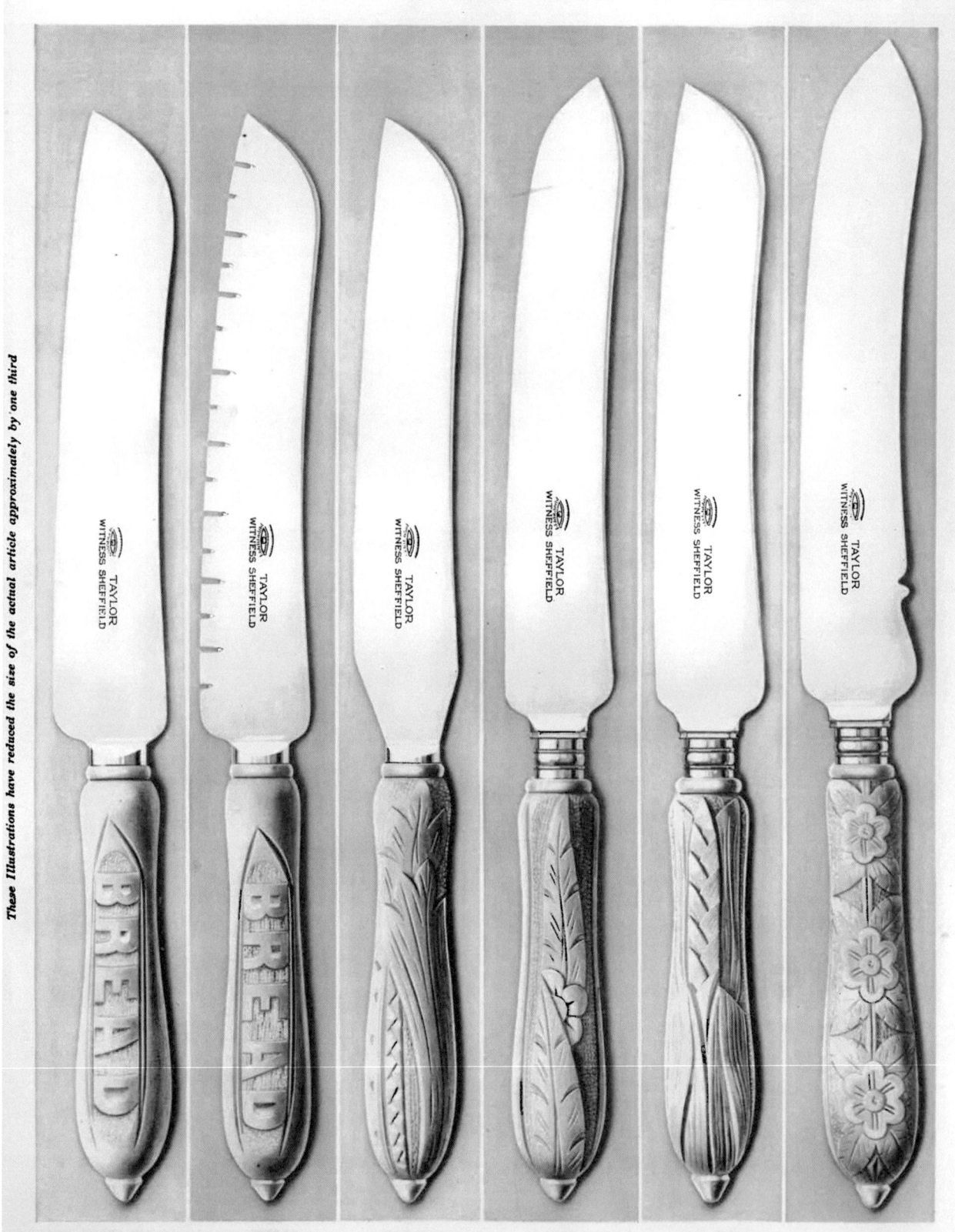

These Illustrations have reduced the size of the actual article approximately by one third

| 6501 | 6502 | 6503 | 6506 | 6507 | 6508 |

Taylor's Witness — Bread Knives

SECTION A — PAGE 27

STEEL BLADES. *Description of handle given under number*

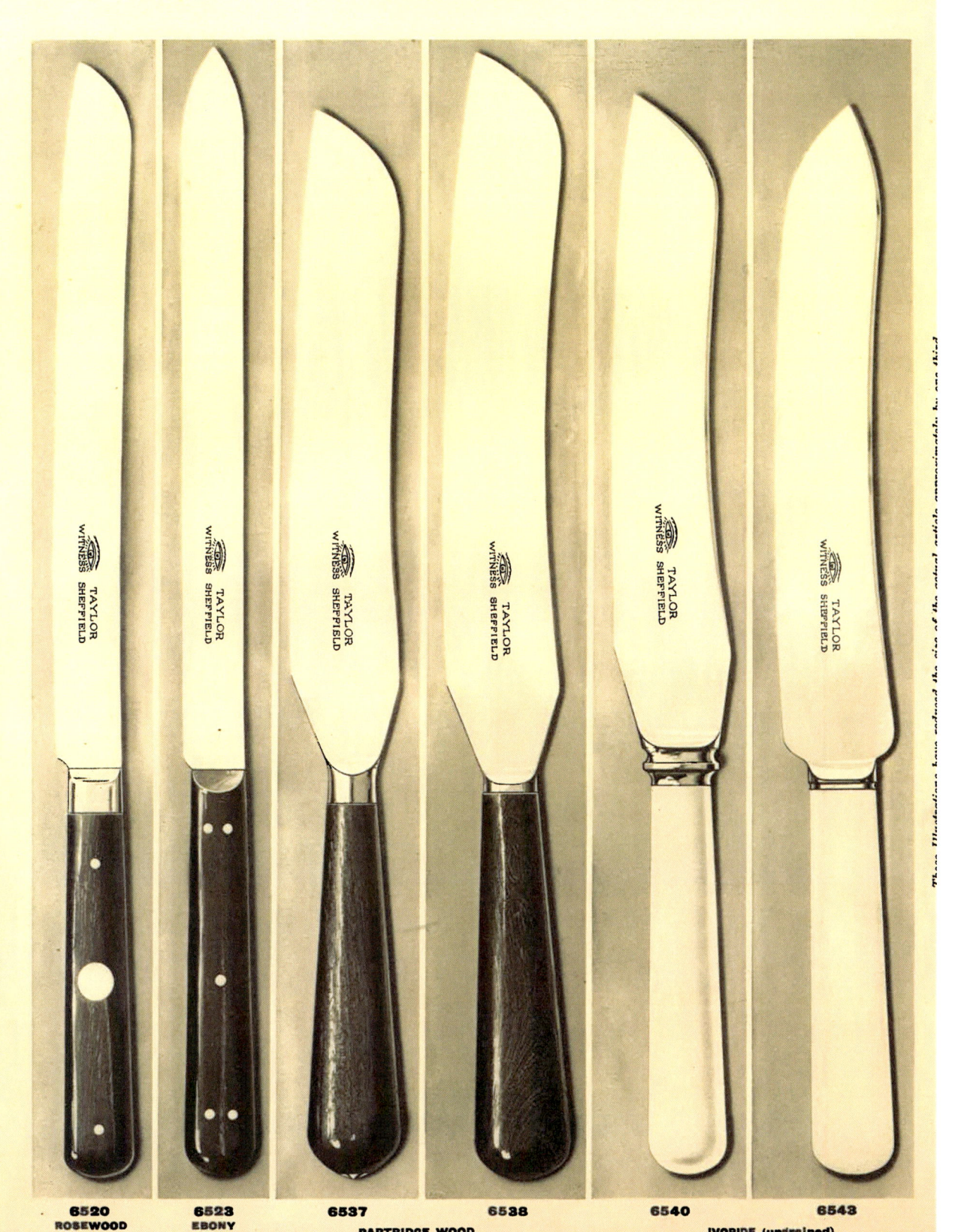

6520	6523	6537	6538	6540	6543
ROSEWOOD	EBONY	PARTRIDGE WOOD		IVORIDE (ungrained)	

SECTION A
PAGE 28

Taylor's Witness Bread Knives

STAINLESS STEEL BLADES. *Description of handle given under number*

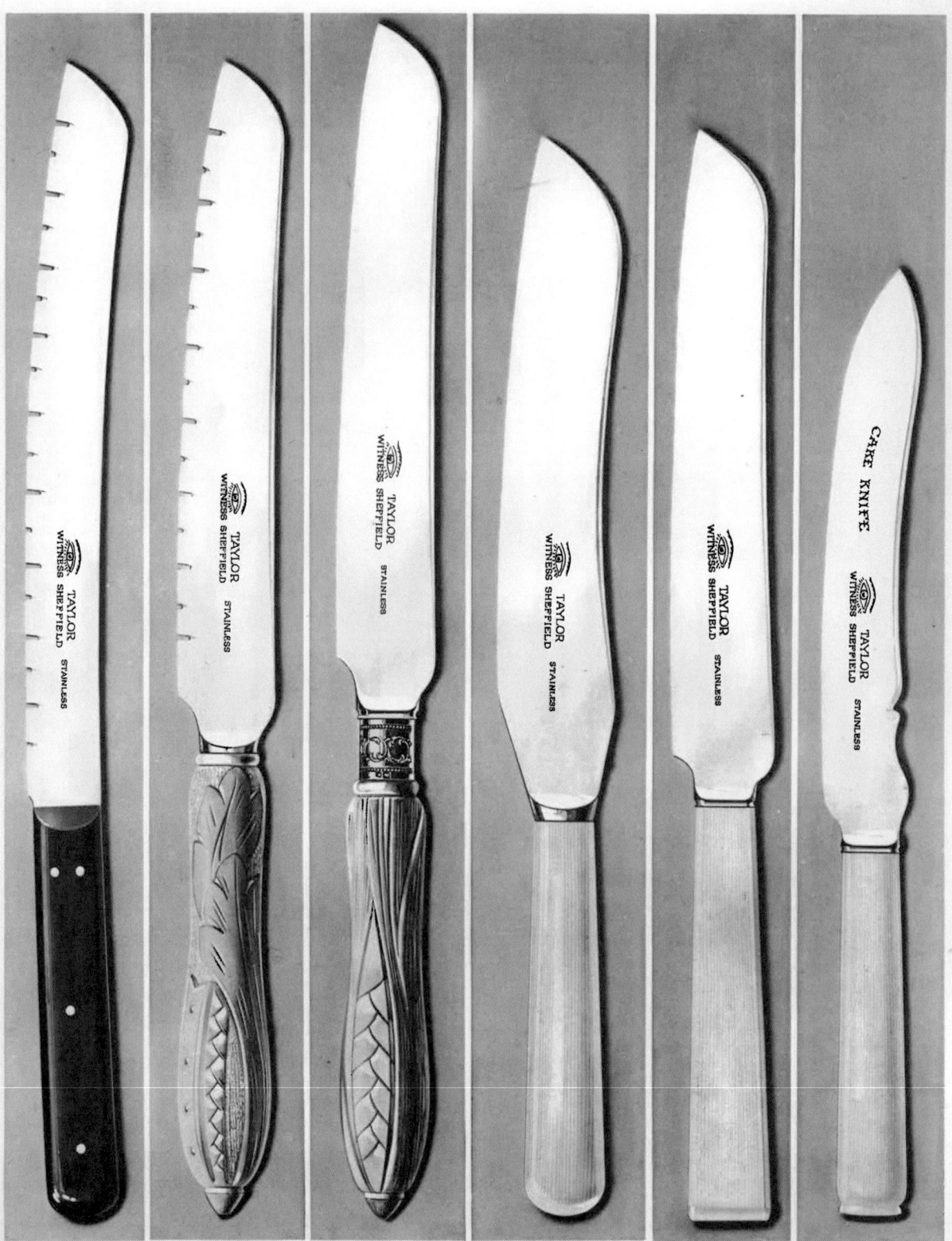

7522	7510	7512 (Silver Ferrule)	7541	7544	7550
EBONY	BOXWOOD (Hand Carved)		IVORIDE (Best African Grained)		

(7550: CAKE KNIFE)

Taylor's Witness

Carving Knives & Forks

SECTION A — PAGE 31

Steel Blades.   Stag Horn Handles
Spring Guard Pattern Forks supplied to match

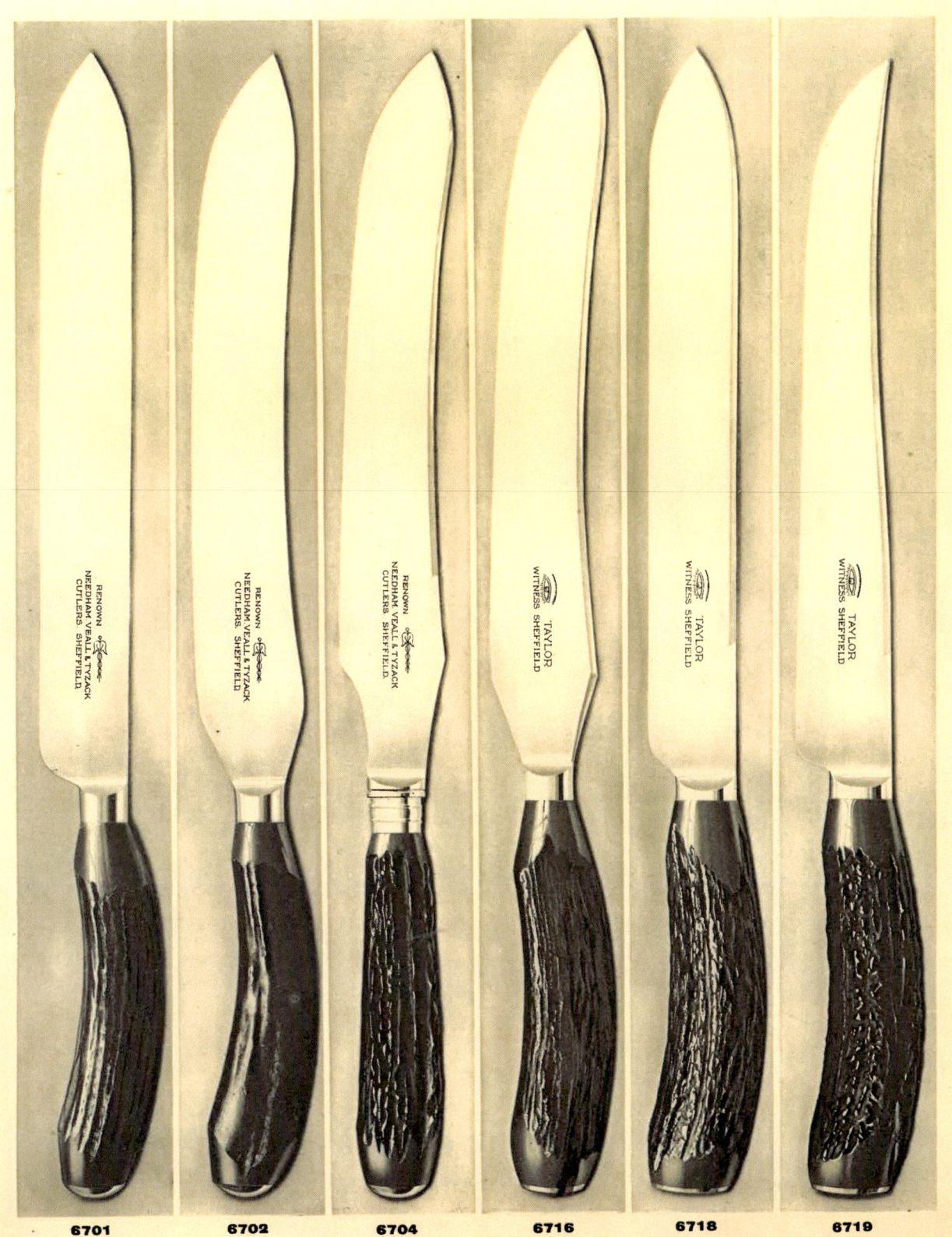

| 6701 | 6702 | 6704 | 6716 | 6718 | 6719 |

These Illustrations have reduced the size of the actual article approximately by one third

SECTION A
PAGE 32

Taylor's Witness Carving Knives

STEEL BLADES.   UNGRAINED IVORIDE HANDLES
SPRING GUARD PATTERN FORKS SUPPLIED TO MATCH

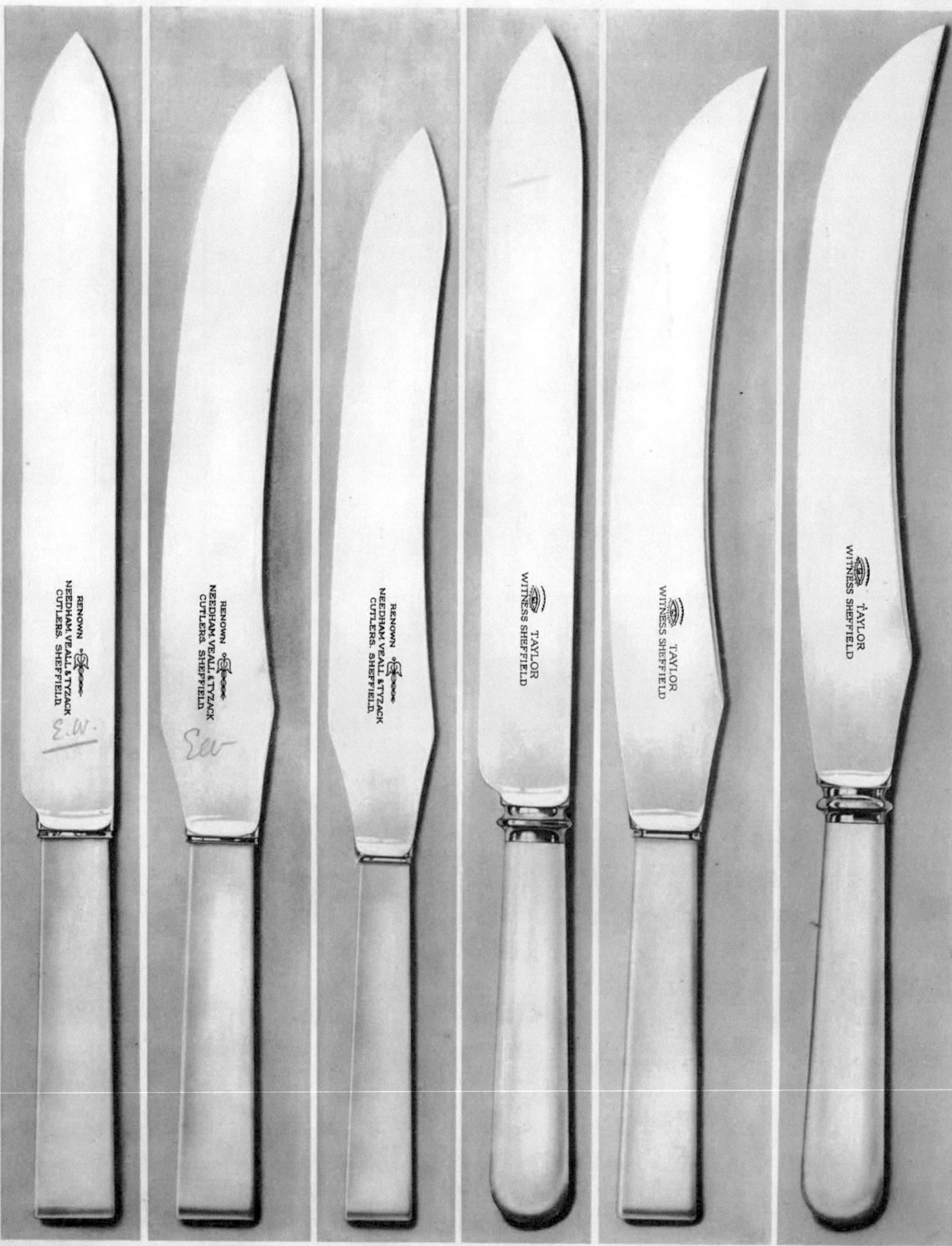

| 6802 | 6803 | 6804 | 6810 | 6813 | 6814 |

SECTION A
PAGE 35

Taylor's Witness Carving Knives
AND FORKS

The "VEALL" CARVER FORK GUARD

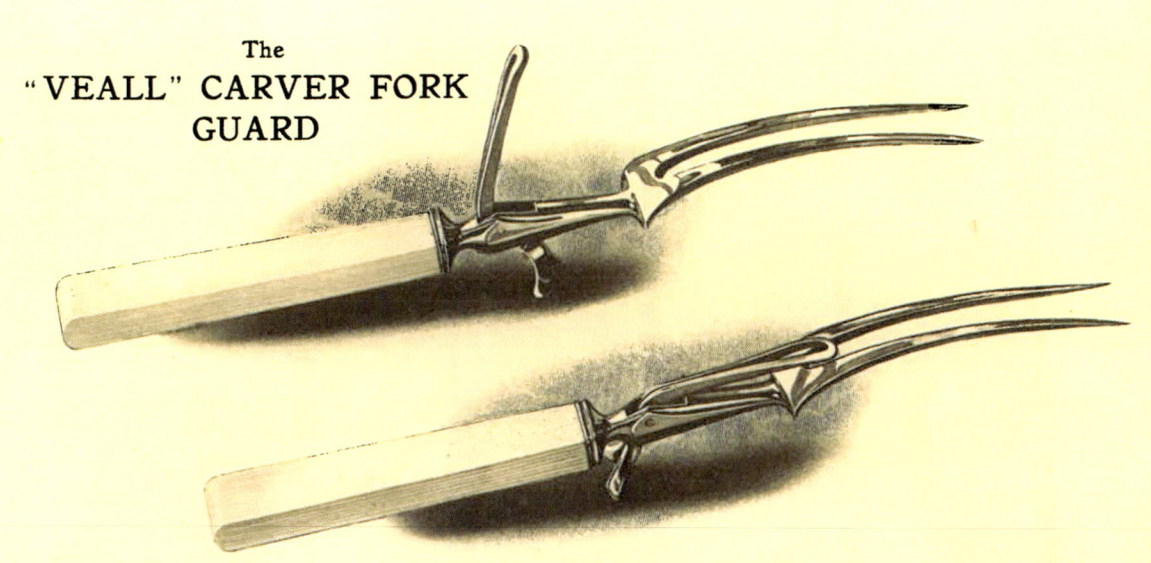

THE "VEALL" Carver Fork Guard serves a double purpose. Besides being a perfectly rigid guard, there is a divided extension through the Fork to the underpart, forming a Rest, which protects the table linen from stain. The Rest being divided forms a spring, so that when the Guard is either up or down it always remains firm in position. The arrangement is simple, but unique, and is a distinct advance on former styles.

DISCARD THE OLD-FASHIONED KNIFE-AND-FORK TABLE REST

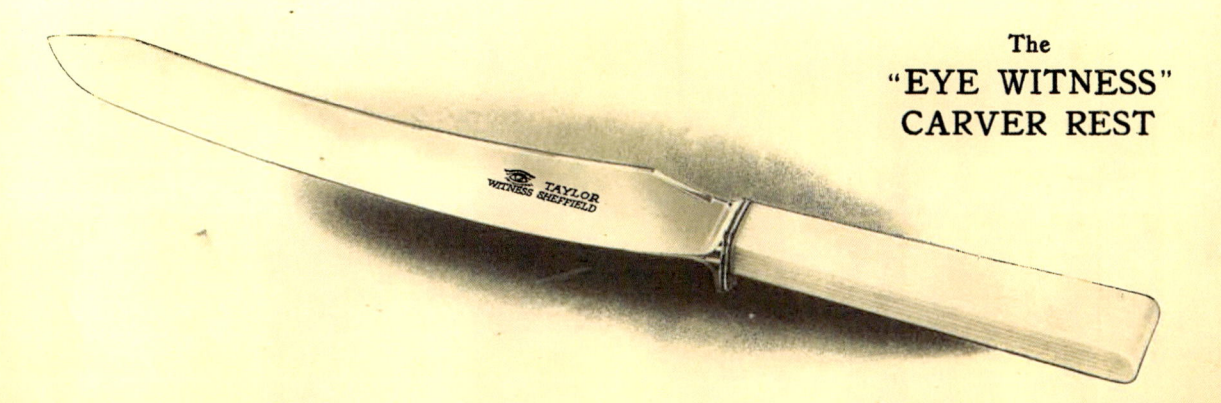

The "EYE WITNESS" CARVER REST

ALL "EYE WITNESS" Carving Knives illustrated on the following pages are fitted with a Rest, which serves a similar purpose to that on the Carver Fork. This again is a simple device, and is widely appreciated, as it keeps the blade clear of the table linen. Cannot get out of order, and easily kept clean.

SECTION A
PAGE 36

TAYLOR'S WITNESS Carving Knives & Forks

STEEL BLADES, WITH "EYE WITNESS" PATENT REST.   STAG HORN HANDLES
NICKEL-PLATED FORKS, FITTED WITH "VEALL'S" PATENT GUARD, SUPPLIED TO MATCH

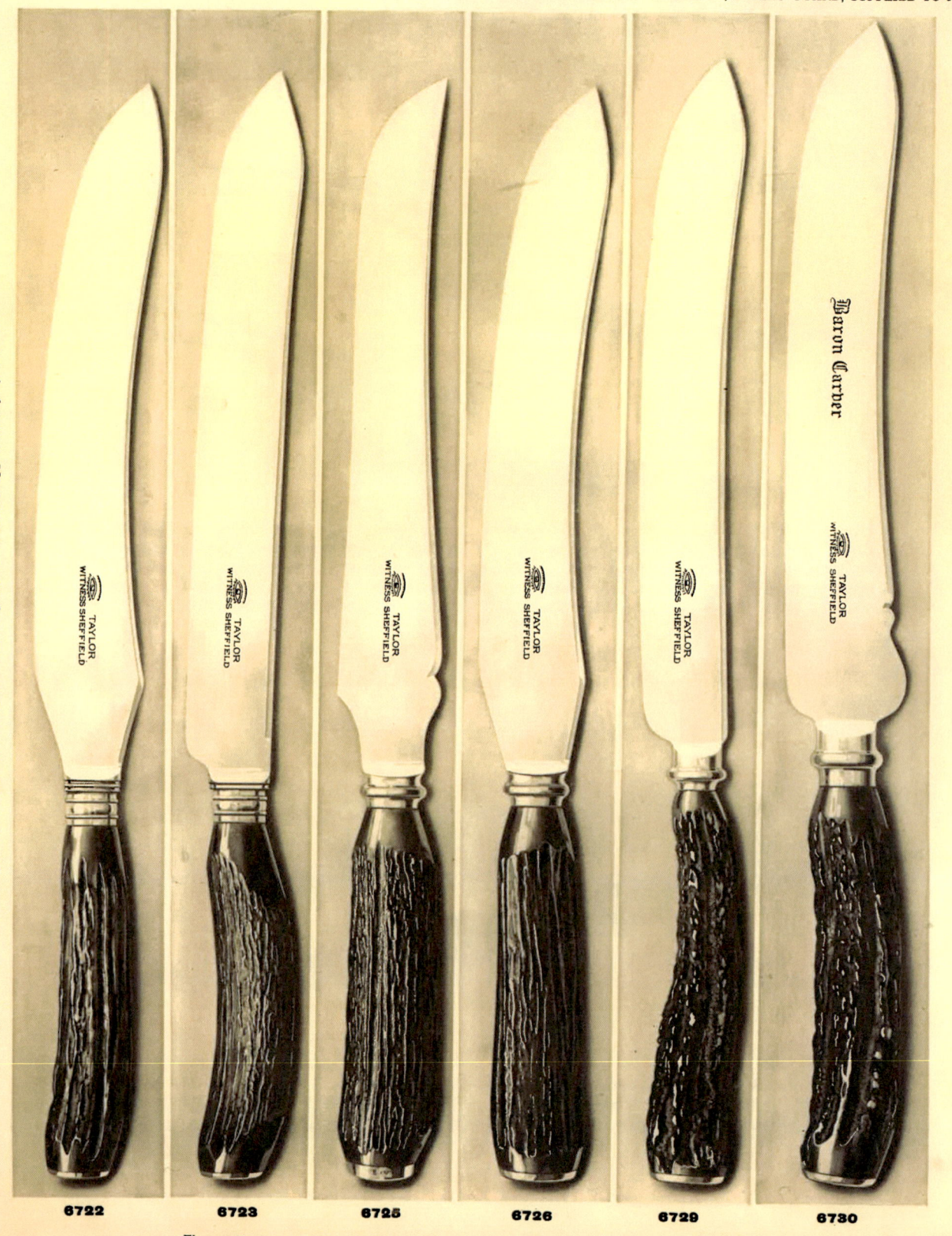

| 6722 | 6723 | 6725 | 6726 | 6729 | 6730 |

These patterns can also be supplied in Stainless Steel; for numbers and prices see Price List

TAYLOR'S WITNESS — Carving Knives & Forks

SECTION A — PAGE 37

STEEL BLADES, WITH "EYE WITNESS" PATENT REST.   STAG HORN HANDLES
NICKEL-PLATED FORKS, FITTED WITH "VEALL'S" PATENT GUARD, SUPPLIED TO MATCH

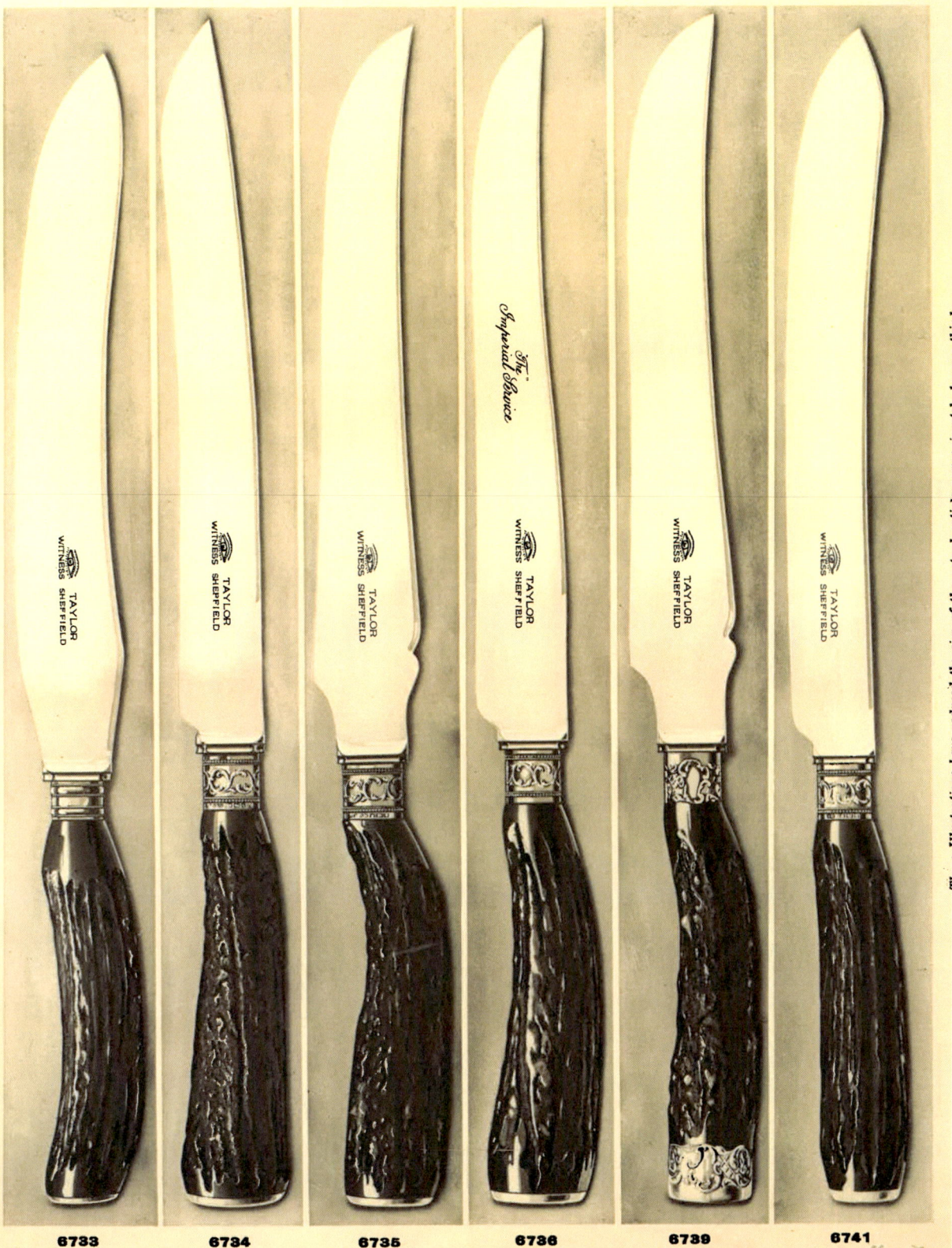

| 6733 | 6734 | 6735 | 6736 | 6739 | 6741 |

These patterns can also be supplied in Stainless Steel; for numbers and prices see Price List

SECTION A
PAGE 28

ᴛaylor's WITNESS Carving Knives

STEEL BLADES, WITH "EYE WITNESS" PATENT REST.   BEST AFRICAN GRAINED IVORIDE HANDLES
NICKEL-PLATED FORKS, FITTED WITH "VEALL'S" PATENT GUARD. SUPPLIED TO MATCH

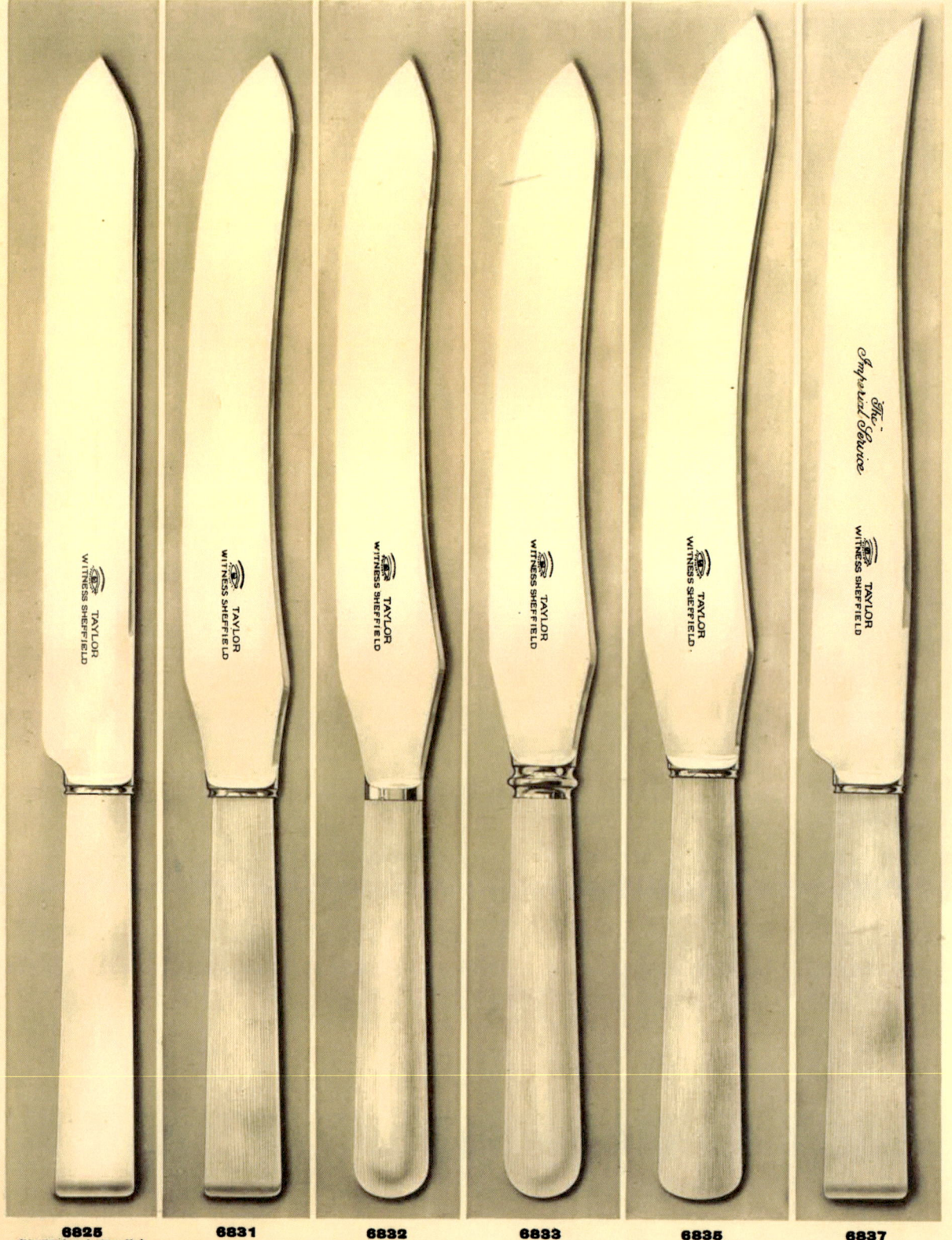

| 6825 (Ungrained Handle) | 6831 | 6832 | 6833 | 6835 | 6837 |

These patterns can also be supplied in Stainless Steel; for numbers and prices see Price List

Taylor's Witness — Carving Knives & Forks

SECTION A — PAGE 39

Steel Blades, with "Eye Witness" Patent Rest. Best African Grained IVORIDE Handles
Nickel-plated Forks, fitted with "Veall's" Patent Guard. Supplied to match

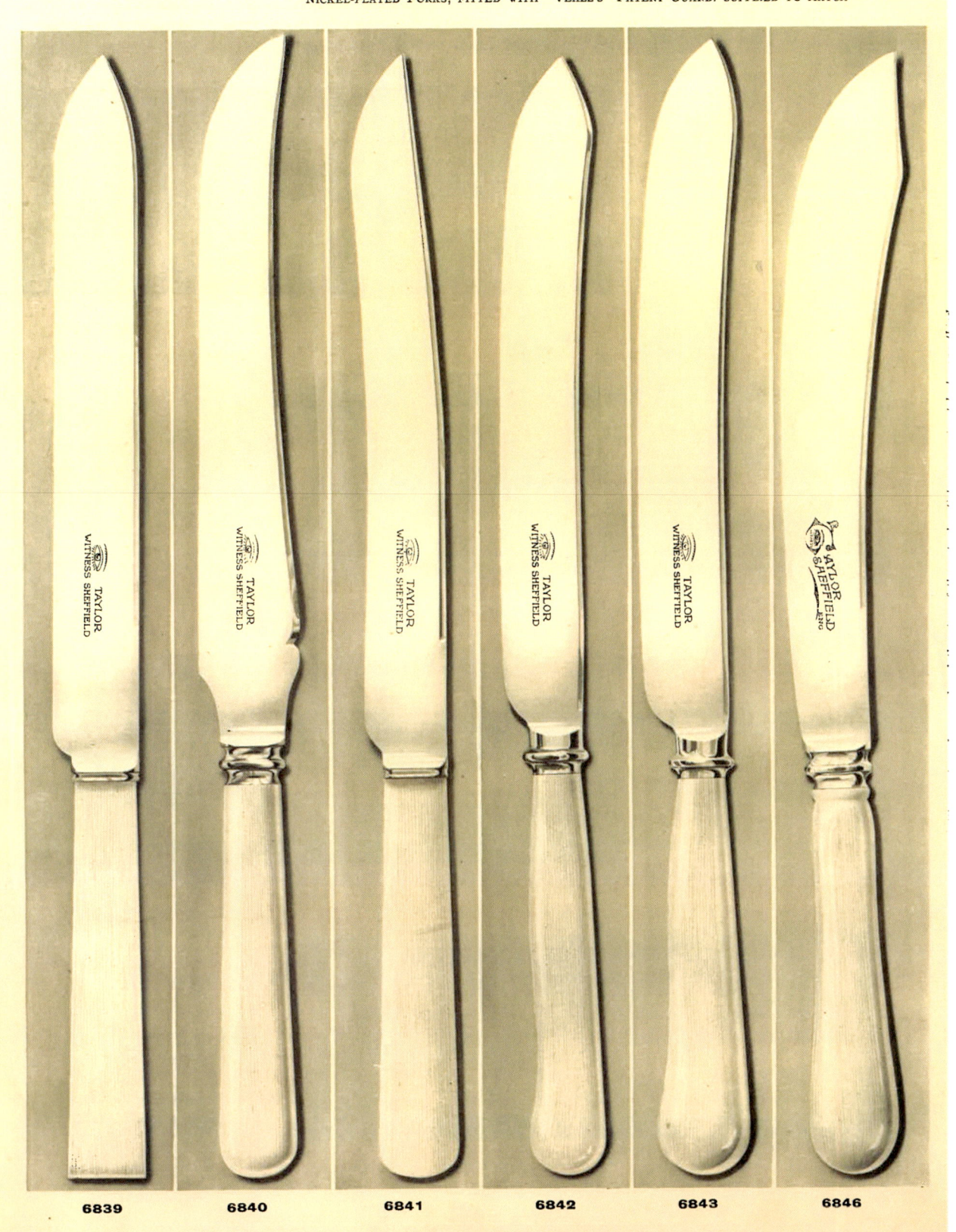

| 6839 | 6840 | 6841 | 6842 | 6843 | 6846 |

These patterns can also be supplied in Stainless Steel; for numbers and prices see Price List

Taylor's Witness — Sets of Carvers

IN BLACK AND CROCODILE LEATHERETTE COVERED CASES, LINED WITH CHOICE COLOURED SATIN AND SILK

CASE No. 600/3 piece
Fitted with
  Good quality Forged Steel Carving Knife.
  Carving Fork with Spring Guard.
  Forged Sharpening Steel.
  Stag Horn Handles mounted with iron caps.

CASE No. 600/5 piece
Fitted as above
  with one pair of Game Carvers to match in addition.

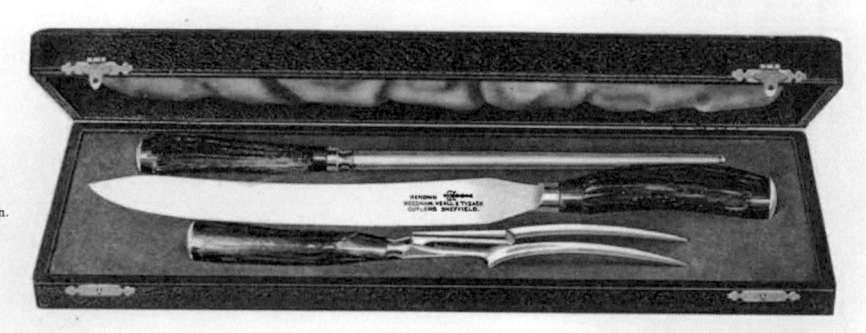

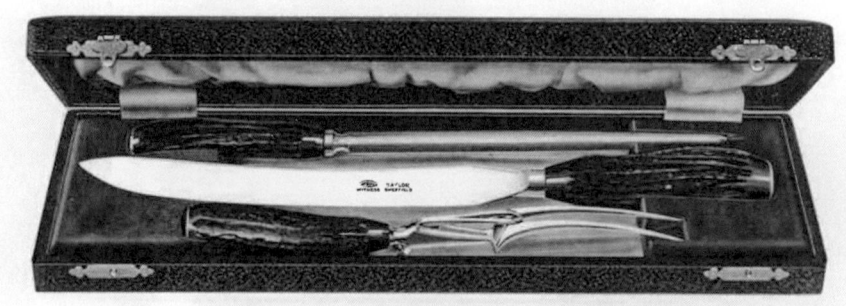

CASE No. 603/3 piece
Fitted with
  Good quality Forged Steel Carving Knife.
  Nickel-plated Carving Fork with Patent Guard.
  Forged Sharpening Steel.
  Stag Horn Handles mounted with iron caps.

CASE No. 603/5 piece
Fitted as above
  with one pair of Game Carvers to match in addition.

CASE No. 606/3 piece
Fitted with
  Best quality Forged Steel Carving Knife with "Eye-Witness" Patent Rest.
  Nickel-plated Carving Fork with Patent Guard.
  Forged Sharpening Steel.
  Stag Horn Handles mounted with Nickel-Silver Caps.

CASE No. 606/5 piece
Fitted as above
  with one pair of Game Carvers to match in addition

CASE No. 706/3 and 5 piece
Fitted as above
  but with **Stainless Steel Blades.**

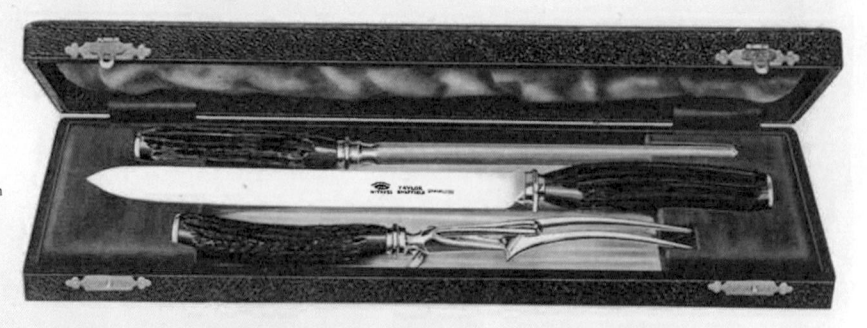

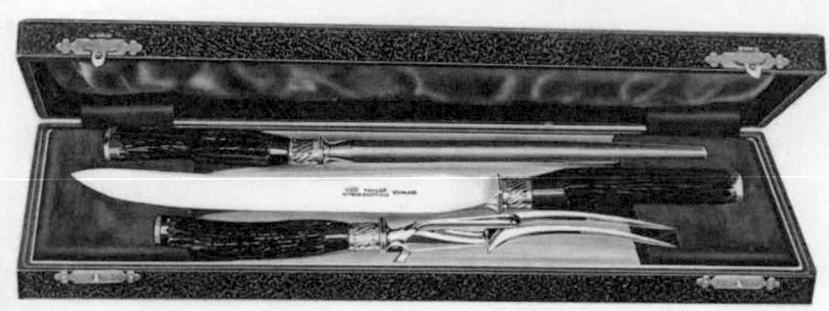

CASE No. 608/3 piece
Fitted with
  Best quality Forged Steel Carving Knife with "Eye-Witness" Patent Rest.
  Nickel-plated Carving Fork with Patent Guard.
  Forged Sharpening Steel.
  Stag Horn Handles mounted with Silver-plated Ferrules and Nickel-Silver Caps.

CASE No. 608/5 piece
Fitted as above
  with one pair of Game Carvers to match in addition.

CASE No. 708/3 and 5 piece
Fitted as above
  but with **Stainless Steel Blades.**

These illustrations have reduced the size of the actual article approximately to one third

SECTION A
PAGE 41

Taylor's Witness

Sets of Carvers

IN BLACK AND CROCODILE LEATHERETTE COVERED CASES, LINED WITH CHOICE COLOURED SATIN AND SILK

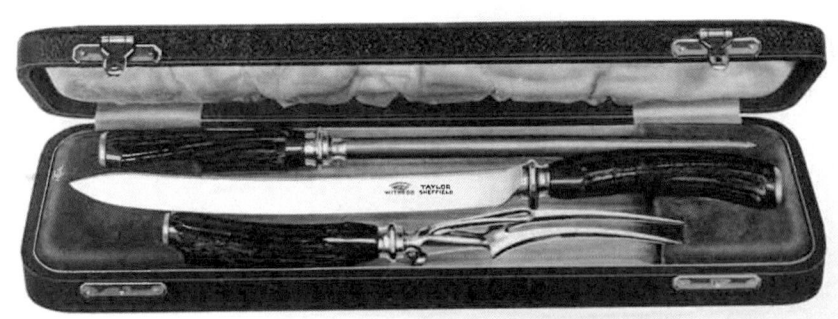

CASE No. 610/3 piece
Fitted with
Best quality Forged Steel Carving Knife with "Eye-Witness" Patent Rest.
Nickel-plated Carving Fork with Patent Guard.
Forged Sharpening Steel.
Stag Horn Handles mounted with Nickel-Silver Caps.

CASE No. 610/5 piece
Fitted as above
with one pair of Game Carvers to match in addition.

CASE No. 710/3 and 5 piece
Fitted as above
but with **Stainless Steel Blades**.

CASE No. 711/3 and 5 piece
Fitted as above
with **Stainless Steel Blades** and **Stainless Steel Forks**.

CASE No. 612/3 piece
Fitted with
Best quality Forged Steel Carving Knife
Nickel-plated Carving Fork with Patent Guard.
Forged Sharpening Steel.
Stag Horn Handles mounted with Silver-plated Caps and Ferrules.

CASE No. 612/5 piece
Fitted as above
with one pair of Game Carvers to match in addition.

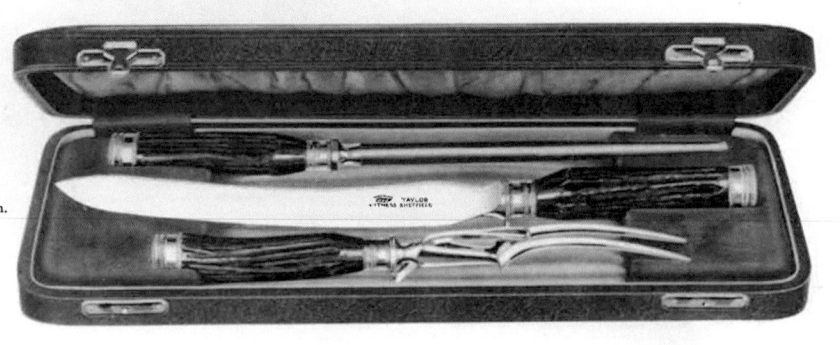

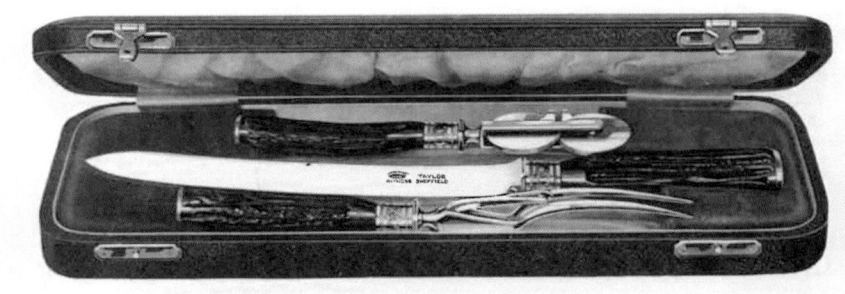

CASE No. 615/3 piece
Fitted with
Best quality Forged Steel Carving Knife with "Eye-Witness" Patent Rest.
Nickel-plated Carving Fork with Patent Guard.
Two-wheel Knife Sharpener.
Stag Horn Handles mounted with Sterling Silver Ferrules and Nickel-Silver Caps.

CASE No. 615/5 piece
Fitted as above
with one pair of Game Carvers to match in addition.

CASE No. 715/3 and 5 piece
Fitted as above
but with **Stainless Steel Blades**.

CASE No. 716/3 and 5 piece
Fitted as above
with **Stainless Steel Blades** and **Stainless Steel Forks**.

CASE No. 618/5 piece
Fitted with
Best quality Forged Steel 9" Meat and Game Carving Knives with "Eye-Witness" Patent Rests.
Nickel-plated Carving Fork with Patent Guard.
Forged Sharpening Steel.
Stag Horn Handles mounted with Sterling Silver Caps.

CASE No. 618/3 piece
Fitted as above
but with one pair 9" Meat Carvers and Sharpening Steel only.

CASE No. 718/3 and 5 piece
Fitted as above
but with **Stainless Steel Blades**.

CASE No. 719/3 and 5 piece
Fitted as above
with **Stainless Steel Blades** and **Stainless Steel Forks**.

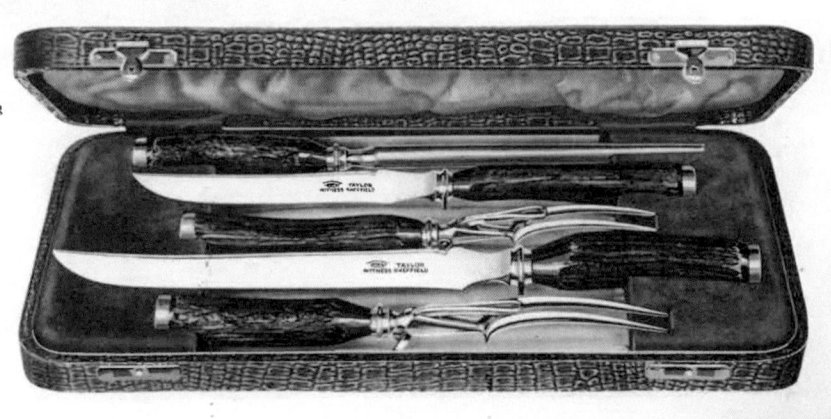

SECTION A
PAGE 42

Taylor's Witness

Sets of Carvers

IN BLACK AND CROCODILE LEATHERETTE COVERED CASES, LINED WITH CHOICE COLOURED SATIN AND SILK

These illustrations have reduced the size of the actual article approximately to one third

CASE No. 630/3 piece
Fitted with
Good quality Forged Steel Carving Knife.
Carving Fork with Spring Guard.
Forged Sharpening Steel.
Square Ivoride Handles.

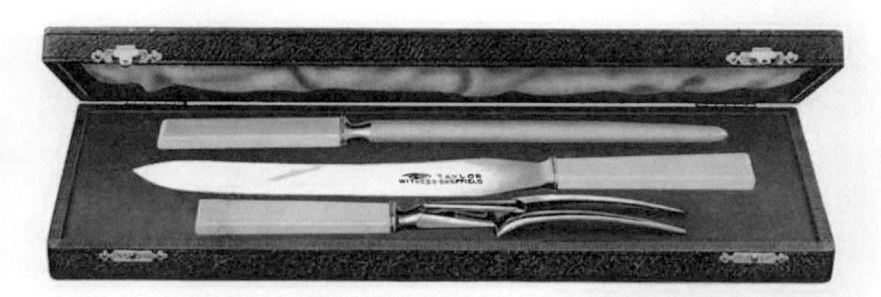

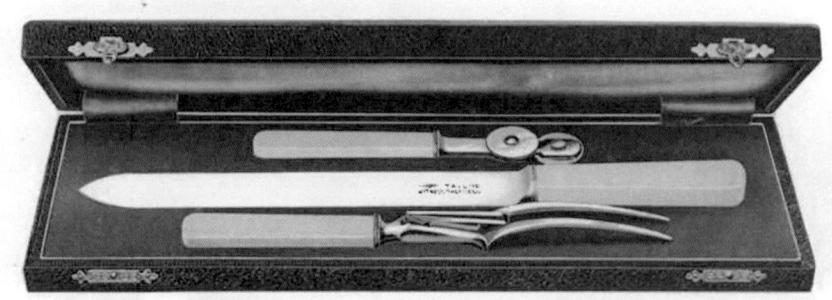

CASE No. 632/3 piece
Fitted with
Good quality Forged Steel Carving Knife.
Carving Fork with Spring Guard
Two-Wheel Knife Sharpener.
Square Ivoride Handles.

CASE No. 636/3 piece
Fitted with
Good quality Forged Steel Carving Knife with
"Eye-Witness" Patent Rest.
Nickel-plated Carving Fork with Patent Guard.
Forged Sharpening Steel.
Round Ivoride Handles.

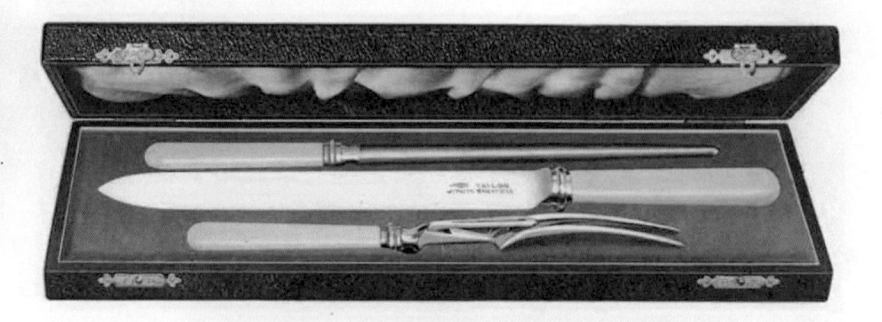

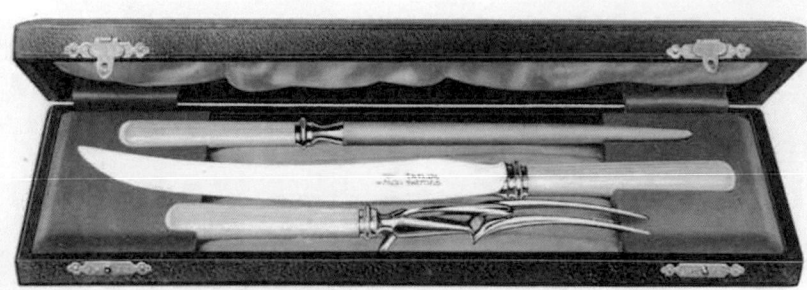

CASE No. 638/3 piece
Fitted with
Good quality Forged Steel Carving Knife.
Nickel-plated Carving Fork with Patent Guard.
Forged Sharpening Steel.
Round Ivoride Handles.

SECTION A
PAGE 43

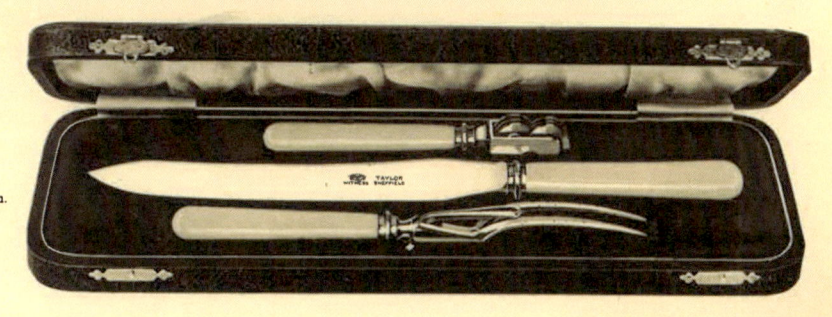

Taylor's Witness

Sets of Carvers

IN BLACK AND CROCODILE LEATHERETTE COVERED CASES,
LINED WITH CHOICE COLOURED SATIN AND SILK

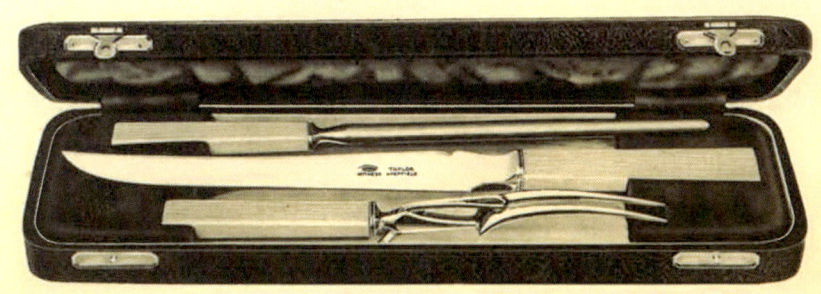

CASE No. 640/3 piece
Fitted with
  Best quality Forged Steel Carving Knife with
    "Eye-Witness" Patent Rest.
  Nickel-plated Carving Fork with Patent Guard.
  Forged Sharpening Steel.
  Best African Grained Ivoride Square handles.

CASE No. 640/5 piece
Fitted as above
  with one pair of Game Carvers to match in addition.

CASE No. 740/3 and 5 piece
Fitted as above
  but with **Stainless Steel Blades.**

CASE No. 642/3 piece
Fitted with
  Best quality Forged Steel Carving Knife with
    "Eye-Witness" Patent Rest.
  Nickel-plated Carving Fork with Patent Guard.
  Forged Sharpening Steel.
  Grained Ivoride Round Handles.

CASE No. 642/5 piece
Fitted as above
  with one pair of Game Carvers to match in addition.

CASE No. 742/3 and 5 piece
Fitted as above
  but with **Stainless Steel Blades.**

CASE No. 743/3 and 5 piece
Fitted as above
  with **Stainless Steel Blades** and
  Stainless Steel Forks.

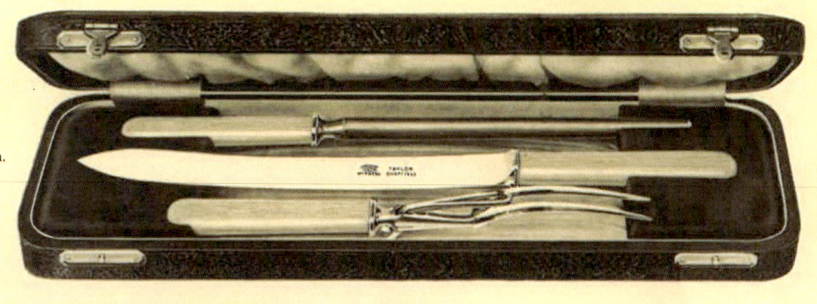

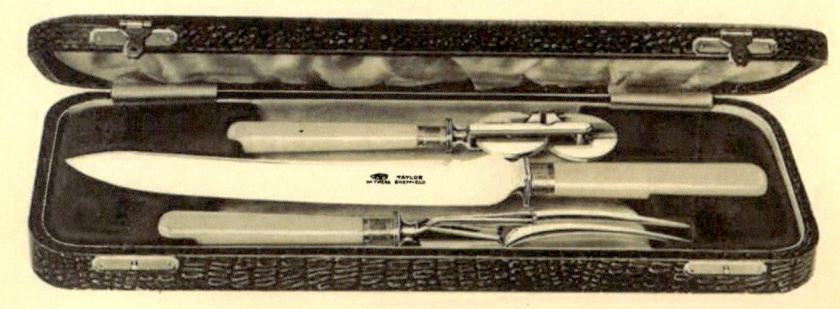

CASE No. 644/3 piece
Fitted with
  Best quality Forged Steel Carving Knife with
    "Eye-Witness" Patent Rest.
  Nickel-plated Carving Fork with Patent Guard.
  Two-Wheel Knife Sharpener.
  Best ungrained Ivoride Round Handles mounted
    with Sterling Silver Ferrules.

CASE No. 644/5 piece
Fitted as above
  with one pair of Game Carvers to match in addition.

CASE No. 646/3 piece
Fitted with
  Best quality Forged Steel Carving Knife with
    "Eye-Witness" Patent Rest.
  Nickel-plated Carving Fork with Patent Guard.
  Six-Wheel Knife Sharpener.
  Best ungrained Ivoride Round Handles.

CASE No. 646/5 piece
Fitted as above
  with one pair of Game Carvers to match in addition.

CASE No. 746/3 and 5 piece
Fitted as above
but with **Stainless Steel Blades.**

These Illustrations have reduced the size of the actual article approximately to one third

SECTION A
PAGE 44

TAYLOR'S WITNESS

Sets of Carvers

IN BLACK AND CROCODILE LEATHERETTE COVERED CASES,
LINED WITH CHOICE COLOURED SATIN AND SILK

CASE No. 648/3 piece
Fitted with
Best quality Forged Steel Carving Knife with "Eye-Witness" Patent Rest.
Nickel-plated Carving Fork with Patent Guard.
Forged Sharpening Steel.
Best African Grained round Ivoride Handles.

CASE No. 648/5 piece
Fitted as above
with one pair of Game Carvers to match in addition.

CASE No. 748/3 and 5 piece
Fitted as above
but with **Stainless Steel Blades**.

CASE No. 749/3 and 5 piece
Fitted as above
with **Stainless Steel Blades** and **Stainless Steel Forks**.

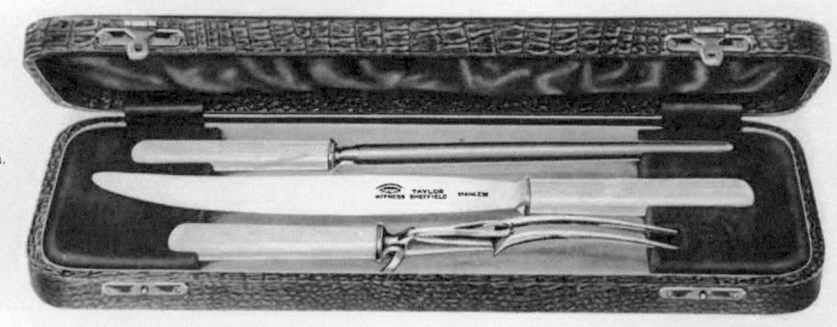

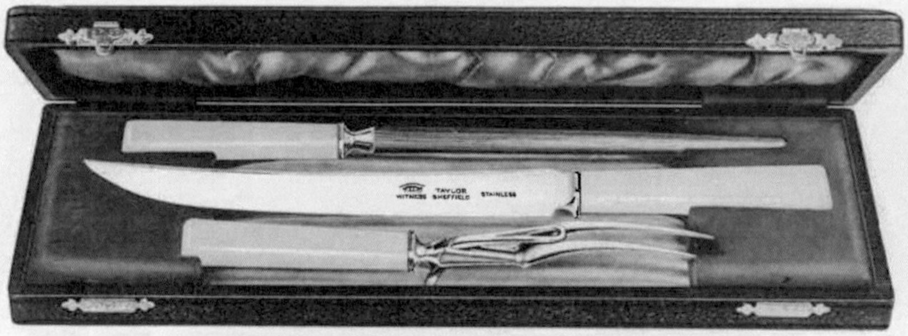

CASE No. 651/3 piece
Fitted with
Best quality Forged Steel Carving Knife with "Eye-Witness" Patent Rest.
Nickel-plated Carving Fork with Patent Guard.
Forged Sharpening Steel.
Ivoride Square Handles.

CASE No. 651/5 piece
Fitted as above
with one pair of Game Carvers to match in addition.

CASE No. 751/3 and 5 piece
Fitted as above
but with **Stainless Steel Blades**.

CASE No. 655/3 piece
Fitted with
Best quality Forged Steel Carving Knife with "Eye-Witness" Patent Rest.
Nickel-plated Carving Fork with Patent Guard.
Forged Sharpening Steel.
Best African Grained Ivoride square Handles with round ends.

CASE No. 655/5 piece
Fitted as above
with one pair of Game Carvers to match in addition.

CASE No. 755/3 and 5 piece
Fitted as above
but with **Stainless Steel Blades**.

CASE No. 756/3 and 5 piece
Fitted as above
with **Stainless Steel Blades** and **Stainless Steel Forks**.

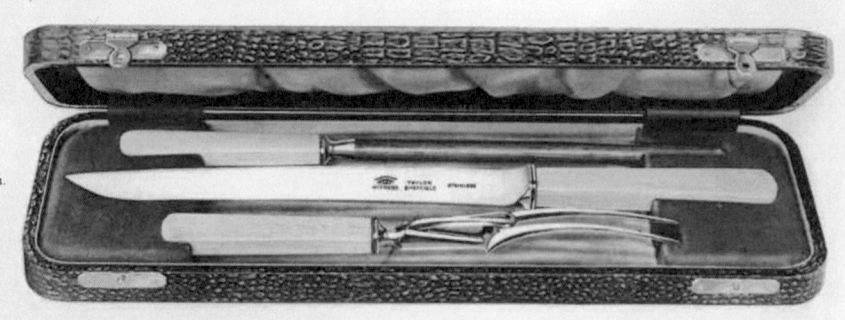

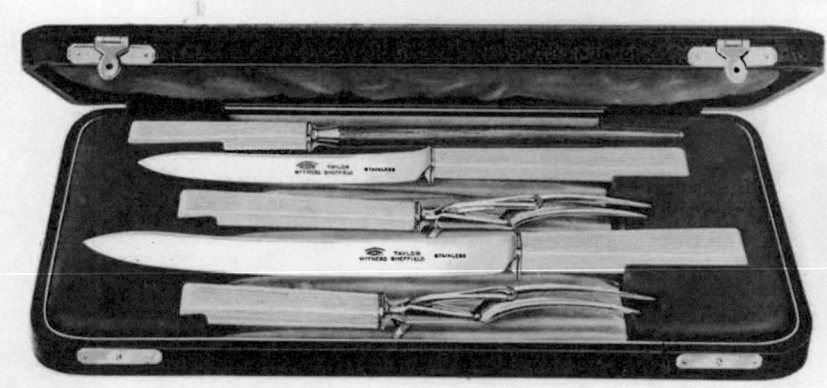

CASE No. 658/5 piece
Fitted with
Best quality Forged Steel 9″ Meat and Game Carving Knives with "Eye-Witness" Patent Rests.
Nickel-plated Carving Forks with Patent Guards.
Forged Sharpening Steel.
Good quality Grained Ivoride square Handles.

CASE No. 658/3 piece
Fitted as above
but with one pair 9″ Meat Carvers and Sharpening Steel only.

CASE No. 758/3 and 5 piece
Fitted as above
but with **Stainless Steel Blades**.

CASE No. 759/3 and 5 piece
Fitted as above
with **Stainless Steel Blades** and **Stainless Steel Forks**.

SECTION A
PAGE 45

Taylor's Witness

Sets of Carvers

IN BLACK AND CROCODILE LEATHERETTE COVERED CASES,
LINED WITH CHOICE COLOURED SATIN AND SILK

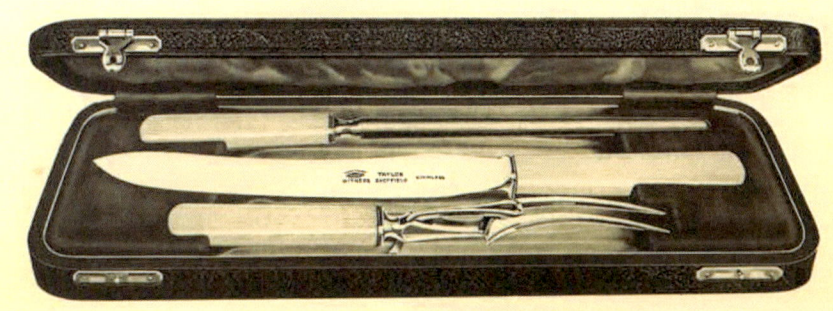

CASE No. 660/3 piece
Fitted with
  Best quality Forged Steel Carving Knife with
    "Eye-Witness" Patent Rest.
  Nickel-plated Carving Fork with Patent Guard.
  Forged Sharpening Steel.
  Best African Grained Ivoride Square Handles with
    round ends.

CASE No. 660/5 piece
Fitted as above
  with one pair of Game Carvers to match in addition.

CASE No. 760/3 and 5 piece
Fitted as above
  but with **Stainless Steel Blades.**

CASE No. 761/3 and 5 piece
Fitted as above
  with **Stainless Steel Blades** and **Stainless Steel Forks.**

CASE No. 663/3 piece
Fitted with
  Best quality Forged Steel Carving Knife with
    "Eye-Witness" Patent Rest.
  Nickel-plated Carving Fork with Patent Guard.
  Two-Wheel Knife Sharpener.
  Best African Grained Ivoride Round Handles.

CASE No. 663/5 piece
Fitted as above
  with one pair of Game Carvers to match in addition.

CASE No. 763/3 and 5 piece
Fitted as above
  but with **Stainless Steel Blades.**

CASE No. 764/3 and 5 piece
Fitted as above
  with **Stainless Steel Blades** and
  Stainless Steel Forks.

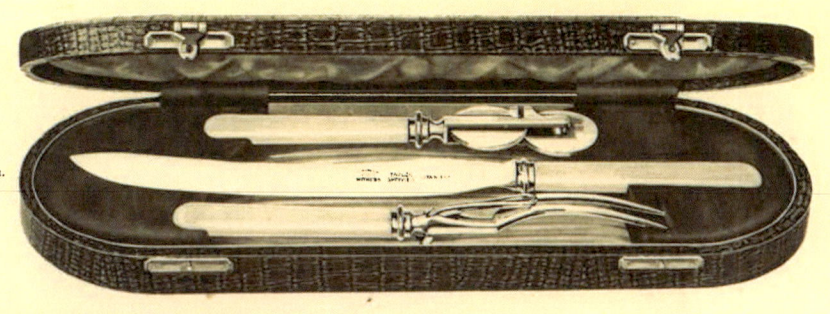

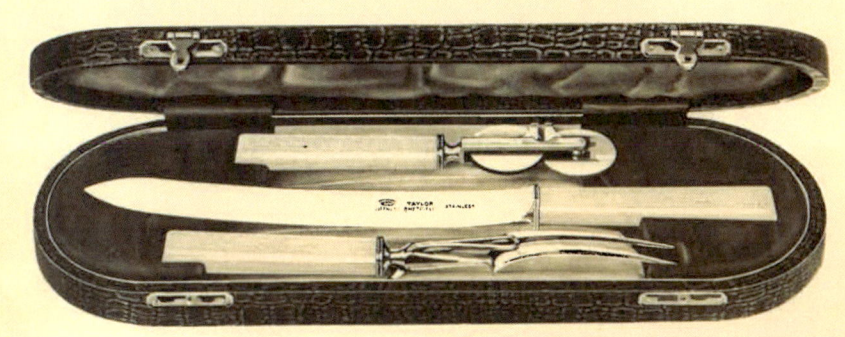

CASE No. 666/3 piece
Fitted with
  Best quality Forged Steel Carving Knife with
    "Eye-Witness" Patent Rest.
  Nickel-plated Carving Fork with Patent Guard.
  Two-Wheel Knife Sharpener.
  Best African Grained Ivoride Square Handles.

CASE No. 666/5 piece
Fitted as above
  with one pair of Game Carvers to match in addition.

CASE No. 766/3 and 5 piece
Fitted as above
  but with **Stainless Steel Blades**

CASE No. 767/3 and 5 piece
Fitted as above
  with **Stainless Steel Blades** and
  Stainless Steel Forks.

CASE No. 670/3 piece
Fitted with
  Best quality Forged Steel Carving Knife with
    "Eye-Witness" Patent Rest.
  Nickel-plated Carving Fork with Patent Guard.
  Forged Sharpening Steel.
  Best African Grained Ivoride Handles—shaped
    to the grip of the Hand.

CASE No. 670/5 piece
Fitted as above
  with one pair of Game Carvers to match in addition.

CASE No. 770/3 and 5 piece
Fitted as above
  but with **Stainless Steel Blades.**

CASE No. 771/3 and 5 piece
Fitted as above
  with **Stainless Steel Blades** and
  Stainless Steel Forks.

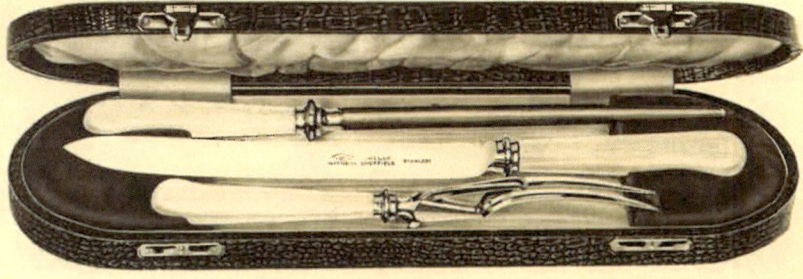

These Illustrations have reduced the size of the actual article approximately to one third

SECTION A
PAGE 46

Taylor's Witness Presentation Cases

IN BLACK AND CROCODILE LEATHERETTE COVERED CASES, LINED WITH CHOICE COLOURED SATIN AND SILK

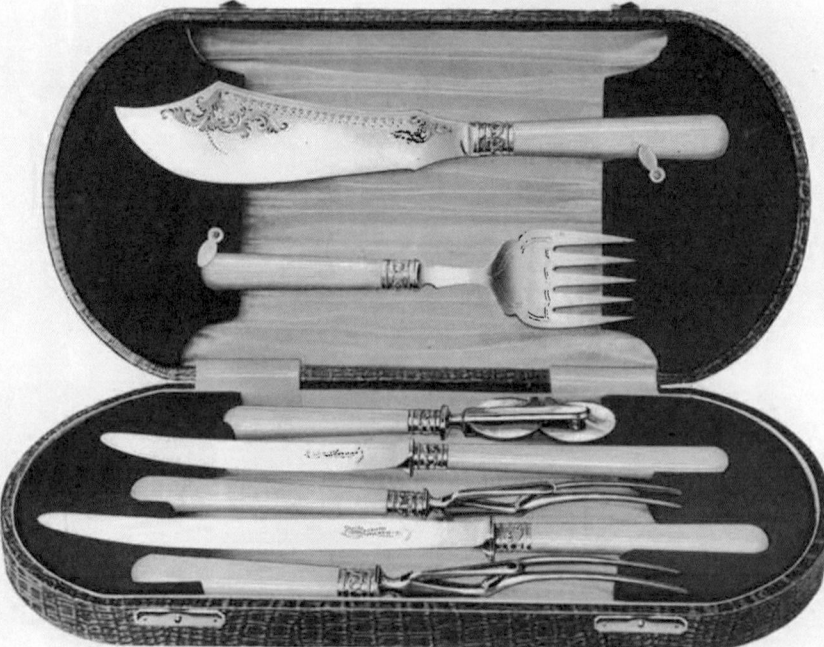

These illustrations have reduced the size of the actual article approximately to one third

CASE No. 775/7 piece
Fitted with
Stainless Steel 9" Meat and Game Carving Knives with "Eye-Witness" Patent Rests.
Nickel-plated Carving Forks with Patent Guards
Two-Wheel Knife Sharpener.
One pair of Silver-plated Fish Carvers.
Best African Grained Ivoride Round Handles mounted with Sterling Silver Ferrules.

CASE No. 775/5 piece
Fitted as above
with one pair of 9" Meat and Game Carving Knives and Forks as above and Two-Wheel Knife Sharpener only.

CASE No. 775/3 piece
Fitted as above
with one pair of 9" Meat Carvers and Two-Wheel Knife Sharpener only

CASE No. 776/3, 5 and 7 piece
Fitted as above
but with **Stainless Steel** Forks.

BREAKFAST CARVERS
CASE No. 790
Fitted with
Stainless Steel Breakfast Carving Knife.
Nickel-plated Carving Fork.
Best African Grained Square Ivoride Handles.

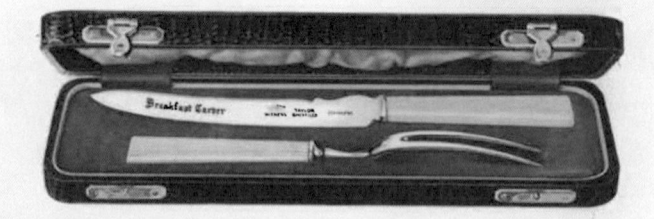

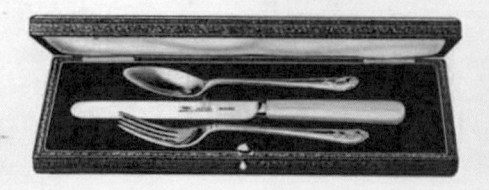

CHILD'S SET
CASE No. 802
Fitted with
Stainless Steel Knife with Best African Grained Ivoride Round Handle and Silver-plated Spoon and Fork.

FISH SERVERS
CASE No. 810
Fitted with
One pair of Fish Carvers with Silver-plated Blades
Best African Grained Ivoride Round Handles.

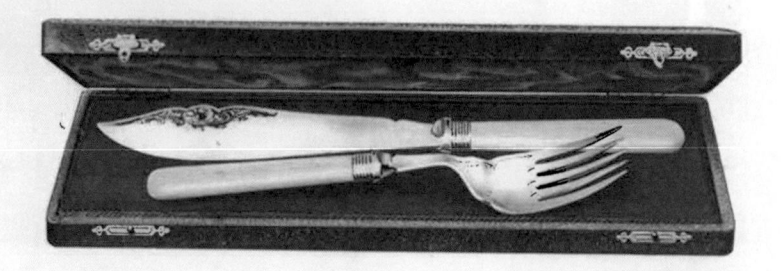

Taylor's Witness Sheffield — Table Cutlery — Scale Tang

SECTION A
PAGE 47

SHELL BOLSTER.   **SOLID BOLSTER.**

3201	3202	3222	3223	3224	3225	3243	3244	3220	3278	3272
EBONY.	BONE.	EBONY.	BONE.	EBONY.	BONE.	EBONY.	BONE.	BLACK BUFFALO.	BONE.	FORBUCK.

SECTION A
PAGE 48

Table Cutlery

TAYLOR'S WITNESS SHEFFIELD

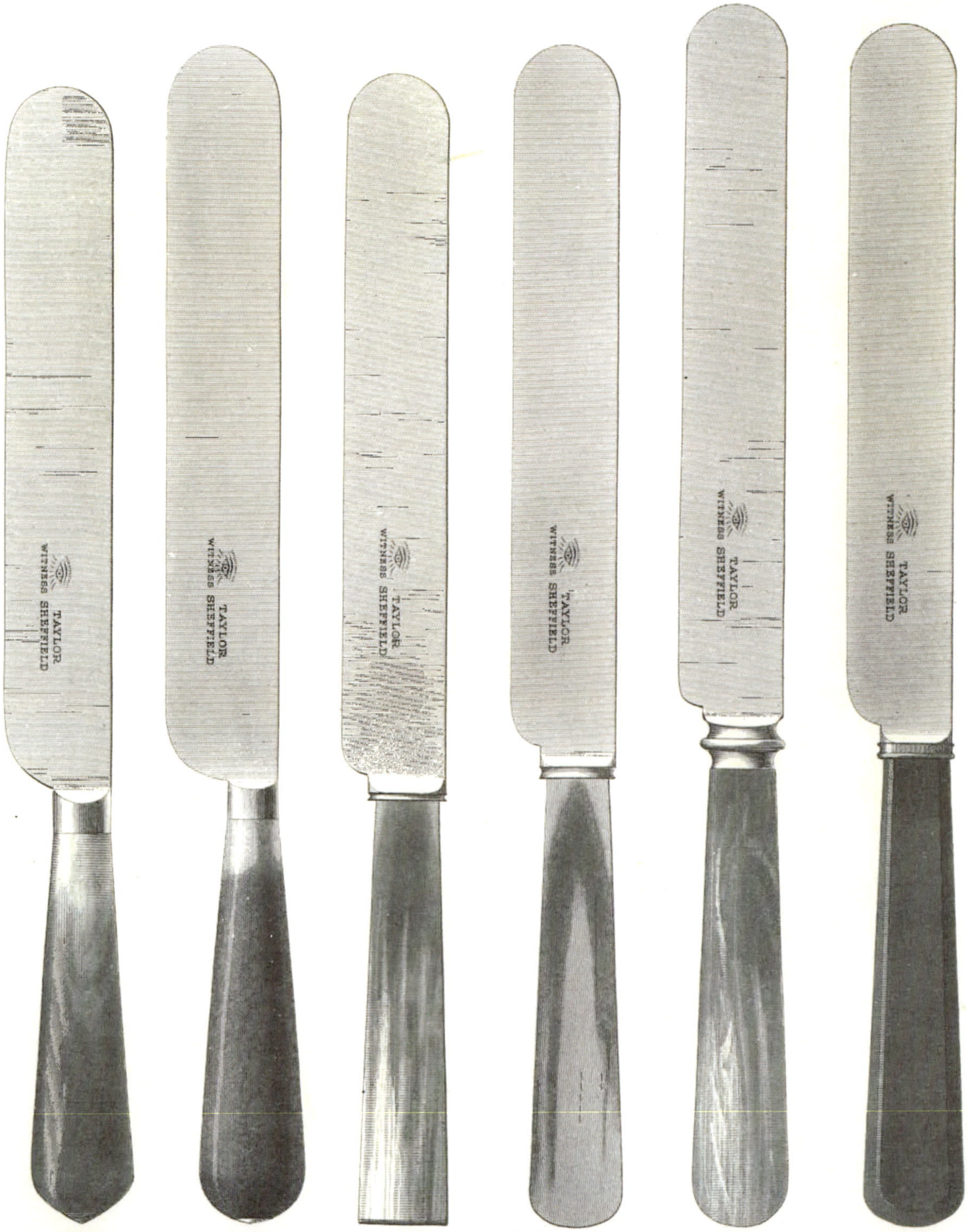

| 8725 | 8729 | 8704 | 8713 | 8705 | 8711 | 8678 |
| BUFFALO. | BUFFALO. | BUFFALO. | BUFFALO. | HAS SHAPE HANDLE, AS 8704 | BUFFALO. | BUFFALO. |

Taylor's Witness-Sheffield

SECTION A
PAGE 49

Table Cutlery

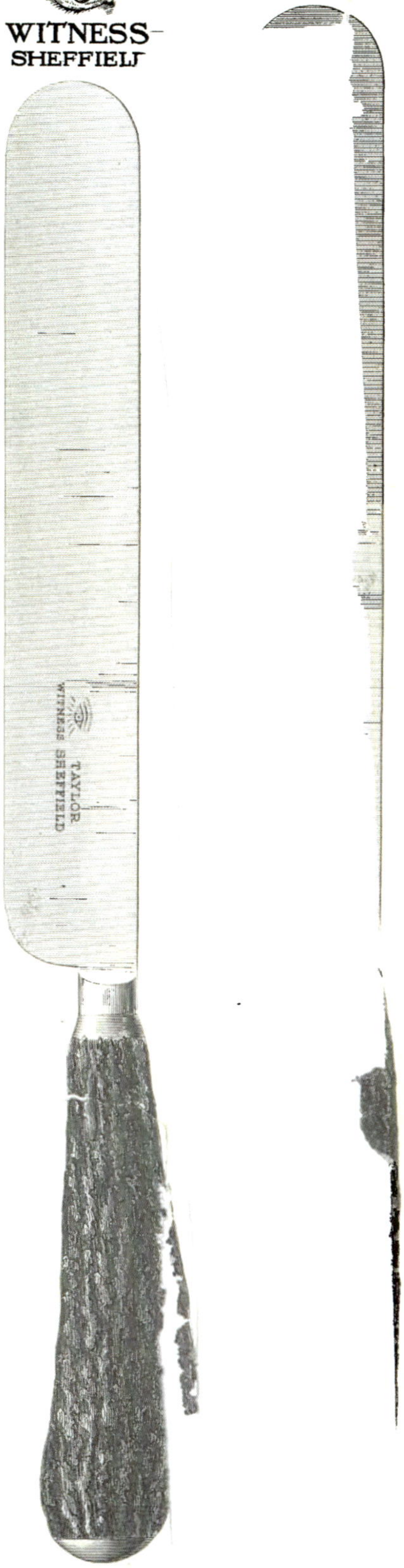

| 8767 STAG. | 8765 STAG, IS CHEAPER FINISH. | 8626 BEST HARD WHITE BONE. | 8648 BEST HARD WHITE BONE. | 8619 BEST HARD WHITE BONE. |

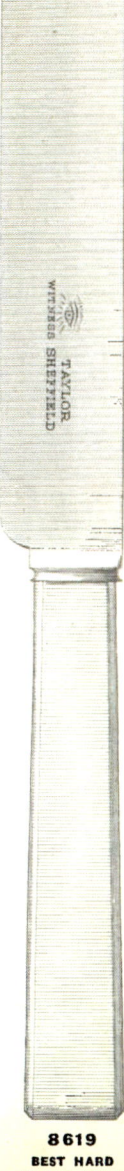

SECTION A
PAGE 50

Butchers' Knives

Taylor's WITNESS SHEFFIELD

THICK-BACK FISH CHOPPING KNIFE.

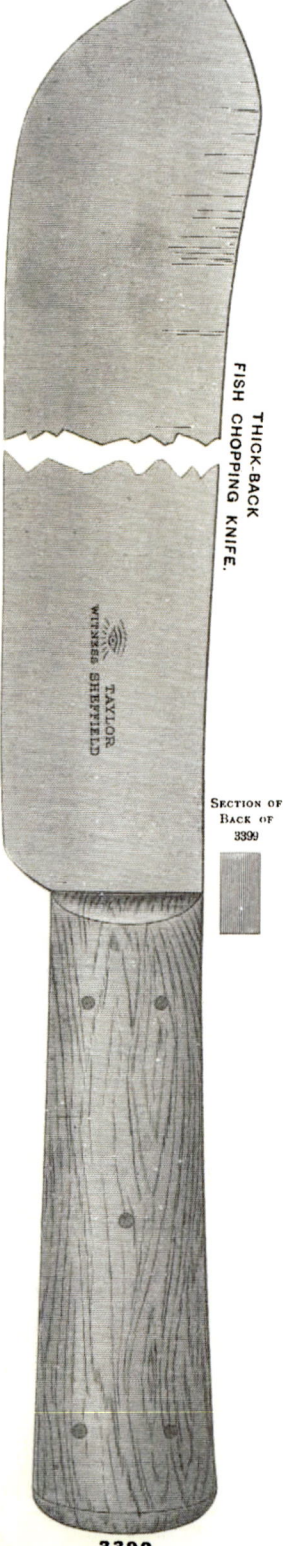

SECTION OF BACK OF 3399

3399
10 in. to 14 in.
FISH CHOPPING.
BEECH AND LEATHER.
5 Iron Pins.

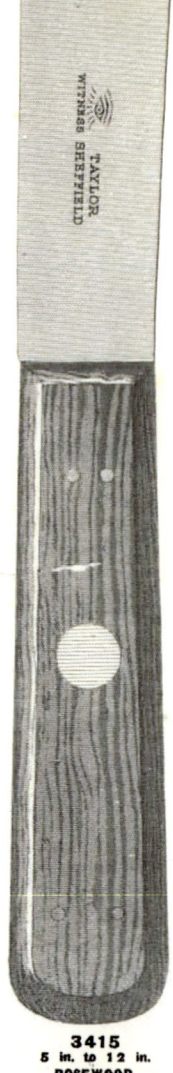

3403
5 in. to 12 in.
BEECH.
3 Iron Pins.
2nd Quality is 3400

3404
5 in. to 12 in.
BEECH.
5 Iron Pins.

3415
5 in. to 12 in.
ROSEWOOD.
4 Brass Pins and Screw.
3414 Do. Narrower Blade.

TAYLOR'S WITNESS SHEFFIELD

Butchers' Knives

SECTION A
PAGE 51

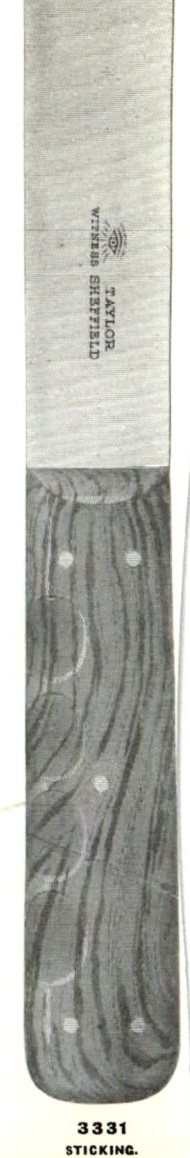

3430 SG
ROSEWOOD.

7089 SG
ROSEWOOD.

3482
ROSEWOOD.

THE "SAFETY GRIP" HANDLE.

Insures perfect hold, non-slip and comfort in use.

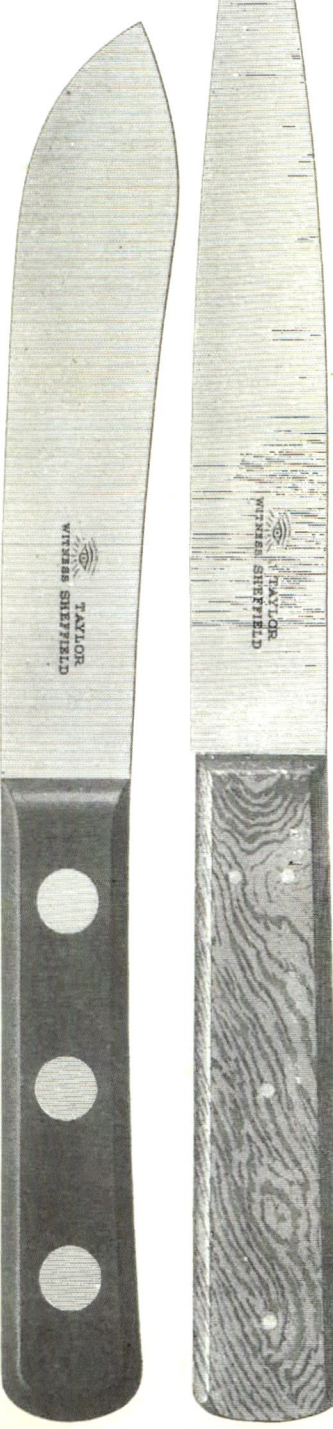

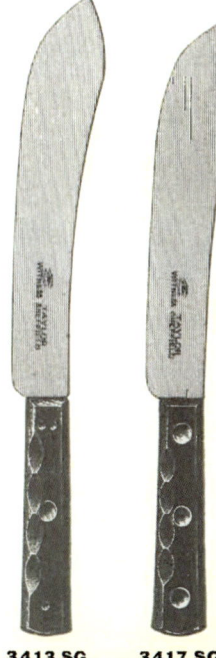

3417
5 in. to 12 in.
WORKING.
EBONY.
3 Brass Screws.

3430
5 in. to 7 in.
STICKING.
ROSEWOOD.
5 Iron Pins.

3433
5 in. to 12 in.
SPEAR.
ROSEWOOD.
4 Brass Pins and Screw.

3331
STICKING.
5 in. to 12 in.
ROSEWOOD.
5 Iron Pins.

3413 SG
ROSEWOOD.

3417 SG
EBONY.

SECTION A
PAGE 52

Butchers' Knives

Taylor's
WITNESS
SHEFFIELD

3382
BEECH.

7091
BEECH.

THE "SAFETY GRIP" HANDLE.

Insures perfect hold, non-slip and comfort in use.

3502
BONING.
5 in. to 6 in.
BEECH.
5 Iron Pins.

3332
BONING.
5 in. to 7 in.
ROSEWOOD.
5 Iron Pins.

3330
BONING.
5 in. to 7 in.
EBONY.
4 Brass Pins and Screw.

7090 SG
ROSEWOOD.

7088 SG
ROSEWOOD.

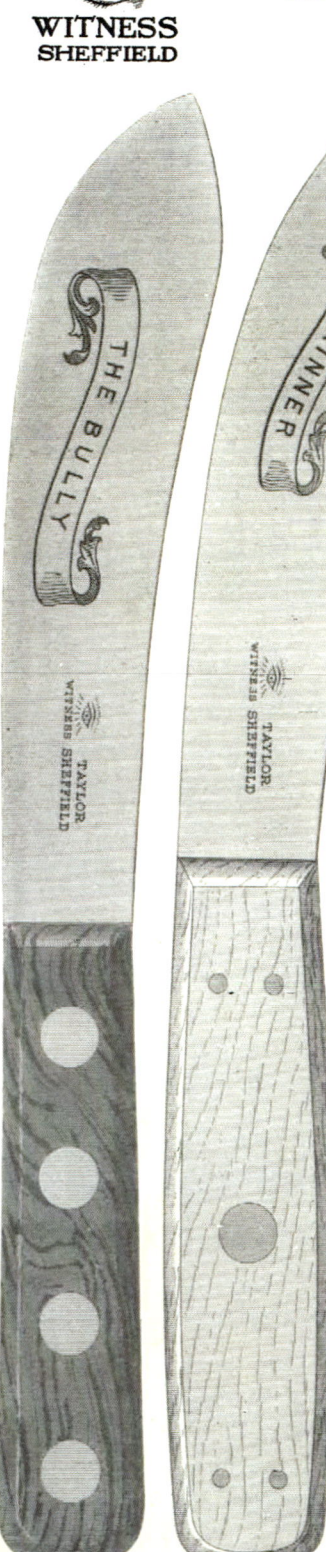

Taylor's Witness Sheffield — Butchers' Knives

SECTION A
PAGE 53

3467	3333	3425	3423	3443
5 in. to 12 in.	SKINNING.	5 in. to 7 in.	4¼ in.	10 in. to 12 in.
ROSEWOOD.	6 in. to 7 in.	SKINNING.	SKINNING.	EBONY.
4 Brass Screws.	BEECH.	ROSEWOOD.	BEECH.	BRASS BOLSTER.
	4 Brass Pins and Screw.	4 Brass Pins and Screw.	5 Iron Pins.	4 Brass Pins and Screw.

SECTION A
PAGE 54

Cooks' Knives, Slicers, &c.

Taylors WITNESS SHEFFIELD

3453	3456	3460	3461	3480	3481
COOKS'.	COOKS'.	HAM or BEEF.	SLICER.	PROVISION.	PROVISION.
5 in. to 12 in.	5 in. to 12 in.	10 in. to 16 in.	10 in. to 12 in.	6 in. to 12 in.	6 in. to 12 in.
BLACK.	EBONY.	ROSEWOOD.	EBONY.	ROSEWOOD.	EBONY.
Through Tang	3 Iron Pins.	¼ in. Narrower, 3459		3 Brass Pins and Screw.	4 Brass Pins and Screw.

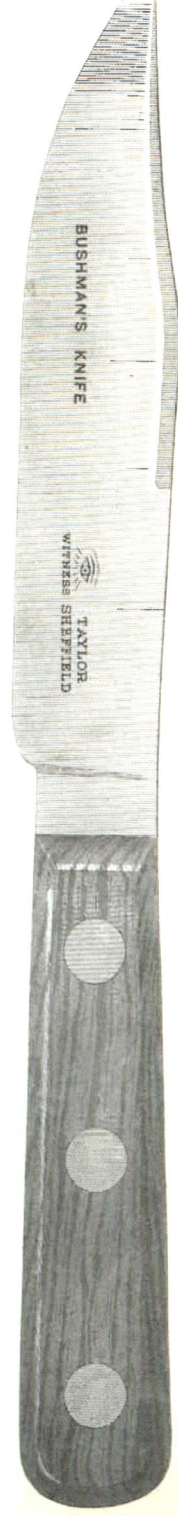

TAYLOR'S WITNESS SHEFFIELD

Sheath Knives

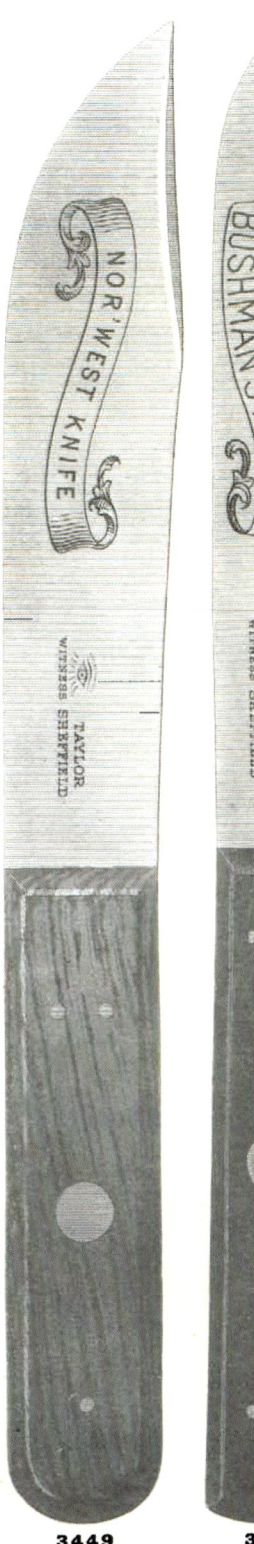

SECTION A
PAGE 55

3449	3486	3450	3444	3476	3235
5 in. to 6 in.	5 in. to 6 in.	5 in. to 6 in.	5 in. to 6 in.	5½ in.	5 in. to 6½ in.
ROSEWOOD.	EBONY.	ROSEWOOD.	EBONY.	EBONY.	ROSEWOOD.

SECTION A
PAGE 56

Butcher and Sheath Knives
COMMON QUALITY FOR THE NATIVE TRADE.

Needham, Veall & Tyzack Ltd
WITNESS
SHEFFIELD

9280	9289	9281	9282	9284	9252
4½ in. to 12 in.	4½ in. to 12 in.	4½ in. to 12 in.	4½ in. to 10 in.	4½ in. to 10 in.	5 in. to 6 in.
BEECH.	REDWOOD.	ROSE or EBONY.	ROSE, EBONY or BEECH.	EBONY.	REDWOOD.
CLIP POINT.		Brass Screws.	Brass Screws.	Brass Screws and Eye.	Iron Screws.

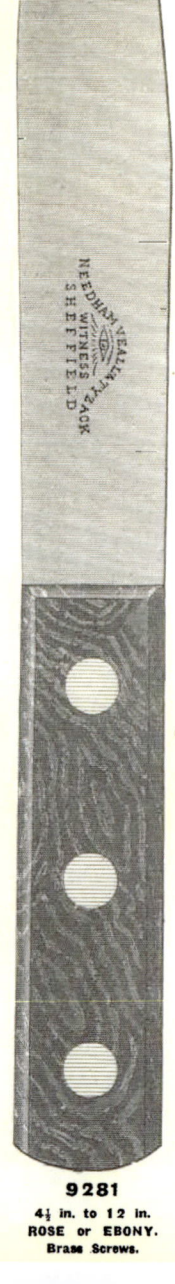

TAYLOR'S WITNESS SHEFFIELD

Rabbiters' Sets & Sheaths

SECTION A
PAGE 57

3470
STEEL.

LEATHER SHEATH.
With Two Loops.
Copper Rivets.
Used for the Four Patterns
Illustrated hereon.

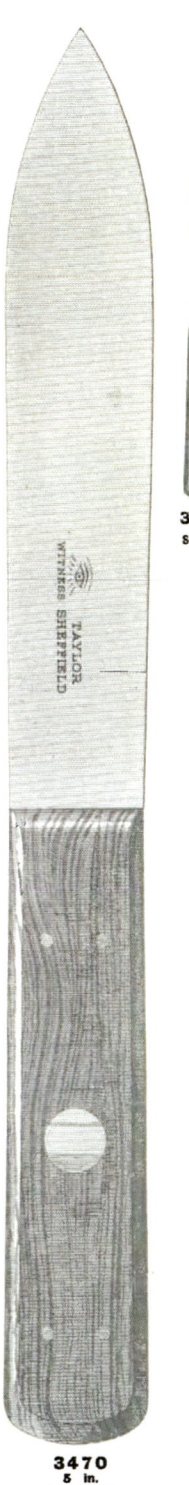

3470
5 in.
ROSEWOOD.

3472
ALL STEEL.

3472
5½ in.
EBONY.

3474
5 in.
ROSEWOOD.
Steel Handled to Match.

3478
STAG.
Steel Handled to Match.

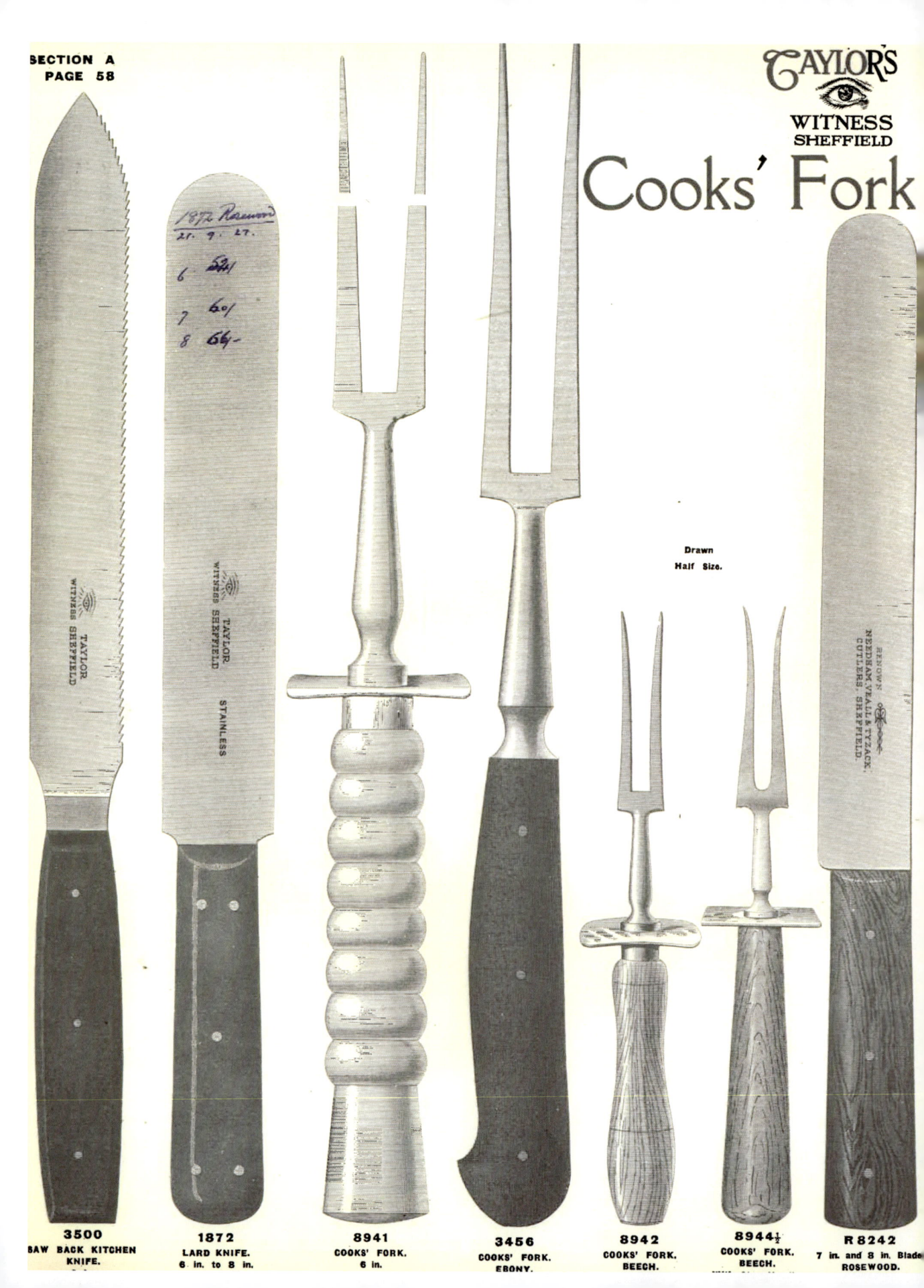

SECTION A
PAGE 58

Taylor's
WITNESS SHEFFIELD
Cooks' Fork

Drawn Half Size.

3500	1872	8941	3456	8942	8944½	R 8242
SAW BACK KITCHEN KNIFE.	LARD KNIFE. 6 in. to 8 in.	COOKS' FORK. 6 in.	COOKS' FORK. EBONY.	COOKS' FORK. BEECH.	COOKS' FORK. BEECH.	7 in. and 8 in. Blade. ROSEWOOD.

Taylor's Witness Sheffield

Butchers' Steels

SECTION A
PAGE 59

9013	9016	8770R	9006	9005	8995
IRON SWIVEL. BRASS GUARD. 10 in. to 13 in. REDWOOD.	IRON SWIVEL. BRASS GUARD. 10 in. to 13 in. REINDEER.	IRON SWIVEL. 9 in. to 12 in. STAG.	IRON SWIVEL. BRASS GUARD. 10 in. to 13 in. BUFFALO.	IRON SWIVEL. BRASS GUARD. 10 in. to 13 in. BUFFALO.	KITCHEN STEEL. 8 in. and 9 in. POLISHED BEECH.

SECTION A
PAGE 60

Butchers' Steels

**TAYLOR'S
WITNESS
SHEFFIELD**

9003	9019	9051	9011 9012	9017	9022
IRON SWIVEL. BRASS GUARD. 10 in. to 13 in. STAG.	IRON SWIVEL. 10 in. to 13 in. BUFFALO.	All Brass Fittings. 10 in. to 13 in. COCOWOOD.	BRASS SWIVEL. BRASS GUARD. 10 in. to 13 in. ROSEWOOD. BUFFALO.	All Brass Fittings. BRASS GUARD. 10 in. to 13 in. EBONY.	IRON SWIVEL. 10 in. to 13 in. INLAID EBONY.

9053
IRON SWIVEL.
10 in. to 13 in.
INLAID REDWOOD.

SECTION A
PAGE 61

Pruning or Linoleum Knife

**THE REGISTERED No. 522152
RENEWABLE BLADE
LINOLEUM or PRUNING KNIFE.**

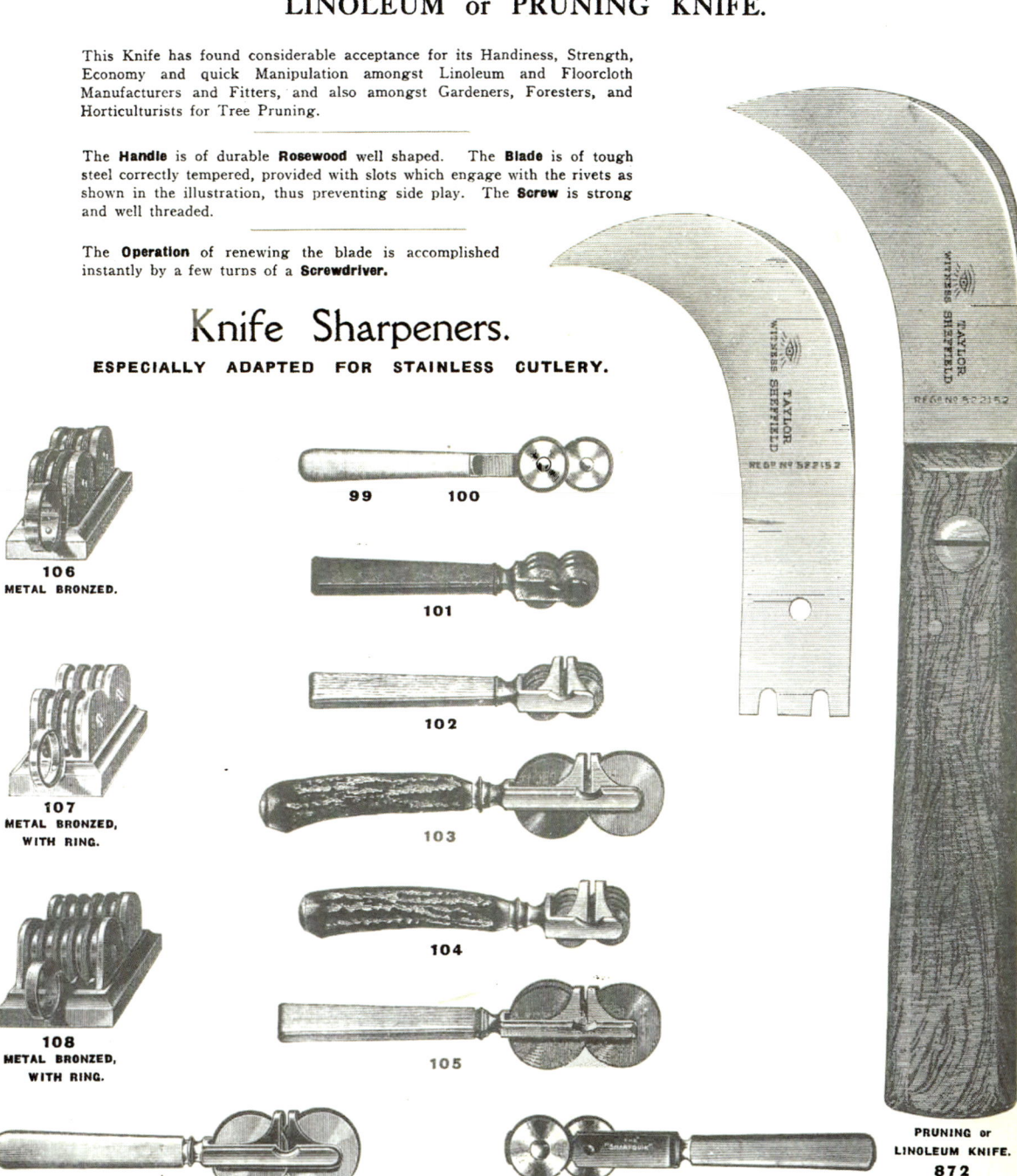

This Knife has found considerable acceptance for its Handiness, Strength, Economy and quick Manipulation amongst Linoleum and Floorcloth Manufacturers and Fitters, and also amongst Gardeners, Foresters, and Horticulturists for Tree Pruning.

The **Handle** is of durable **Rosewood** well shaped. The **Blade** is of tough steel correctly tempered, provided with slots which engage with the rivets as shown in the illustration, thus preventing side play. The **Screw** is strong and well threaded.

The **Operation** of renewing the blade is accomplished instantly by a few turns of a **Screwdriver**.

Knife Sharpeners.

ESPECIALLY ADAPTED FOR STAINLESS CUTLERY.

106 METAL BRONZED.

107 METAL BRONZED, WITH RING.

108 METAL BRONZED, WITH RING.

99   100

101

102

103

104

105

109

THE "SHARPQUIK."

THE "TWIN WHEEL."

PRUNING or LINOLEUM KNIFE.
872

SECTION A
PAGE 62

Pruning, Hop and Linoleum Knives

TAYLOR'S
WITNESS
SHEFFIELD

8976	8977	8925	875	8920	8924
BEECH.	BEECH.	4 in. BEECH.	BEECH.	4 in. and 4½ in. BEECH.	4 in. and 4½ in. BEECH.

TAYLOR'S WITNESS SHEFFIELD

SECTION A
PAGE 63

Putty and Painters' Knives

IN CLIP POINT
As 8901 is 8886

IN SQUARE POINT
As 8909 is 8908

IN CLIP POINT
As 8901 is 8897

IN SPEAR POINT
As 8895 is 8905

WITH CLIP, SPEAR, SQUARE OR SKEW POINT.

8885
SPEAR POINT.
3½ in., 4 in. and 4½ in.
COCOWOOD.

8895
SPEAR POINT.
IRON FERRULE.
4 in., 4½ in. and 5 in.
EBONY.

8900
CLIP POINT.
4 in., 4½ in. and 5 in.
EBONY.

8901
CLIP POINT.
4½ in.
COCOWOOD.

8909
SQUARE POINT.
IRON FERRULE.
4 in., 4½ in. and 5 in.
EBONY.

SECTION A
PAGE 64

Painters' Knives

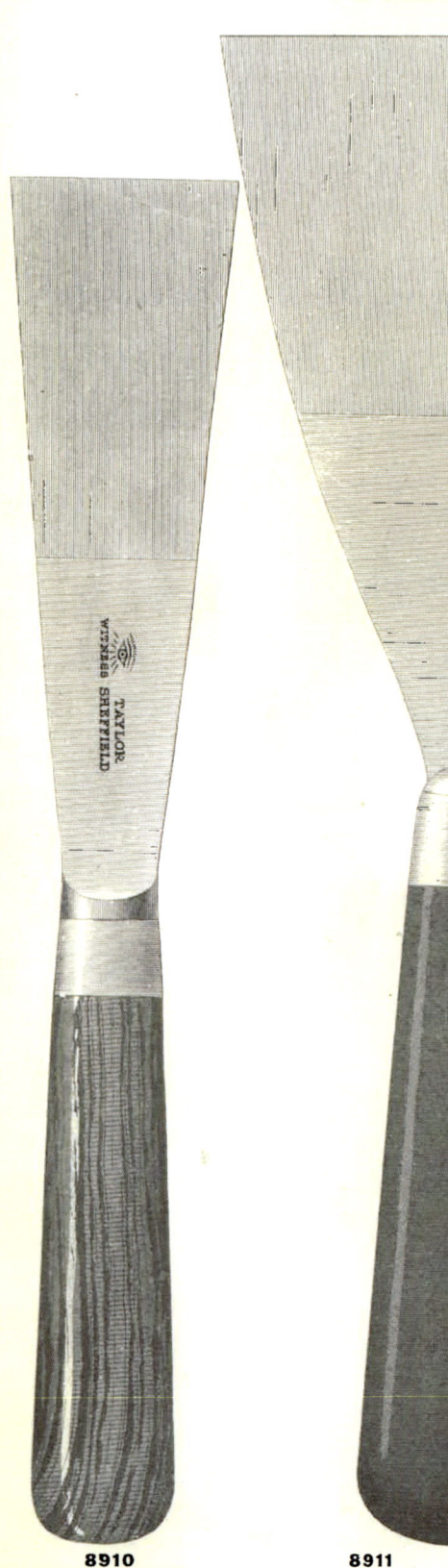

TAYLOR'S
WITNESS
SHEFFIELD

8910
BRASS FERRULE.
4 in., 4½ in., and 5 in.
COCOWOOD.

8911
5½ in.
2 in. to 4 in.
EBONY.

8912½
WITH SKEW BLADE.
IRON FERRULE.
4½ in.
REDWOOD.

8916
GLAZIERS' HACK KNIFE.
4 in.
3 Iron Rivets.
FIBRE.

8928 {SCALE TANG HANDLE is 8928½}
PALLETTE.
5 in. to 12 in.

8898
SQUARE POINT.
BEECH.
2 in., 2½ in., 3 in.

TAYLOR'S WITNESS SHEFFIELD

Oyster Knives

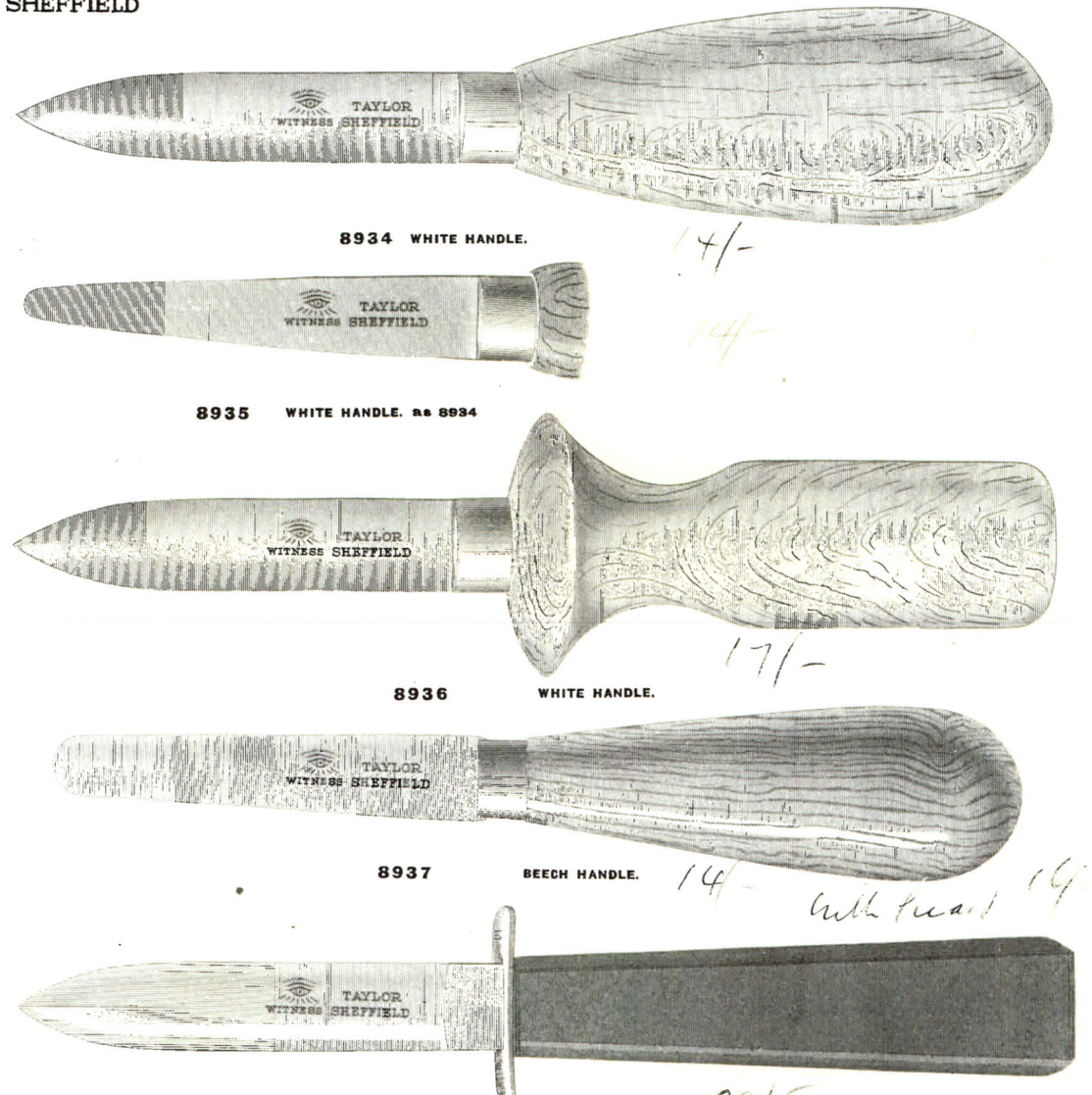

SECTION A
PAGE 65

8934 WHITE HANDLE. 14/-

8935 WHITE HANDLE. as 8934 14/-

8936 WHITE HANDLE. 17/-

8937 BEECH HANDLE. 14/- with guard 16/-

8950 TIP HANDLE. 30/-

Farrier's Knife
SINGLE OR DOUBLE EDGE.

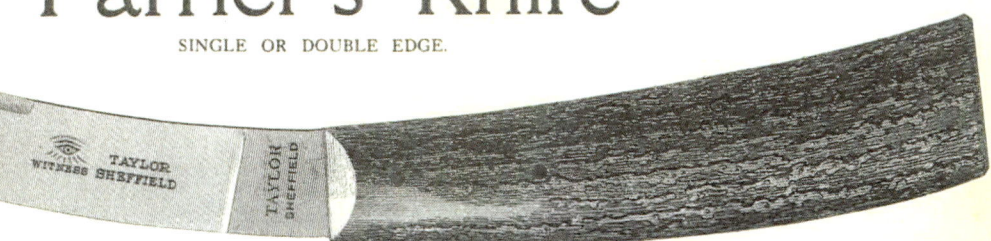

Sizes, SEARCHER, ¼ in., ⅜ in., ½ in.
HANDLE, REINDEER.

27/-

SECTION A
PAGE 66

Vegetable and Grape Fruit Knives

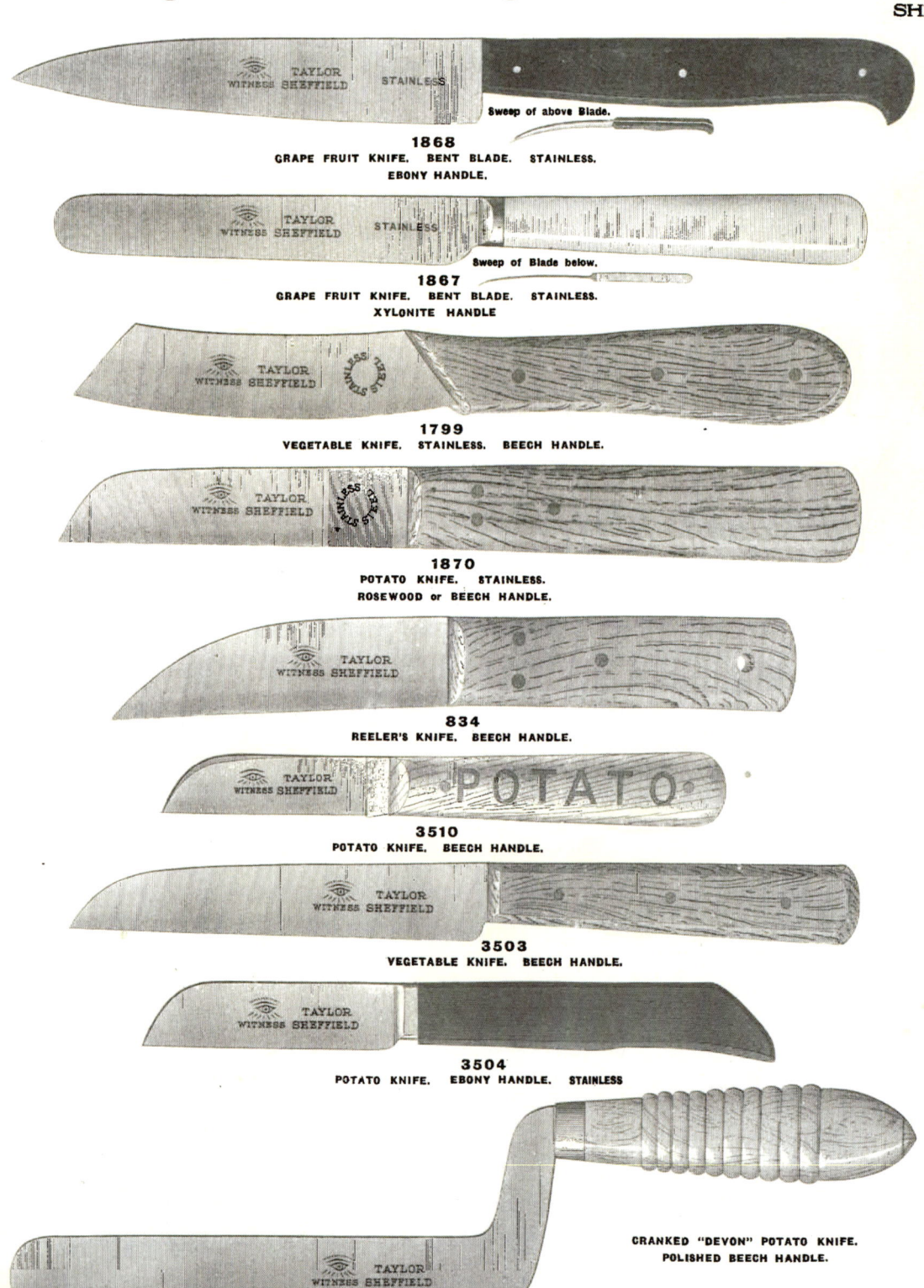

TAYLOR'S WITNESS SHEFFIELD

1868
GRAPE FRUIT KNIFE. BENT BLADE. STAINLESS.
EBONY HANDLE.

Sweep of above Blade.

1867
GRAPE FRUIT KNIFE. BENT BLADE. STAINLESS.
XYLONITE HANDLE

Sweep of Blade below.

1799
VEGETABLE KNIFE. STAINLESS. BEECH HANDLE.

1870
POTATO KNIFE. STAINLESS.
ROSEWOOD or BEECH HANDLE.

834
REELER'S KNIFE. BEECH HANDLE.

3510
POTATO KNIFE. BEECH HANDLE.

3503
VEGETABLE KNIFE. BEECH HANDLE.

3504
POTATO KNIFE. EBONY HANDLE. STAINLESS

CRANKED "DEVON" POTATO KNIFE.
POLISHED BEECH HANDLE.

SECTION A
PAGE 67

Taylor's Witness Sheffield
Shoemakers', Mill, & Kitchen Knives

8929
BEECH HANDLE.

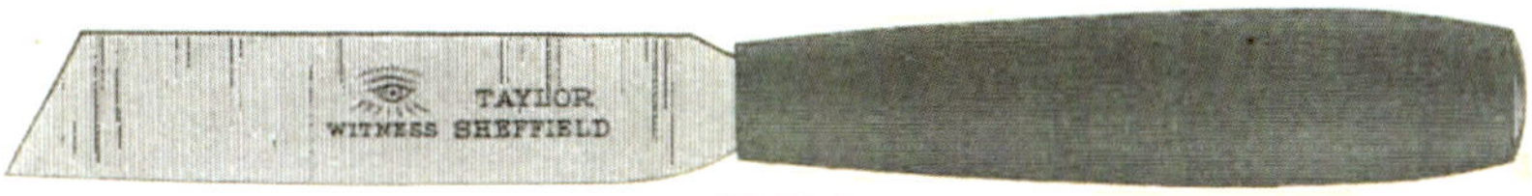

8930 B
WITH WHITE HANDLE, 8930

8930½

8931
WHITE HANDLE.

C 8931½
ROSEWOOD HANDLE.

8953
MILL KNIFE. BEECH HANDLE.

3457
KITCHEN KNIFE.

3451
KITCHEN KNIFE.

SECTION A
PAGE 68

Taylor's
WITNESS
SHEFFIELD
ENGLAND

Latest Cutlery Gadgets

IMPROVED
PAINTER'S SCRAPER
Registered No. 718818

The Painter's Boon, a Practical Tool.

No more burnt hands from the flare of the Lamp.

The Guard keeps the hands clean and free from hot paint sliding down.

The Scraper has good square corners to go well into the crevices of mouldings and panels.

BLADES 4½ in. long by 1¼ in. 2 in. 3 in. wide.

The CUT & CHOP KNIFE
Registered No. 238406

BLADE 9 in. long, 3 in. wide.   BEECH HANDLE, 5 in. long.

THE ADVANTAGES of this new Registered Implement leap to the eye. For Steak and Chop Cutting, Fish Dressing and for Kitchen use, especially in Hotels and Restaurants, the saving of time and particular handiness of having a tool equal to slicing the meat and chopping the bone, will commend itself to every Butcher, Provision Dealer, Fishmonger, Chef, and Cook.

MADE of Fine Sheffield Steel and with the "EYEWITNESS" Guarantee of Perfection this is a distinctly helpful article.

The "EYEJEENIC" BUTCHER KNIFE

Will shortly be put on the Market as a necessary item towards the distribution of clean food.

THE HANDLE is so applied that no steel comes near its surface and it consequently offers the minimum of crevices for the accumulation of deleterious germs and other matter.

ALL "EYEWITNESS" GOODS ARE GUARANTEED PERFECT.

The "PEP" CORK LIFTER PENKNIFE
Registration Applied for

THE HANDLE, which is of Nickel and in one piece, is formed at the tail into a solid and efficient Crown Cork Lifter, Handy, Useful, and an unobtrusive Pocket Companion.

It is particularly adapted for an Advertising Line with the Name of the Donor stamped in the Handle.

MADE ONLY AT TAYLOR'S "EYEWITNESS" CUTLERY & PLATE WORKS, SHEFFIELD, ENGLAND.

Taylor's Witness Sheffield.

SECTION A
PAGE 69

E.P. Fish Eaters and Carvers.

970 E.P.N.S. Xylonite. Silver Ferrule.

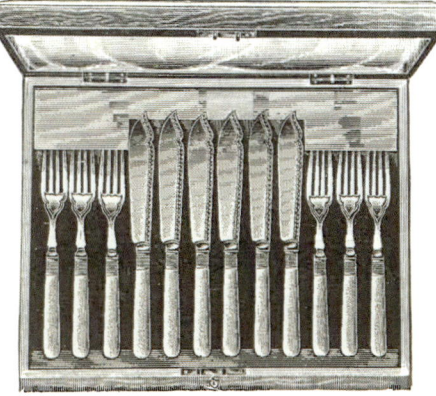

966 E.P.N.S. Grained Xylonite.

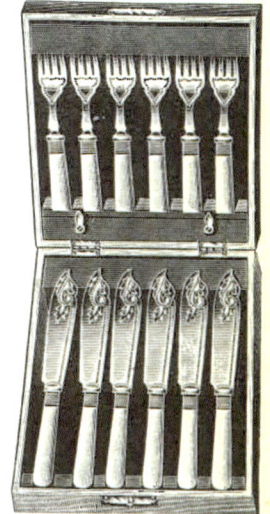

930 E.P.N.S. Grained Xylonite.

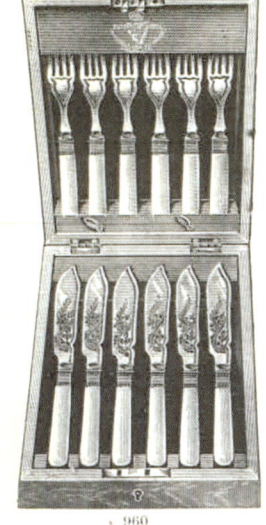

960 E.P.N.S. Grained Xylonite.

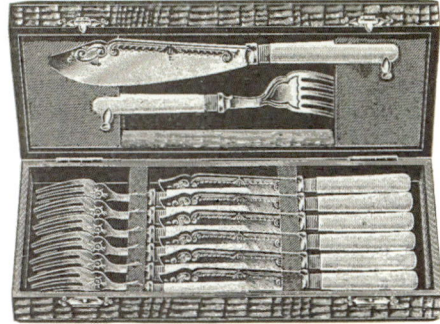

965 E.P.N.S. Grained Xylonite.

969 E.P.N.S. Xylonite Handles.

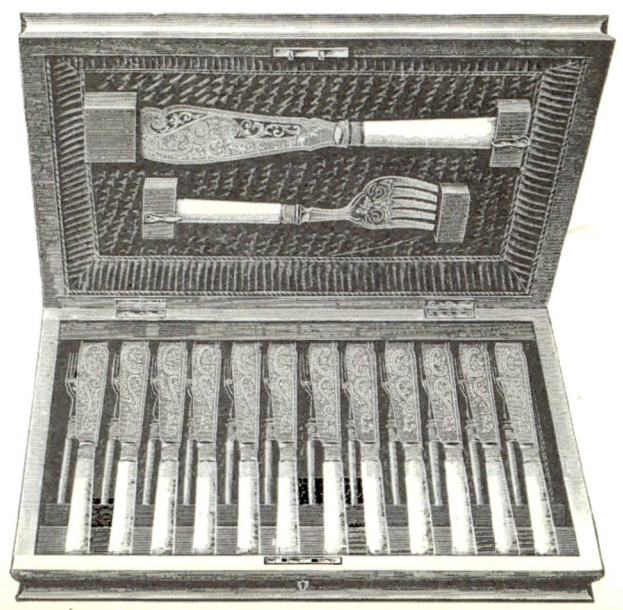

903 E.P.N.S. Xylonite.

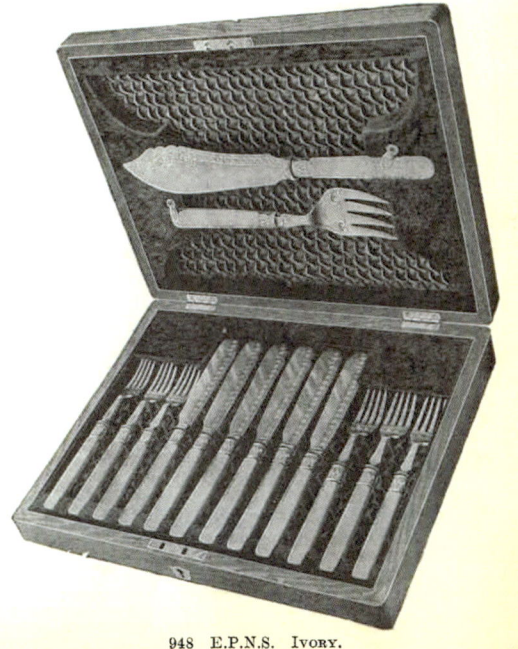

948 E.P.N.S. Ivory.

SECTION A
PAGE 70

Taylor's WITNESS SHEFFIELD.

E.P. Afternoon Tea Spoons.

CLAW SUGAR TONGS. 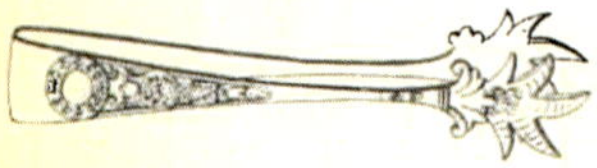
263

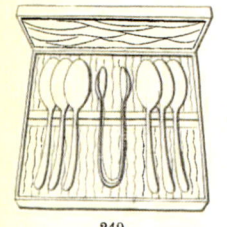

CLAW SUGAR TONGS.
264

249
CASE OF SIX SPOONS AND TONGS.

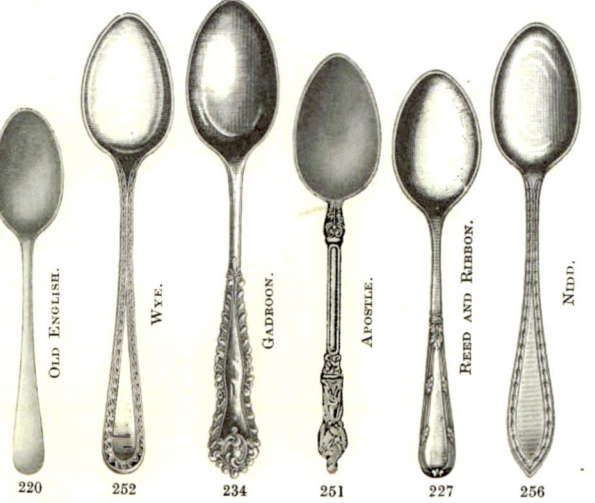

220 Old English.
252 Wye.
234 Gadroon.
251 Apostle.
227 Reed and Ribbon.
256 Ndd.

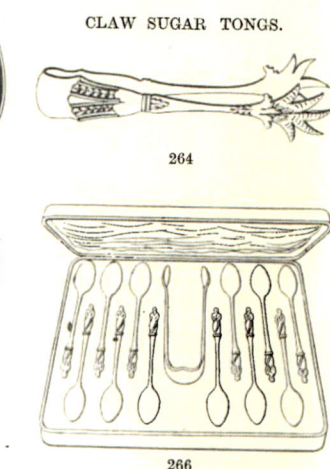

266
CASE OF TWELVE SPOONS AND TONGS.

Fish Eaters and Carvers.

837	913	911	960	989	967	956	972	915	909	947
CAKE FORK. E.P.N.S. NEW LUSTRE.	E.P.N.S. STAINLESS STEEL.	E.P.N.S. XYLONITE.	E.P.N.S. GRAINED XYLONITE.	E.P.N.S. GRAINED XYLONITE.	E.P.N.S. GRAINED XYLONITE.	E.P.N.S. GRAINED XYLONITE.	E.P.N.S. GRAINED XYLONITE.	E.P.N.S. NEW LUSTRE.	E.P.N.S.	E.P.N.S. SOLID HANDLE.

SECTION A
PAGE 71

Taylor's WITNESS SHEFFIELD. E.P. Fruit Knives and Forks.

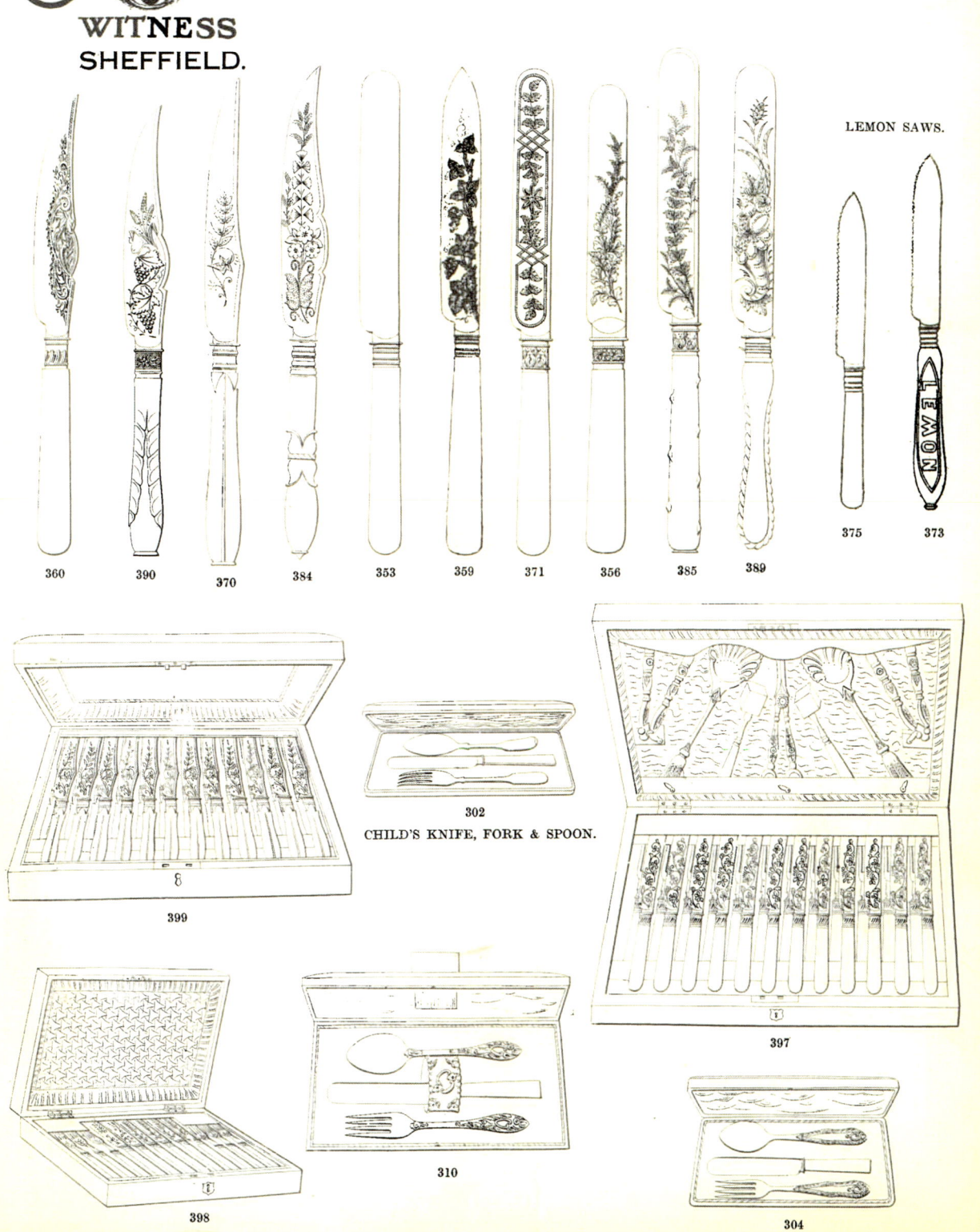

LEMON SAWS.

360   390   370   384   353   359   371   356   385   389   375   373

399

302
CHILD'S KNIFE, FORK & SPOON.

397

398   310   304

SECTION A
PAGE 72

Taylor's WITNESS SHEFFIELD. Electro-plated Butter Knives.

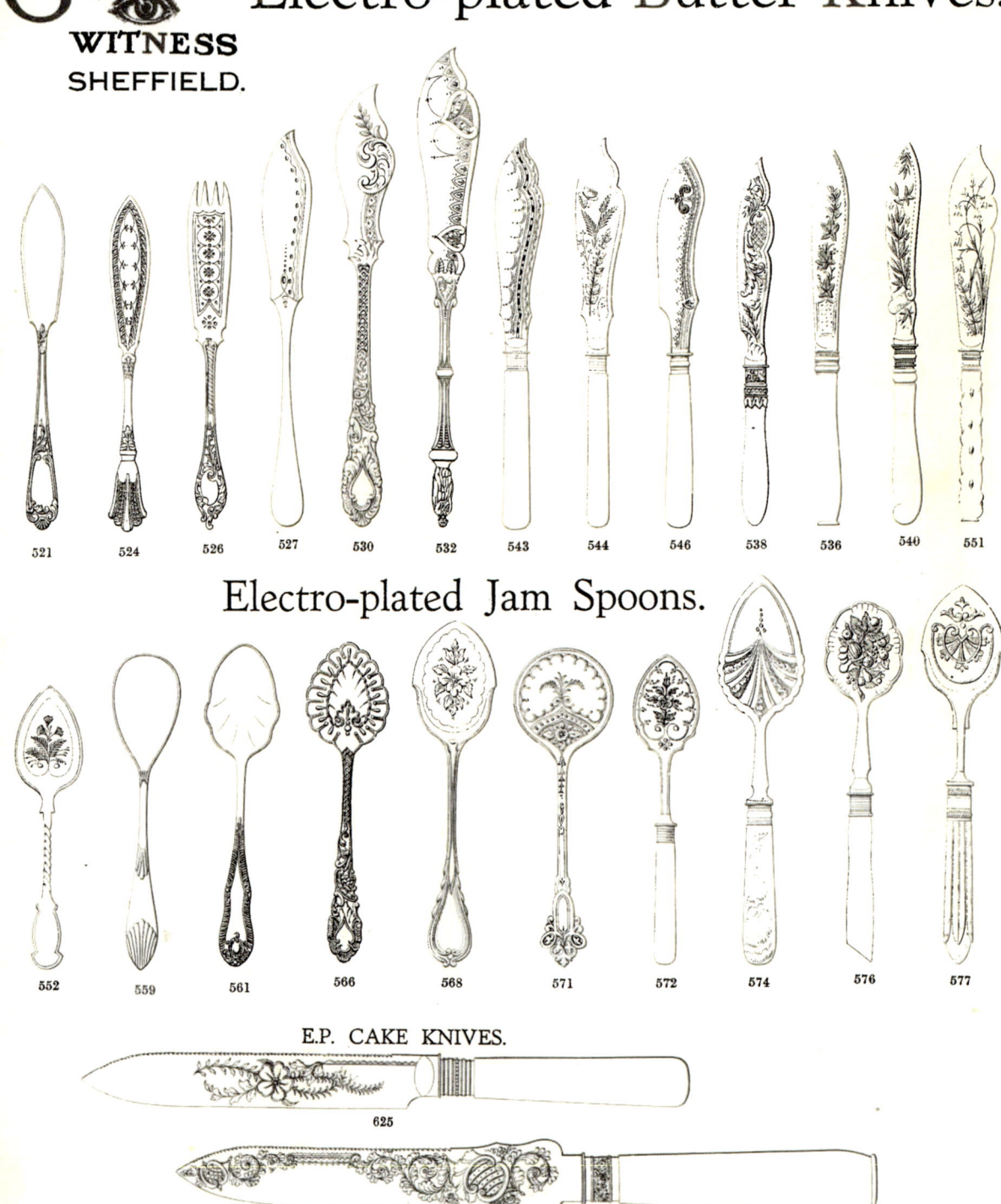

| 521 | 524 | 526 | 527 | 530 | 532 | 543 | 544 | 546 | 538 | 536 | 540 | 551 |

Electro-plated Jam Spoons.

| 552 | 559 | 561 | 566 | 568 | 571 | 572 | 574 | 576 | 577 |

E.P. CAKE KNIVES.

625

623

621

SECTION A
PAGE 73

Taylor's Electro-plated Pickle Forks.
WITNESS SHEFFIELD.

E.P. SARDINE SERVERS.

596

593

592

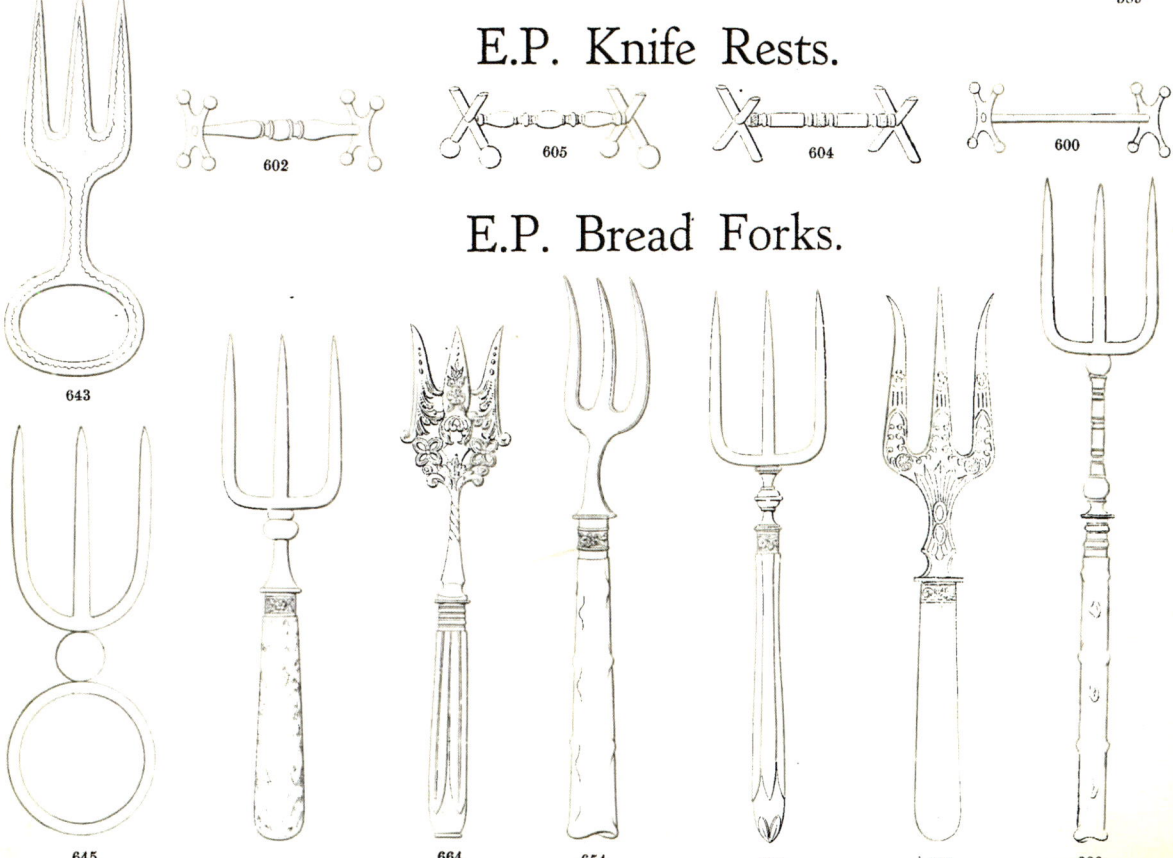

578   579   582   581   583   587   588   589

E.P. Knife Rests.

602   605   604   600

E.P. Bread Forks.

643

645   655   664   654   659   657   666

SECTION A
PAGE 74

Taylor's Witness Sheffield. Electro-plated Sugar Sifters.

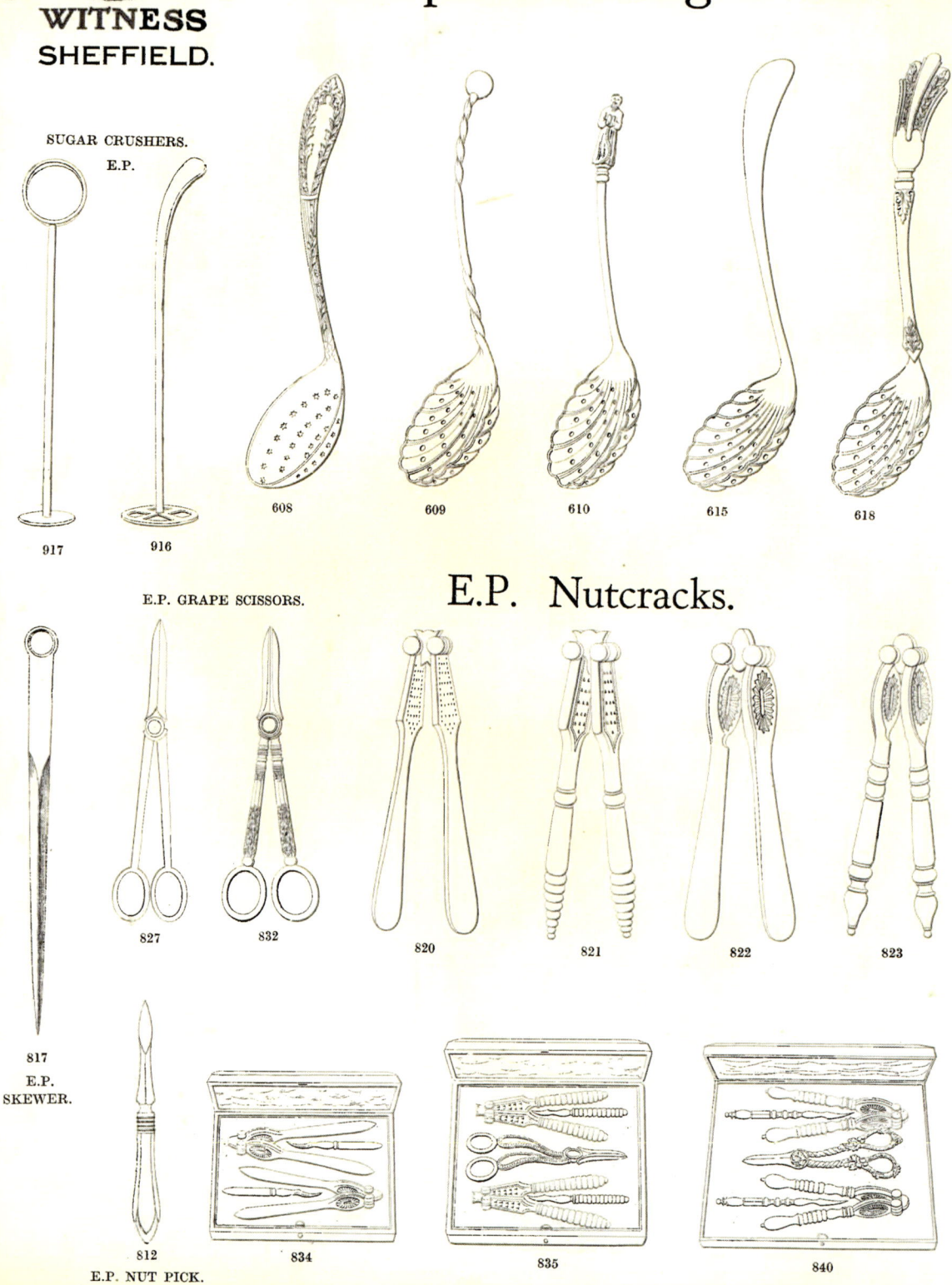

SUGAR CRUSHERS.
E.P.

917   916   608   609   610   615   618

E.P. GRAPE SCISSORS.

E.P. Nutcracks.

827   832   820   821   822   823

817
E.P. SKEWER.

812
E.P. NUT PICK.

834   835   840

Taylor's Witness Sheffield — Combination Cases of E.P.

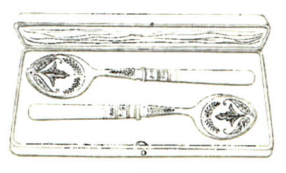

SECTION A
PAGE 75

E.P. BREAD KNIFE & FORK.

626, 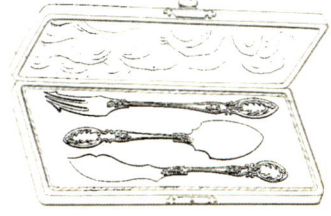 632, 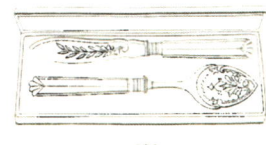 628, 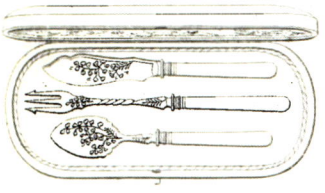 631, 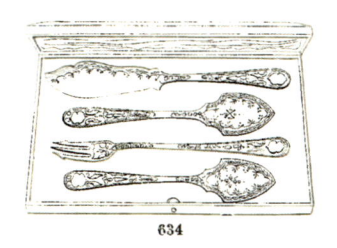 634, 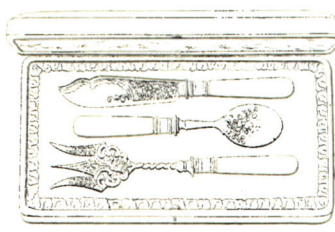 629, 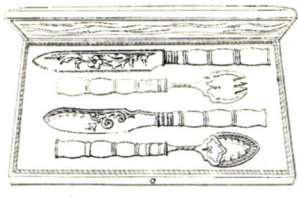 640, 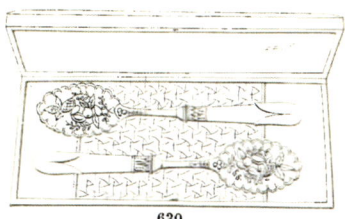 630, 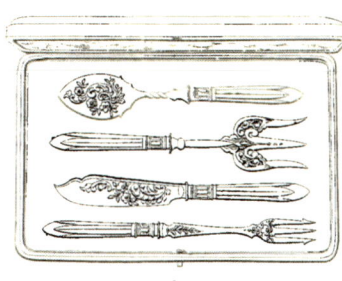 641, 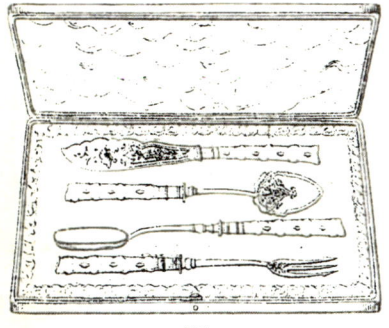 636, 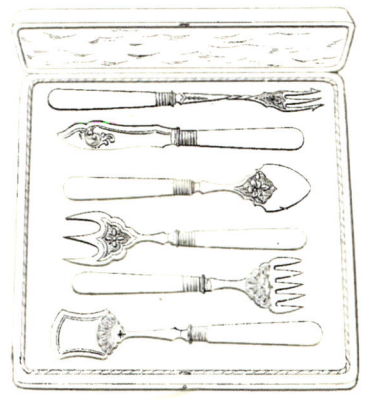 639, 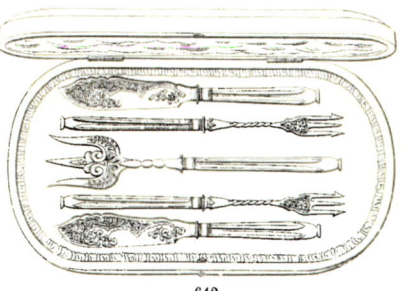 642, 627, 633

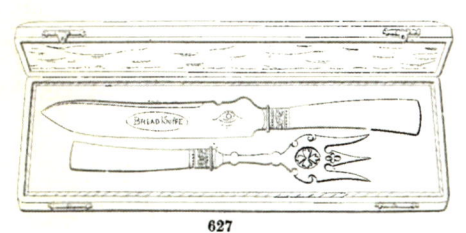

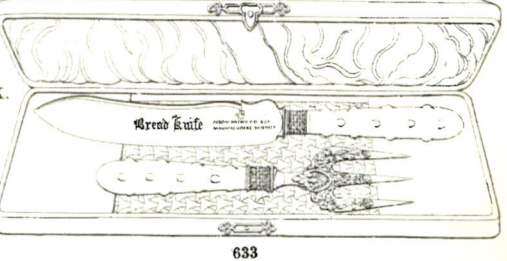

SECTION A
PAGE 76

Taylor's Witness Sheffield.

Spoons and Forks.
Nickel and E.P.N.S.

| FIDDLE. | OLD ENGLISH. | KING'S. | REED AND RIBBON. | BEADED. | GEORGIAN. |

| ROUND BOWL SOUP SPOON. | GADROON. | CHIPPENDALE. | SYLVESTER. | RAT-TAIL. | ALBANY. |

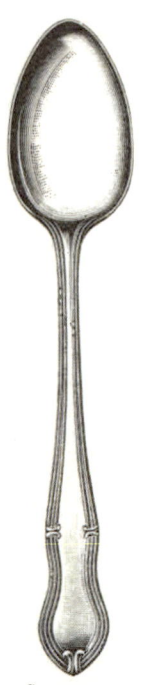

NINETY YEARS' REPUTATION FOR QUALITY!

LONDON 1851.   LONDON 1862.   PARIS 1855.   ANTWERP 1886.   ADELAIDE 1887.

CHRISTCHURCH 1907   GRAHAMSTOWN 1899   MELBOURNE 1888   LONDON 1851   LONDON 1862   PARIS 1855   ANTWERP 1886   ADELAIDE 1887

London Office and Showrooms:
BATH HOUSE,
57, HOLBORN VIADUCT, E.C.1.
Telephone: City 7982.

Scottish Office and Showrooms:
65, BATH STREET, GLASGOW.
Telephone: Douglas 1559.

TAYLOR'S

TRADE MARK: GRANTED 1835.

WITNESS SHEFFIELD.

OFFICES & SHOWROOMS:
Melbourne, Sydney, Georgetown,
Cape Town, Johannesburg,
Nairobi, Calgary, Montreal, Paris.

POCKET KNIVES.

"EYE-WITNESS" STANDS FOR HIGH QUALITY.

EVERY KNIFE IS GUARANTEED PERFECT, and every effort made to back this Guarantee by forethought and application of expert craftsmanship in the selection and make-up of each pattern for its particular use.

Farmers and fishermen, artisans and weavers, horticulturists and hunters, the world over, demand "the knife with the eye on it."

This list is but a selection from the enormous number of patterns made and enquiries for any others not included, will be readily met. The patterns illustrated are stocked ready for immediate delivery.

The assortment of handles in which each pattern is made will be ascertained from the price list.

This list is sent out and accepted on the understanding that it is treated confidentially and not shown to other manufacturers, but used for placing orders with us. Should you not be able to use it for this purpose it is to be returned to us.

NEEDHAM, VEALL & TYZACK, LIMITED,

CUTLERS AND SILVERSMITHS,

TELEGRAMS:
EYE-WITNESS, SHEFFIELD.

TELEPHONE:
CENTRAL 4428 & 4429.

Manufacturers of Table Cutlery, Pocket Cutlery,
Butchers' Knives and Steels,
Scissors, Razors,
Silver and Electro Plated Ware in Designs
to suit all markets.

CODES:
A.B.C. 4TH, 5TH & 6TH EDITIONS.
MARCONI.   BENTLEY'S.
WESTERN UNION, 5 LETTER.
LIEBERS, 1896.

EYE-WITNESS WORKS, SHEFFIELD, ENGLAND.

Taylor's WITNESS SHEFFIELD.

Pocket Cutlery.

NOTE.

For the convenience of buyers, this list shows, in every section, the lowest priced article first, then graduated prices in each section all through.

Shackles for Pocket Knives, 3/- per doz.
Nickel Silver „ Pen „ 6/- „

The different kinds of Handles of Pocket Knives are denoted by a letter prefixed.

When ordering any Handle other than Stag, give the necessary Letter for the Handle required.

Plain No.	denotes	Stag.
A	„	Black.
B	„	White Bone.
C	„	Cocoa.
D	„	Black Chequered.
F	„	Ivory.
G	„	Tortoise Shell.
H	„	Pearl.
M	„	Nickel Silver.
X	„	Xylonite, and description of colour after the No. thus:— X1017 White.
Sterling	„	Sterling Silver.

All Illustrations in this Cutlery List, when not otherwise specified, show the exact size of the article.

NUMERICAL INDEX
Pocket Knives

No.	Page B	No.	Page B	No.	Page B	No.	Page B	No.	Page B	No.	Page B
6 to 28	2	524 to 533	8	1005	28	1108	32	1335	35	1571 1572	48
33 to 46	3	535 536	9	1006	30	1109	24	1339	38	1580	43
50	2	541 to 565	8	1007	27	1112	28	1343	35	1599	46
54½	3			1009	30	1115	30	1348	38	1625½ 1631 1634	44
60 to 97	4	566	18	1010 1011	32	1132	29	1352	36	1647 1648	45
101	3	568	8	1015	29	1138	33	1353	25	1657	46
151 to 159	5	575	9	1016	34	1140	31	1355 1361	36	1658½ 1668	45
161 174	6	591 to 605	8	1017 1017½	26	1140½	33	1363	37	1671	
177 178	5	611	10	1018 1019	31	1143 1146	29	1363½	36	1680½	47
179	6	613 to 642	9	1022 to 1028	28	1150	25	1368	38	1682 1685	48
180 to 188	21	648 to 659	10	1030	34	1156	26	1369	17	1688 to 1695	46
191	5	664 667	19	1032 1033	40	1157	25	1370	38	1696 1699	47
206 212	6	681	11	1035	28	1158	32	1371 to 1375	17	1722	46
224		693	12	1036	31	1159	31	1376	18	1723	47
239	5	704	13	1039	29	1160	32	1377	36	1724 1729	48
241 247	6	722	17	1040	34	1162	26	1379	37	1742 to 1755	43
256 258	10	752 to 760	22	1041 1046	31	1163	27	1381 to 1383	18	1764 1769	47
269	6	763	18	1047	32	1165 1166	24	1388	37	1780 to 1786	44
276 to 293	19	765 766	22	1048	30	1169		1393	38	1788	45
311 to 318	11	782 to 788	23	1049	29	1174	29	1397	36	1789	44
321 to 327	12	813	20	1052	34	1183	30	1398	37	2173	27
331 to 333	11	822 to 847	14	1054	30	1195	27	1408 1421	38	2245	25
339	22	901	24	1055	32	1196	26	1435 1438	37 38	2246	27
347	12	947 to 953	E9	1056	30	1197	24	1443	36	2249 2253	24
353 to 377	13	971	26	1059	31	1199	26	1449	40	2256	29
381 382	11	975	25	1060	28	1200	24	1471	39	2259	27
392		977	26	1061	34	1201	25	1472	40	2263 2263½	24
397	12	978	24	1062 1063	33	1207½	25	1474	39	2264	29
401 to 410	15	983	26	1066	34	1214	29	1480 1481	40	2288	35
411	16	985	26	1067	33	1218	25	1484 to 1499	39	2327	45
414	15	986½	28	1068	30	1226 1230	27	1496	36	3516 to 3529	20
418 to 424	16	987 988	27	1069	33	1261	37	1504 1509	40	3532, 3533	Avi
425	17	989	26	1070	30	1262	25	1515 1516	39	4138	44
426 to 495	7	996	28	1073	34	1264	37	1522	40	4140 to 4156	49
		998	27	1074	30	1278	35	1527 to 1530	41	4158	A68
		1001	26	1076	28	1292	38	1536	42	**RAZORS** are in numerical order excepting:—	
		1001½	26	1077 1080	32	1295½ 1296	37	1543½ to 1546	41	1000	E2
		1002	27	1083	31	1301		1548 to 1559	42	2000	E8
		1004	27	1086 1087	32	1302 to 1306	35	1566 1568	43	3000	E8
				1087½ 1089	33	1314	38	1570	46		
				1091	31	1315	36				
				1093	33	1321	29				
				1096	30	1329 1330	35				
						1331	36				
						1333	37				
						1334	36				

Taylor's WITNESS SHEFFIELD

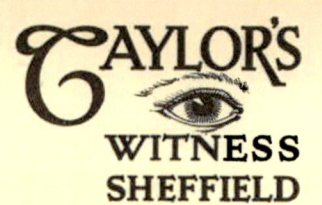

Safety Razor Blades

So insistent has been the demand for a safety razor blade at a moderate price that could be relied on to give a clean shave and service of fair duration, that we have decided to introduce one under our "Eyewitness" mark, which is a guarantee that the quality will be all right.

TYPE A   **TYPE G**

Packed in Envelopettes and then in cartons of six or twelve blades as desired, with a sample card of mounted packets. The blades commend themselves by smart appearance and justify their appearance by perfect service.

Personal trial has proved the "Eyewitness" blade to give a smooth and comfortable shave, and the lasting properties of the edge to be most satisfactory, so that these blades may be offered with confidence. The two shapes illustrated are supplied. Both steel and blade are Sheffield made by experts.

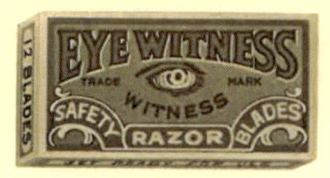

ENVELOPE and CARTON

Flower Gathering Scissor

THIS flower-gathering scissor has just been patented and will be found a very handy and efficient help to easy flower cutting. After the cut the spring holds the flower stalk fast so that it may be conveyed to the basket and then released. Only one hand therefore is required for gathering. Nickel-plated and of attractive appearance, they make a very handsome and acceptable present.

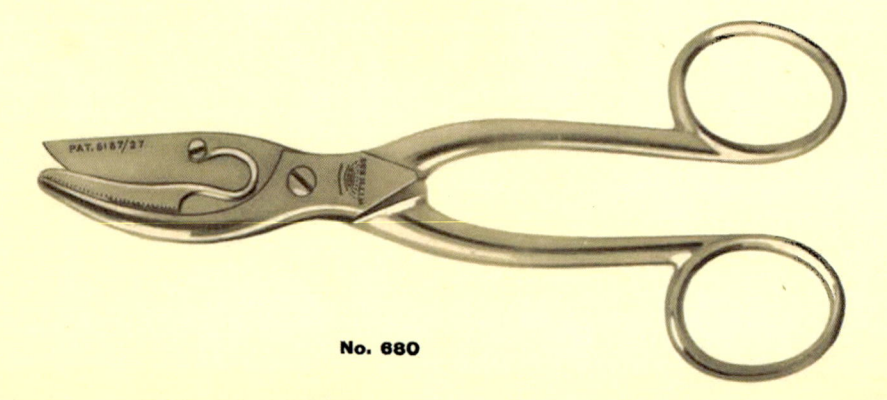

No. 680

SECTION B
PAGE 2

Taylor's Lamb Foot Knives.

WITNESS SHEFFIELD.

ILLUSTRATIONS ARE ACTUAL SIZE OF ARTICLES.

When ordering, prefix the LETTER to the Pattern Number to denote the kind of Handle required, viz:—
PLAIN **No.** IS STAG.   **A**—BLACK.   **B**—WHITE BONE.   **C**—COCO.

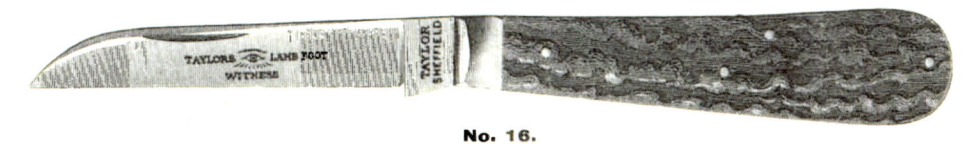

No. 16.

No. 22.   Also made in Sizes $3\frac{1}{2}''$ and $3\frac{3}{4}''$

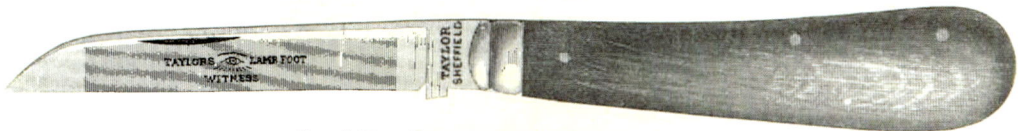

No. A17.   Also made in Size 4", **No. 18**

No. 18½

No. 6.   Also made in Size $3\frac{1}{2}''$ **No. 21.**

No. 28.

No. 8.   Cheaper Quality **No. 18.**

No. 50.   POLISHED BLADE.

SECTION B
PAGE 3

Taylor's Witness Sheffield

Scotch Shepherds Knives.

ILLUSTRATIONS ARE ACTUAL SIZE OF ARTICLES.

When ordering, prefix the LETTER to the Pattern Number to denote the kind of Handle required, viz:—
PLAIN **No.** IS STAG.   **A**—BLACK.   **B**—WHITE BONE.   **C**—COCO.

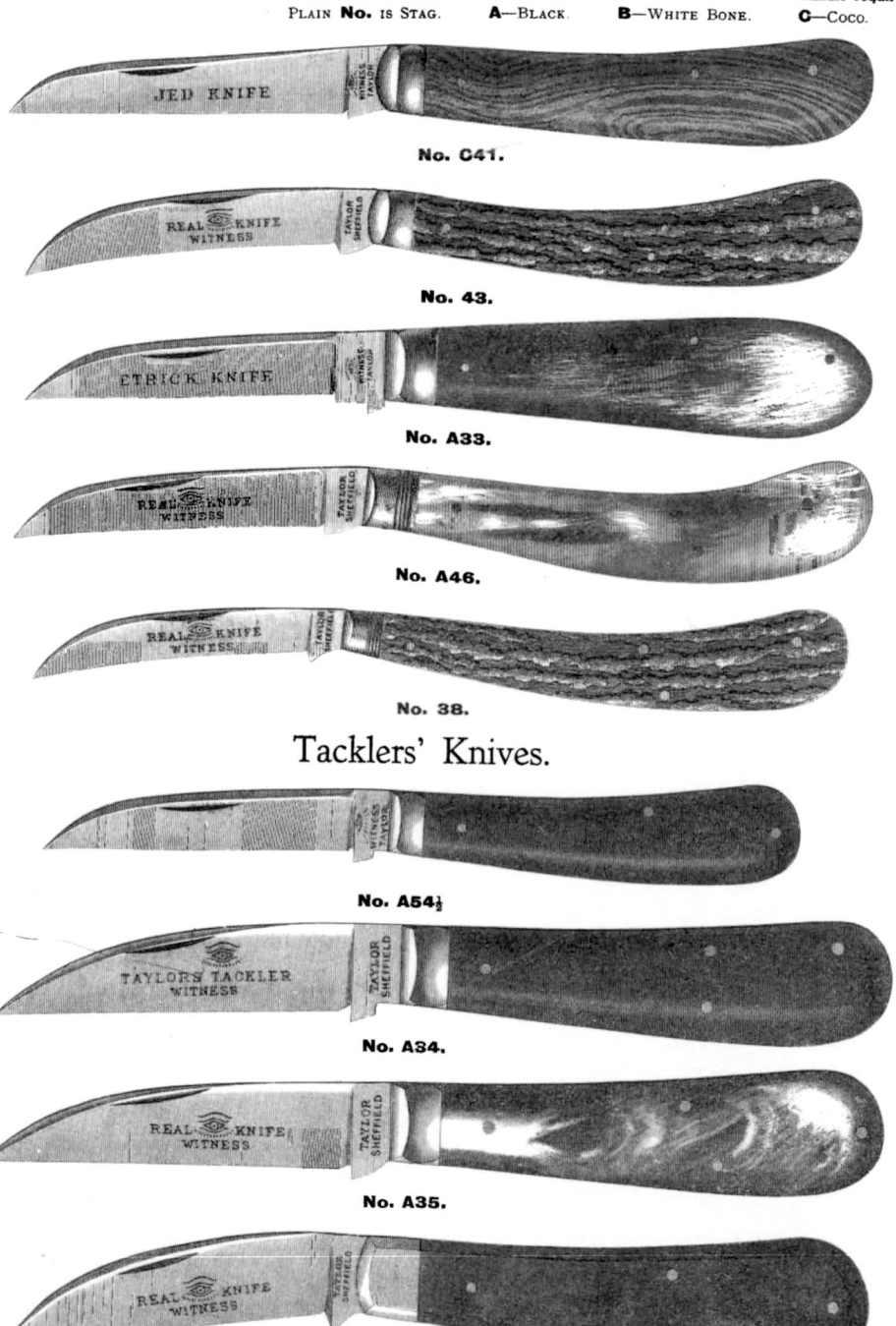

No. C41.

No. 43.

No. A33.

No. A46.

No. 38.

Tacklers' Knives.

No. A54½

No. A34.

No. A35.

No. A101.   BRASS LINED, NICKEL BOLSTER.

SECTION B
PAGE 4

Taylor's Sheep Foot Knives.

WITNESS SHEFFIELD.

ILLUSTRATIONS ARE ACTUAL SIZE OF ARTICLES.

When ordering, prefix the LETTER to the Pattern Number to denote the kind of Handle required, viz:—
PLAIN **No.** IS STAG.   **A**—BLACK.   **B**—WHITE BONE.   **C**—COCO.

No. 64.

No. A70.   SIZES $2\frac{3}{4}''$, $3''$, $3\frac{1}{4}''$, $3\frac{1}{2}''$, $3\frac{3}{4}''$

No. B62.

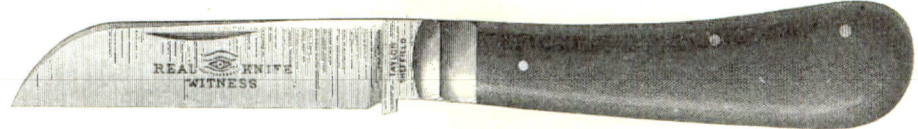

No. A60.

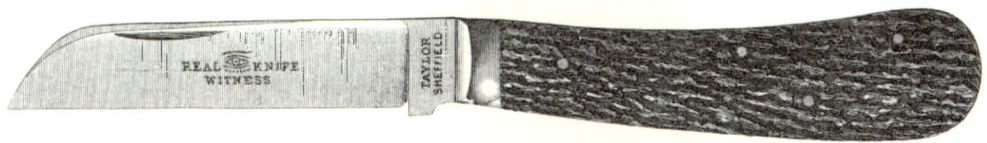

No. 69.

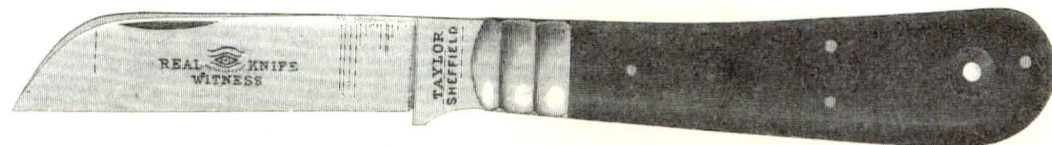

No. A72.   DRILLED FOR LANYARD.

No. A89.

No. A75.   DRILLED FOR LANYARD.

No. 97.

SECTION B
PAGE 5

TAYLOR'S WITNESS SHEFFIELD.

Spear Blade Pocket Knives.

ILLUSTRATIONS ARE ACTUAL SIZE OF ARTICLES.

When ordering, prefix the LETTER to the Pattern Number to denote the kind of Handle required, viz:—
PLAIN **No.** IS STAG.   **A**—BLACK.   **B**—WHITE BONE.   **C**—COCO.

No. C157.

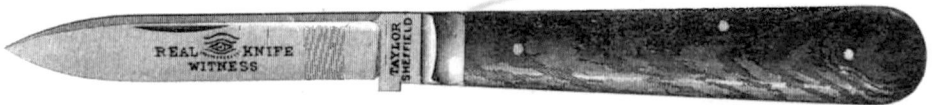

No. C151.

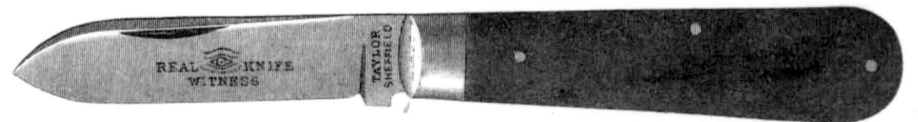

No. A152.

No. 155.

No. C156**

No. A159.

No. A177.   Also made in Size 4¼″ **No. 178.**

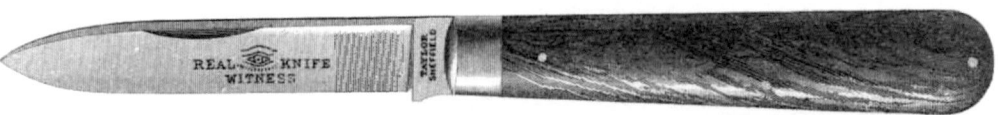

No. C191**

No. 239**   SIZE 4″   Also made in Sizes 3¼″, 3½″ and 3¾″
KNIVES MARKED "**" ARE BRASS LINED WITH NICKEL BOLSTER.

SECTION B
PAGE 6

Taylor's Witness Sheffield — Spear Blade Pocket Knives.

ILLUSTRATIONS ARE ACTUAL SIZE OF ARTICLES.

When ordering, prefix the LETTER to the Pattern Number to denote the kind of Handle required, viz:—
PLAIN **No.** IS STAG.   **A**—BLACK.   **B**—WHITE BONE.   **C**—COCO.

No. B241½   SIZE 3¾″   Also made in Size 3½″ **No. 241.** NICKEL BOLSTER.

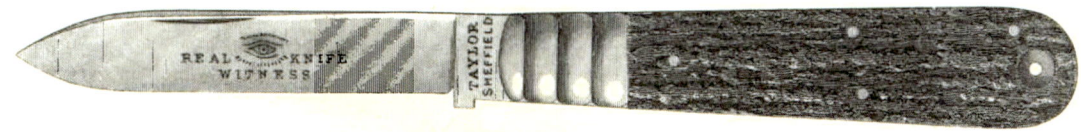

No. 269. DRILLED FOR LANYARD.

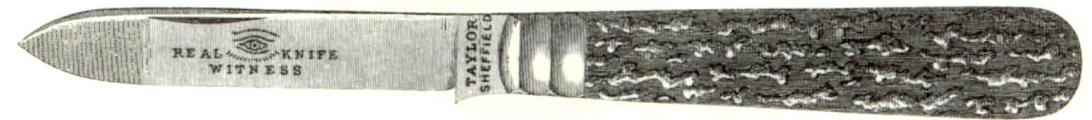

No. 161.

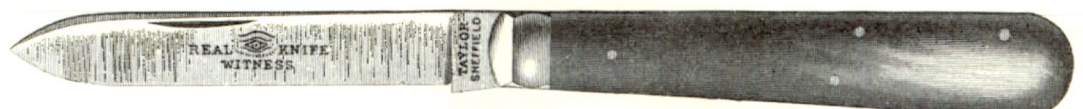

No. A174.

No. A212✶✶

No. A247✶✶   Also made in Size 3¼″

No. A206✶✶   DRILLED FOR LANYARD.

No. 179.

No. B224✶✶

KNIVES MARKED "✶✶" ARE BRASS LINED WITH NICKEL BOLSTER.

SECTION B
PAGE 7

Taylor's Witness Sheffield.

Lamb Foot Knives.

Two Blades.
ILLUSTRATIONS ARE ACTUAL SIZE OF ARTICLES.

When ordering, prefix the LETTER to the Pattern Number to denote the kind of Handle required, viz:—
PLAIN **No.** IS STAG. **A**—BLACK. **B**—WHITE BONE. **C**—COCO.

No. 426.

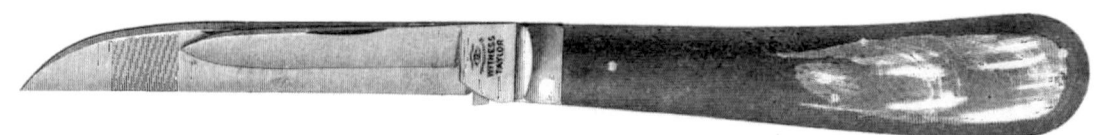

No. A429. Also made in Size 3⅜" No. 428.

No. 482.

Sheep Foot Blades.

No. A451.

No. 470.

No. A453.

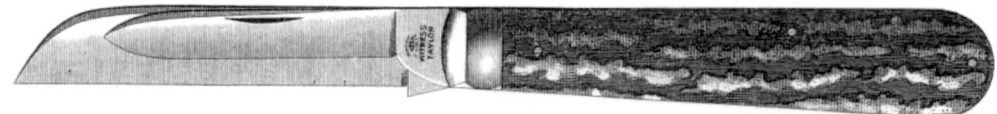

No. 472.

No. A495.

SECTION B
PAGE 8

TAYLOR'S WITNESS SHEFFIELD. Spear Blade Pocket Knives.

Two Blades.

ILLUSTRATIONS ARE ACTUAL SIZE OF ARTICLES.

When ordering, prefix the LETTER to the Pattern Number to denote the kind of Handle required, viz:—
PLAIN **No.** IS STAG.   **A**—BLACK.   **B**—WHITE BONE.   **C**—COCO.

No. A524✸✸

No. A549.

No. A560.   Also made in Sizes 3", 3¼" and 3½"

No. A565✸
✸✸

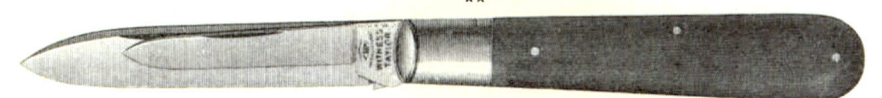

No. A605.   NICKEL BOLSTER.

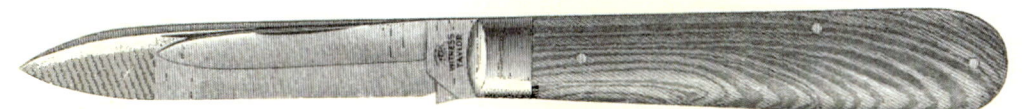

No. C533.

No. A568✸✸   Also made in Size 3½"

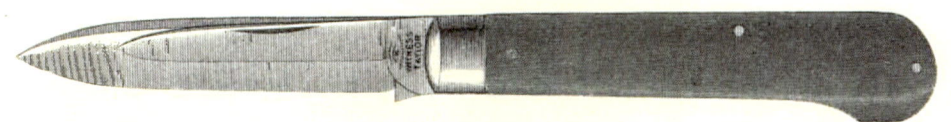

No. A591✸   Also made with Large Castrator Blade: **No. A592**✸ or with Clip Point Blade: **No. A593**✸

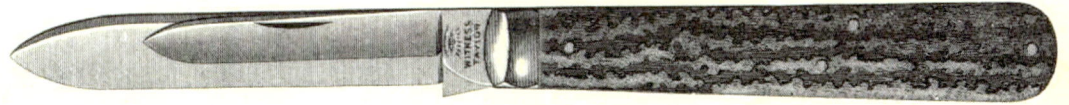

No. 541.

KNIVES MARKED "✸✸" ARE BRASS LINED WITH NICKEL BOLSTER.

✸These patterns can be supplied with Picker and Tweezers. If required add "PT" to the number.

SECTION B
PAGE 9

Taylor's WITNESS SHEFFIELD. Spear Blade Pocket Knives.

Two Blades.

ILLUSTRATIONS ARE ACTUAL SIZE OF ARTICLES.

When ordering, prefix the LETTER to the Pattern Number to denote the kind of Handle required, viz:—
PLAIN No. IS STAG.   A—BLACK.   B—WHITE BONE.   C—COCO.

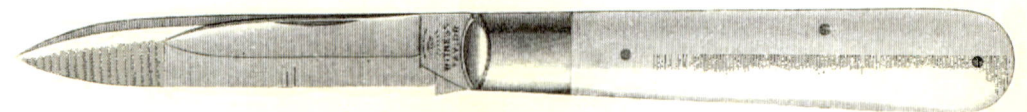

No. B617. NICKEL BOLSTER.

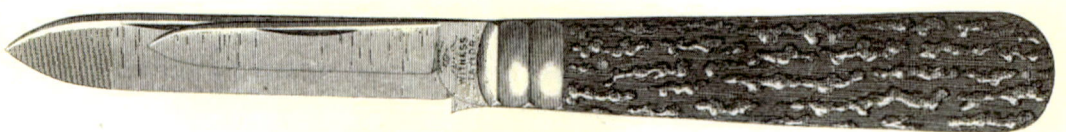

No. 618.

No. A641**   Also made in Sizes $3\frac{1}{4}''$ and $3\frac{1}{2}''$

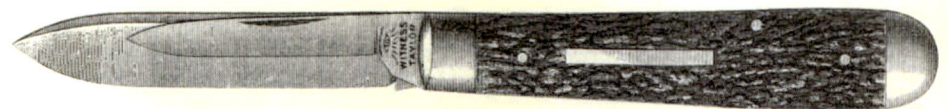

No. 642**   Also made in Size $3\frac{1}{4}''$

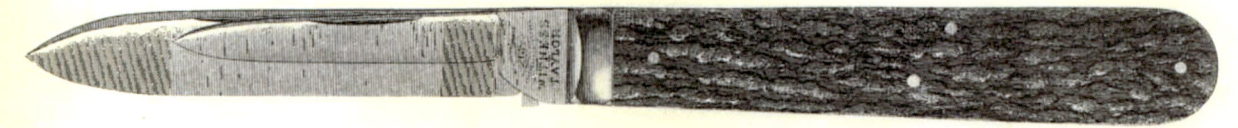

No. 536.   Also made in Size $4\frac{1}{4}''$ **No. 535.**

No. A575.   BRASS LINED.

No. C619**

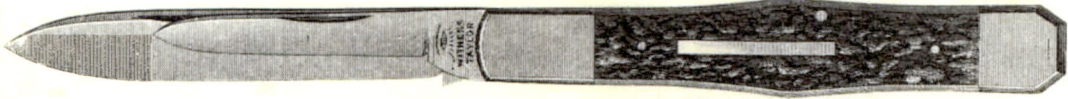

No. 640**   Also made in Size $3\frac{1}{2}''$ **No. 640½**

No. 613PT**   Picker and Tweezer.

KNIVES MARKED "**" ARE BRASS LINED WITH NICKEL BOLSTER.

SECTION B
PAGE 10

Taylor's Witness Sheffield — Clip Point Pocket Knives.

ILLUSTRATIONS ARE ACTUAL SIZE OF ARTICLES.

When ordering, prefix the LETTER to the Pattern Number to denote the kind of Handle required, viz:—
Plain **No.** is Stag.   **A**—Black.   **C**—Coco.

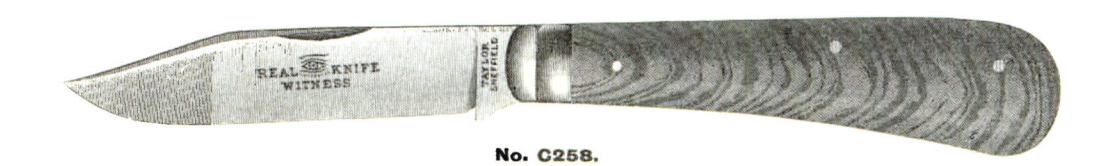

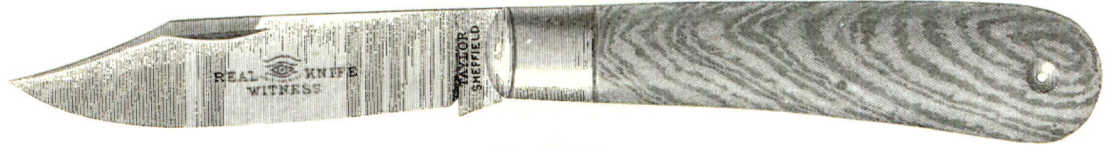

No. C258.

No. C256.

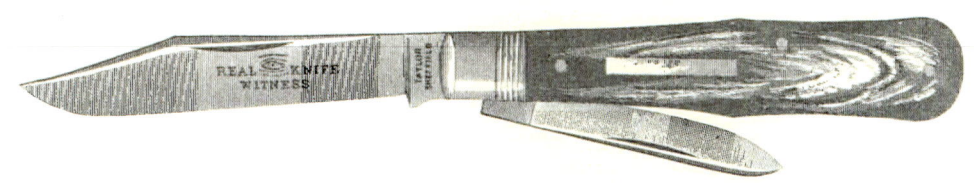

No. A611** POLISHED BLADE.

No. A653.   NICKEL BOLSTER, POLISHED BLADE.

No. 648** POLISHED BLADE.

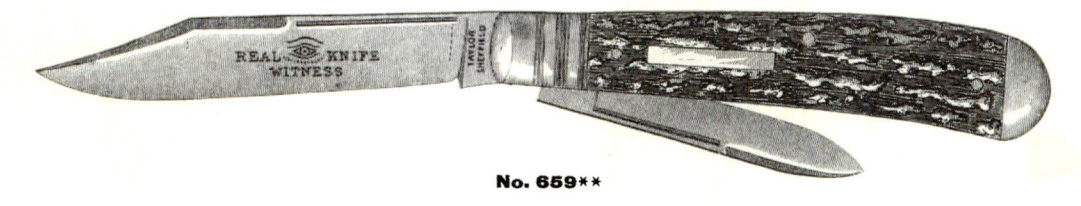

No. 659**

KNIVES MARKED "**" ARE BRASS LINED WITH NICKEL BOLSTER.

SECTION B PAGE 11

Taylor's Witness Sheffield — Pruning Knives.

ILLUSTRATIONS ARE ACTUAL SIZE OF ARTICLES.

When ordering, prefix the LETTER to the Pattern Number to denote the kind of Handle required, viz:—
Plain **No.** is Stag.   **A**—Black.   **C**—Coco.

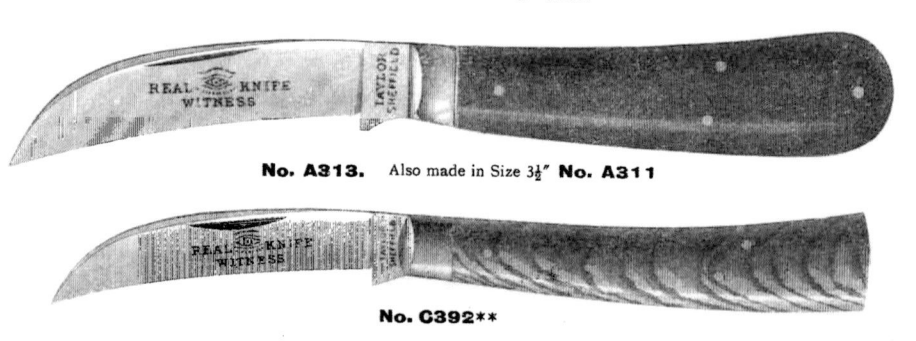

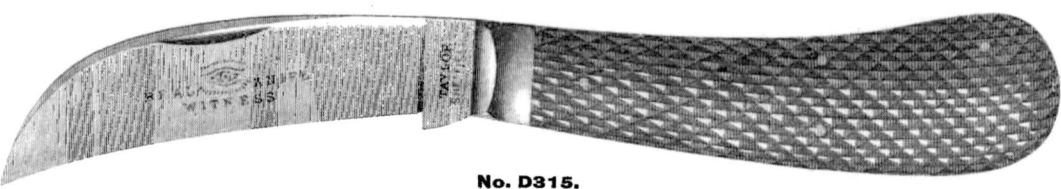

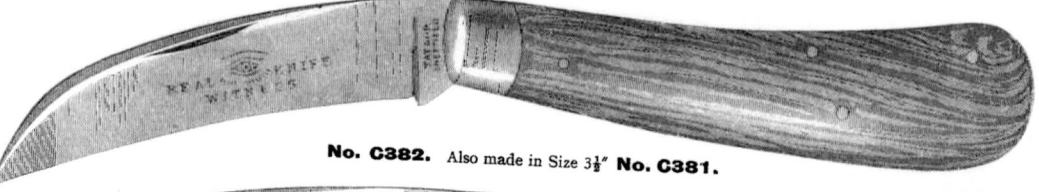

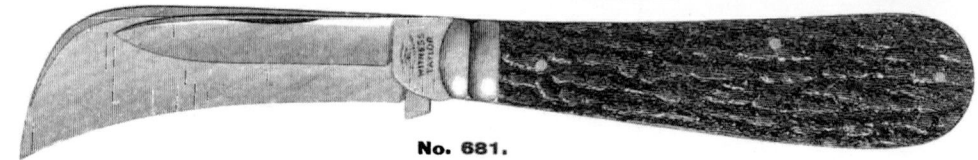

No. A313.   Also made in Size 3½"   **No. A311**

No. C392**

No. D315.

No. A318.

No. C382.   Also made in Size 3½"   **No. C381.**

No. A331.   Nickel Bolster.

No. 332.   Also made with full Pruner Blade, **No. 333.**

No. 681.

Knives marked "**" are Brass Lined with Nickel Bolster.

SECTION B
PAGE 12

Taylor's Witness Sheffield — Pruning Knives.

ILLUSTRATIONS ARE ACTUAL SIZE OF ARTICLES.

When ordering, prefix the LETTER to the Pattern Number to denote the kind of Handle required, viz:—
PLAIN **No.** IS STAG. **A**—BLACK. **C**—COCO. **D**—BLACK DIAMOND CHEQUERED

No. 397. IRON CAP.

No. 321. BRASS CAP.

No. 322. BRASS CAP.

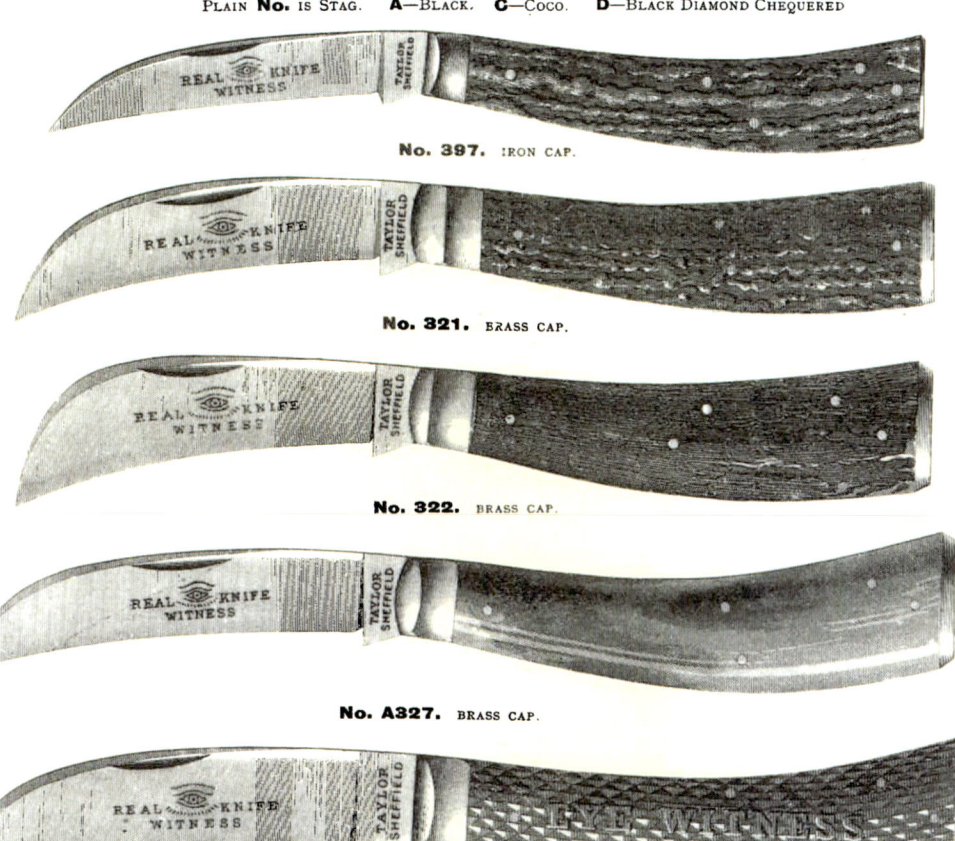

No. A327. BRASS CAP.

No. D325. BRASS CAP. Also made with Full Pruner Blade, **No. 326.**

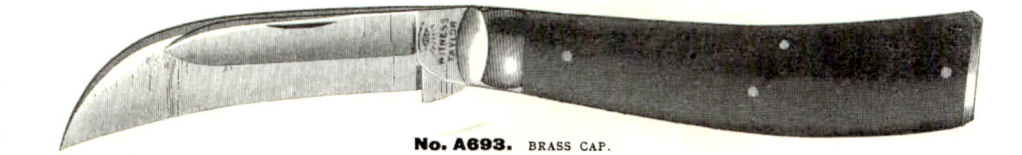

No. A693. BRASS CAP.

No. 347. IRON CAP.

SECTION B
PAGE 13

Taylor's Witness Sheffield.

Pruning Knives.

ILLUSTRATIONS ARE ACTUAL SIZE OF ARTICLES.

When ordering, prefix the LETTER to the Pattern Number to denote the kind of Handle required, viz:—
PLAIN **No.** IS STAG.

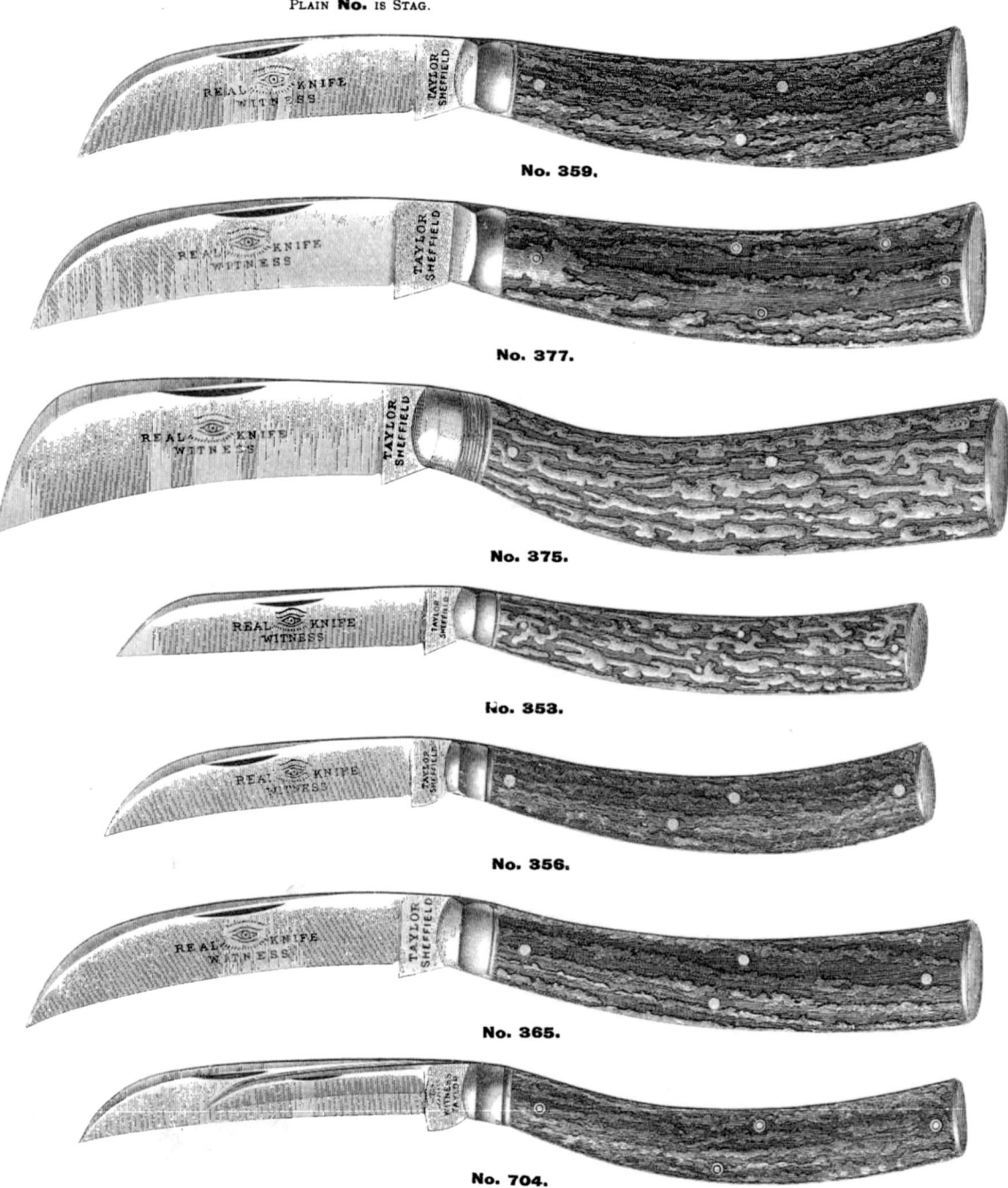

No. 359.

No. 377.

No. 375.

No. 353.

No. 356.

No. 365.

No. 704.

These Knives are all Superior Finish, with End Caps Soldered to Springs.

SECTION B
PAGE 14

Taylor's Witness Sheffield. Budding and Grafting Knives

ILLUSTRATIONS ARE ACTUAL SIZE OF ARTICLES.

When ordering, prefix the LETTER to the Pattern Number to denote the kind of Handle required, viz:—
A—Black.   **F**—Ivory.

No. F822.

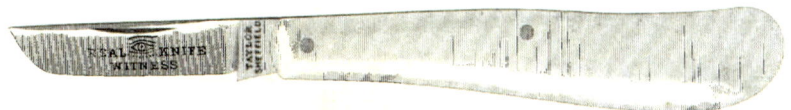

No. F824.

No. F838.

No. A847.

No. F826.   Also made with Nickel Bolster and Brass Lining, **No. F828**✱✱

No. F832.

No. F841.

No. F845✱✱

Knives marked "✱✱" are Brass Lined with Nickel Bolster.

SECTION B
PAGE 15

Taylor's Witness Sheffield.

Castrating Knives.

ILLUSTRATIONS ARE ACTUAL SIZE OF ARTICLES.

When ordering, prefix the LETTER to the Pattern Number to denote the kind of Handle required, viz:—
PLAIN **No.** IS STAG.   **A**—BLACK.

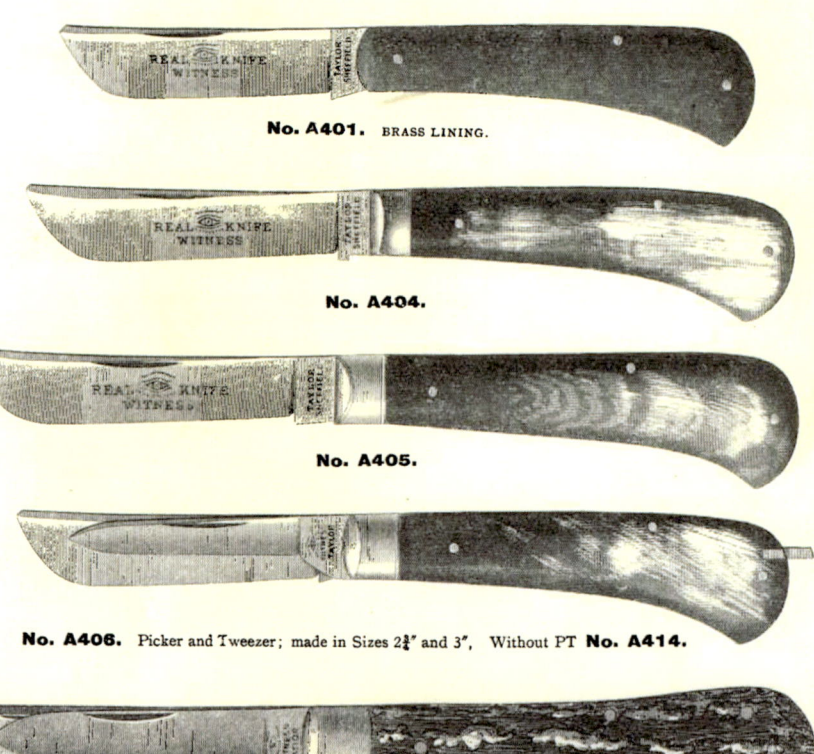

No. A401.   BRASS LINING.

No. A404.

No. A405.

No. A406.   Picker and Tweezer; made in Sizes 2¾" and 3",   Without PT **No. A414.**

No. A407.

No. A403.   Also made in Size 3"   **No. A403-3"**

No. 408.

No. A410.   POLISHED BLADES.

Any of these patterns can be supplied with Picker and Tweezers. If required add "PT" to the number.

SECTION B
PAGE 16

Taylor's WITNESS SHEFFIELD. Castrating and Stock Knives

ILLUSTRATIONS ARE ACTUAL SIZE OF ARTICLES.

When ordering, prefix the LETTER to the Pattern Number to denote the kind of Handle required, viz:—
PLAIN **No.** IS STAG. **A**—BLACK.

Any of these patterns can be supplied with Picker and Tweezers. If required add "PT" to the number.

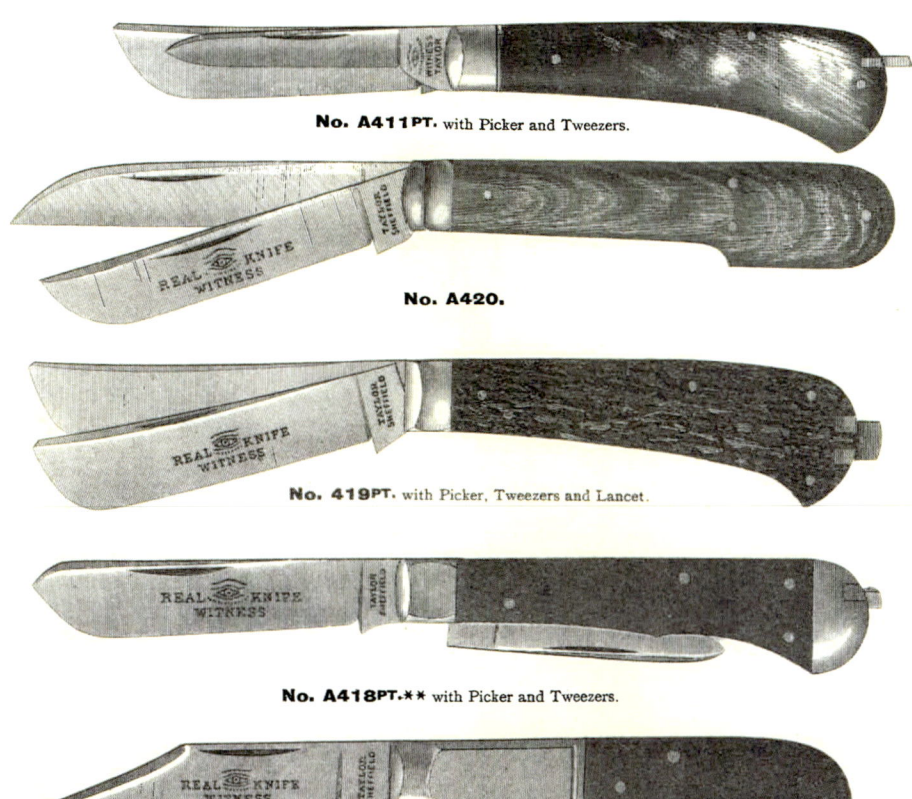

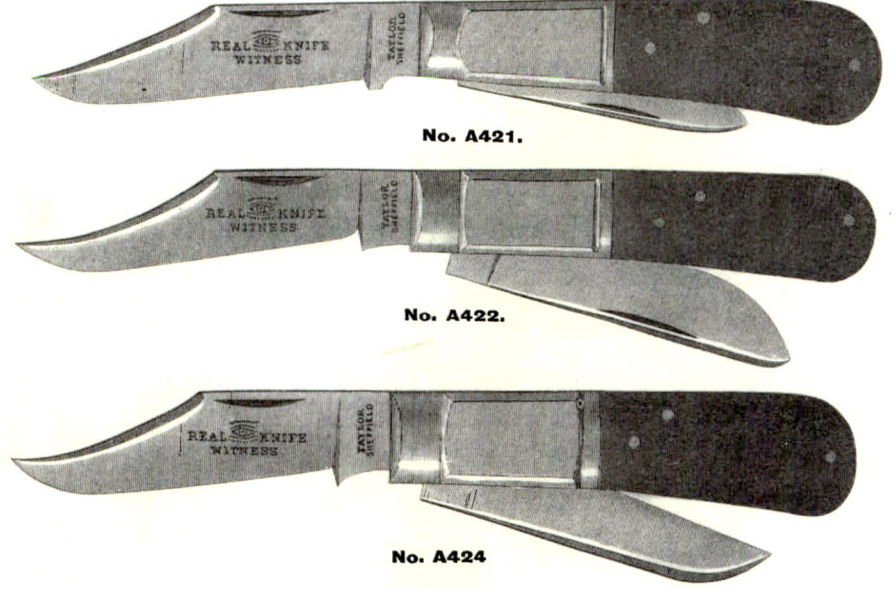

No. A411PT. with Picker and Tweezers.

No. A420.

No. 419PT. with Picker, Tweezers and Lancet.

No. A418PT.✶✶ with Picker and Tweezers.

No. A421.

No. A422.

No. A424

KNIVES MARKED "✶✶" ARE BRASS LINED WITH NICKEL BOLSTER.

SECTION B
PAGE 17

Taylor's Witness Sheffield
Stock and Cattle Knives

ILLUSTRATIONS ARE ACTUAL SIZE OF ARTICLES.

When ordering, prefix the LETTER to the Pattern Number to denote the kind of Handle required, viz:—
PLAIN **No.** IS STAG. **A**—BLACK. **C**—COCO.

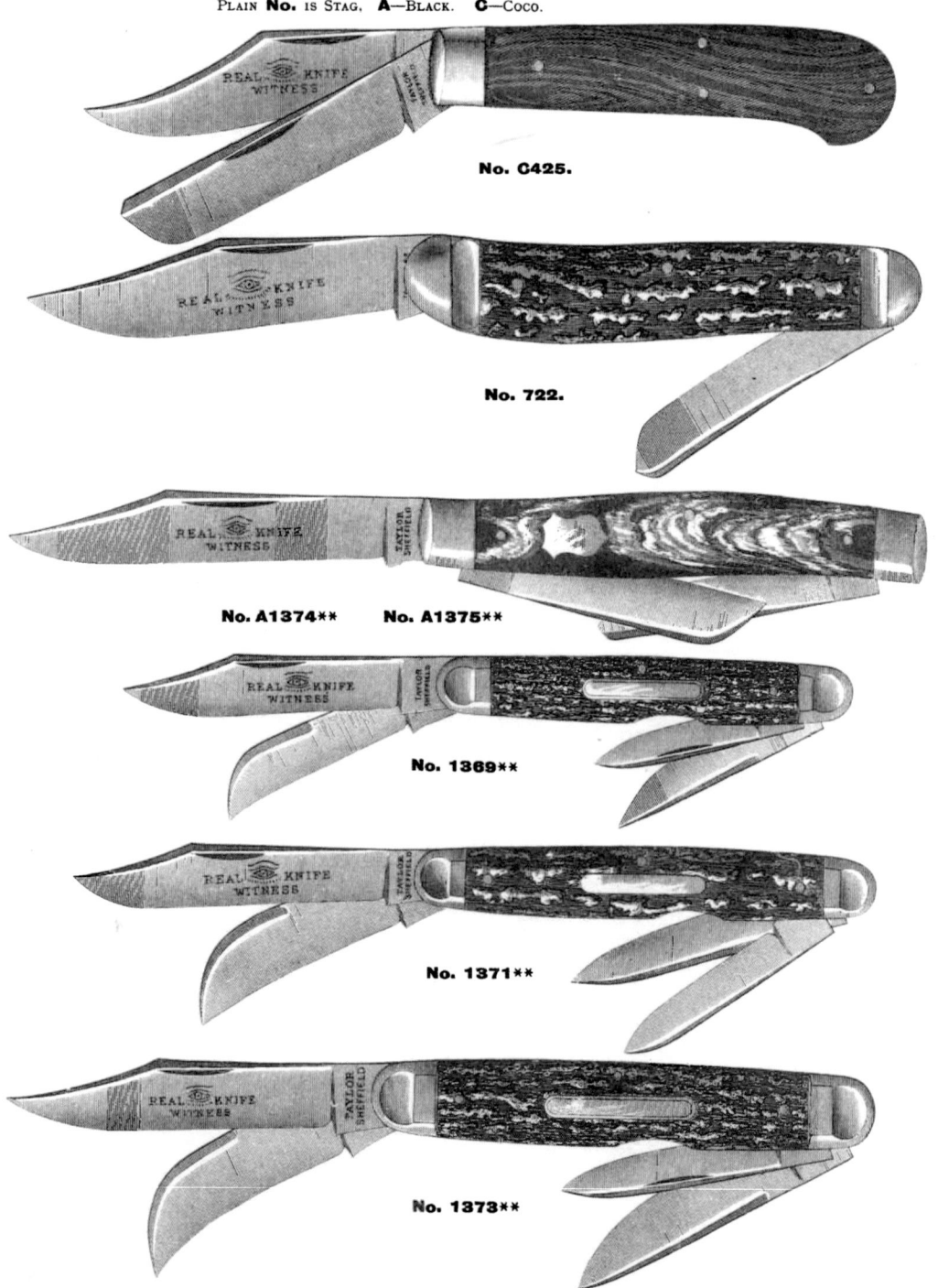

No. C425.

No. 722.

No. A1374✶✶   No. A1375✶✶

No. 1369✶✶

No. 1371✶✶

No. 1373✶✶

KNIVES MARKED "✶✶" ARE BRASS LINED WITH NICKEL BOLSTER.

SECTION B
PAGE 18

Taylor's Witness Sheffield. Castrating and Stock Knives

ILLUSTRATIONS ARE ACTUAL SIZE OF ARTICLES.

When ordering, prefix the LETTER to the Pattern Number to denote the kind of Handle required, viz:—
PLAIN **No.** IS STAG.   **A**—BLACK.   **C**—COCO.

All users of harness or leather belting will appreciate these Knives, which contain a good cutting blade and a leather borer that will make a clean hole of any size that may be required.

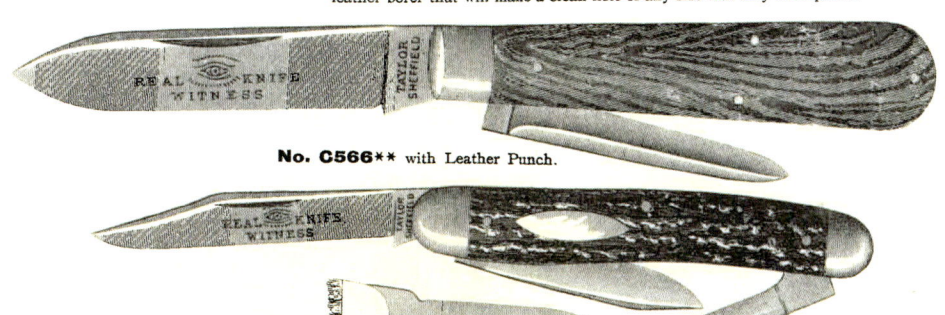

No. C566✶✶ with Leather Punch.

No. 1381✶✶ with Leather Punch.

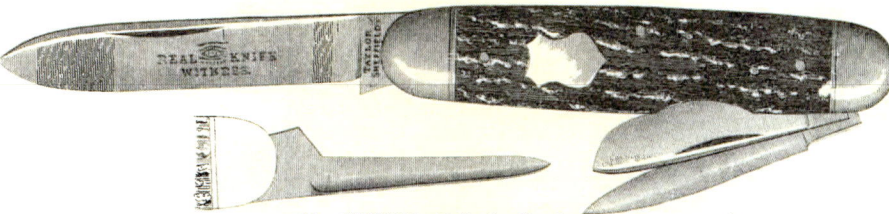

No. 1376✶✶ with Leather Punch.

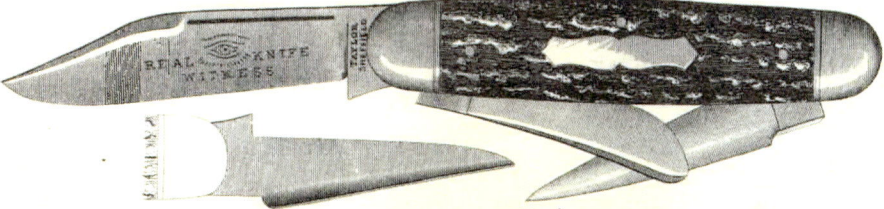

No. 1382✶✶ with Leather Punch.

No. 1383✶✶ with Leather Punch.

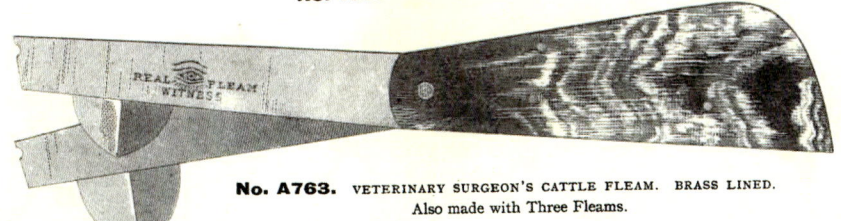

No. A763.   VETERINARY SURGEON'S CATTLE FLEAM.   BRASS LINED.
Also made with Three Fleams.

KNIVES MARKED "✶✶" ARE BRASS LINED WITH NICKEL BOLSTER.

SECTION B
PAGE 19

Taylor's Witness Sheffield.

Lock-Back Knives

No. 276.	No. 286.	No. 284.	No. 293.	No. 290.	No. 664.	No. 667.
4", 4½" & 5"		4½", 5" & 5½"	NICKEL BOLSTER. FOLDING NICKEL GUARD. POLISHED BLADE.	5" & 6" POLISHED BLADE, WITH NICKEL SHACKLE.		NICKEL BOLSTER. POLISHED BLADES.
		POLISHED BLADE, NICKEL BOLSTER.				

SECTION B
PAGE 20

Taylor's Hunting Knives.

WITNESS SHEFFIELD.

When ordering, prefix the LETTER to the Pattern Number to denote the kind of Handle required.

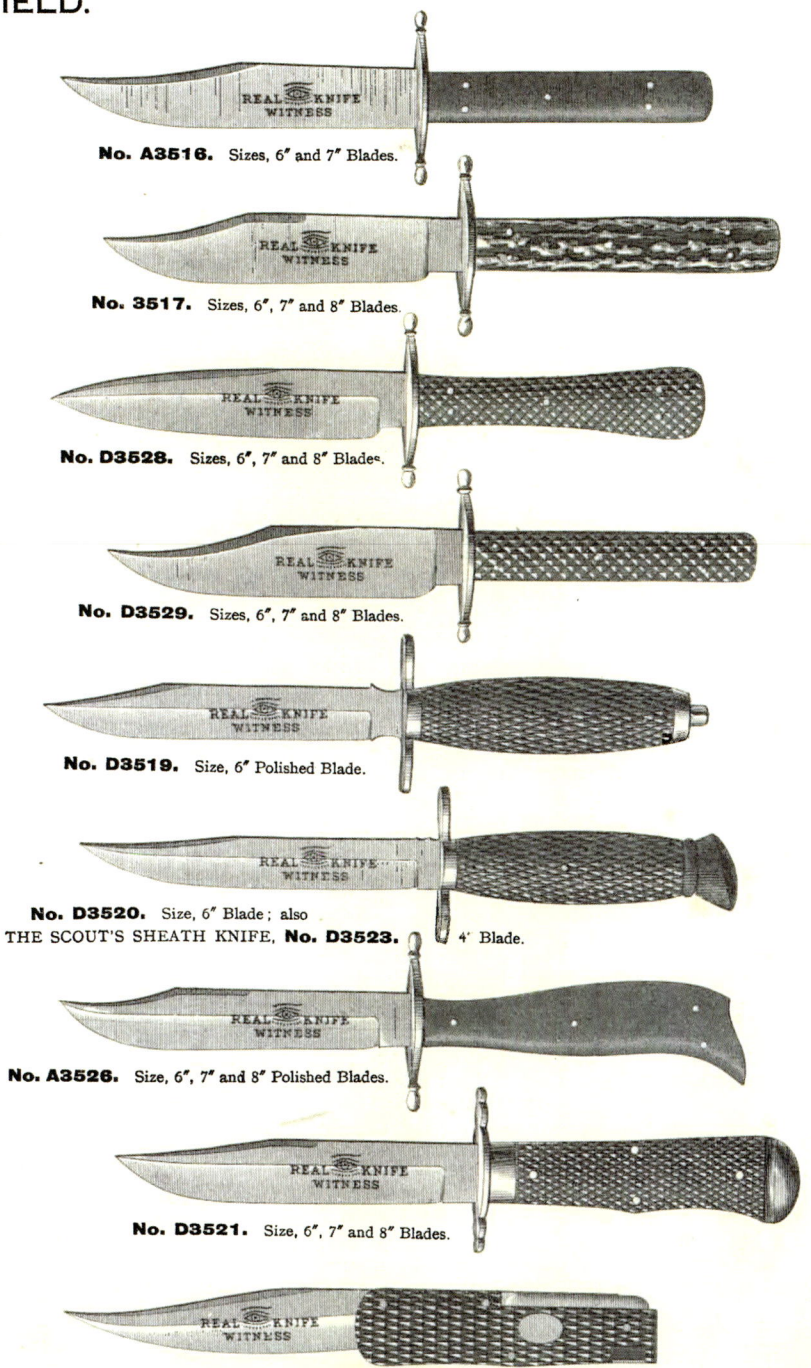

WITH LEATHER SHEATH.

No. A3516. Sizes, 6" and 7" Blades.

No. 3517. Sizes, 6", 7" and 8" Blades.

No. D3528. Sizes, 6", 7" and 8" Blades.

No. D3529. Sizes, 6", 7" and 8" Blades.

No. D3519. Size, 6" Polished Blade.

No. D3520. Size, 6" Blade; also THE SCOUT'S SHEATH KNIFE, **No. D3523.** 4" Blade.

No. A3526. Size, 6", 7" and 8" Polished Blades.

No. D3521. Size, 6", 7" and 8" Blades.

No. D813. Size, 8" Blade. Spring Lock Blade.

SECTION B
PAGE 21

Taylor's Witness Sheffield — Scouts & Sailors Pocket Knives

ILLUSTRATIONS ARE ACTUAL SIZE OF ARTICLES.

When ordering, prefix the LETTER to the Pattern Number to denote the kind of Handle required, viz:—
Plain **No.** is Stag. **A**—Black. **C**—Coco. **D**—Chequered. **M**—Nickel.

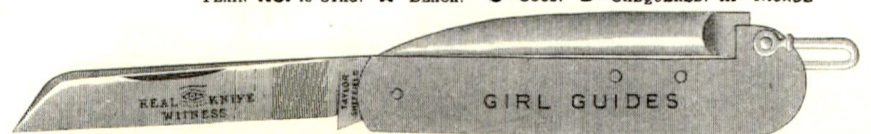

No. M183.

No. D181.

No. D185.

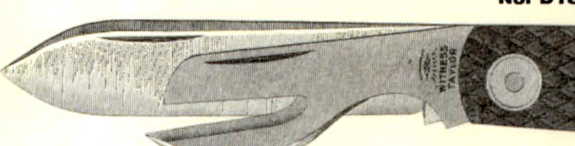

No. D182.

No. A184.

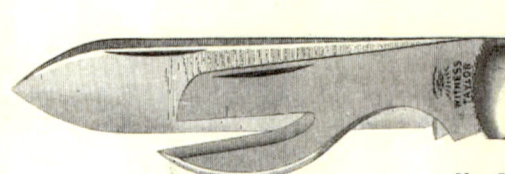

No. D188.

No. D180.

No. A186.

SECTION 8
PAGE 22

TAYLOR'S WITNESS SHEFFIELD
Artisans' Pocket Knives.

ILLUSTRATIONS ARE ACTUAL SIZE OF ARTICLES.

When ordering, prefix the LETTER to the Pattern Number to denote the kind of Handle required, viz:—
PLAIN **No.** IS STAG. **A**—BLACK. **F**—IVORY. **M**—NICKEL.

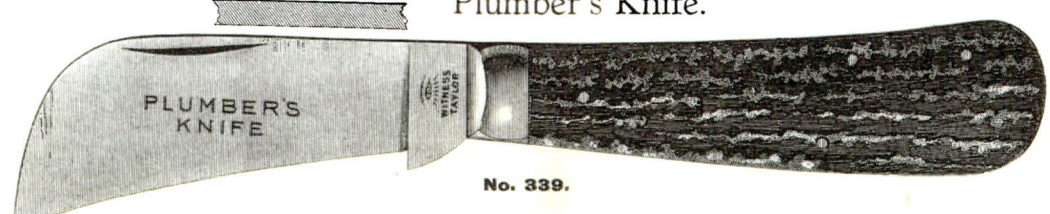

Plumber's Knife.

No. 339.

Timber Scribes.

No. 752.

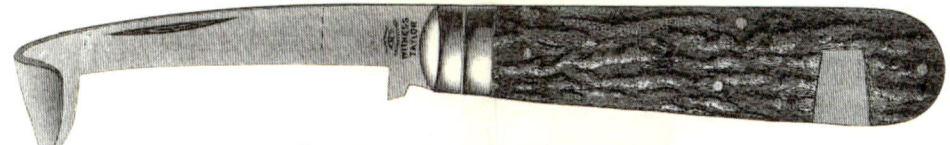

No. 758. Also made with extra Blade, as 760.

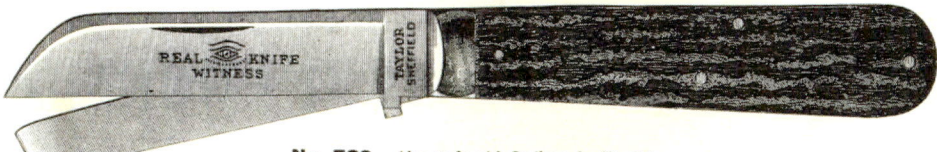

No. 760. Also made with Scribe only, No. 761.

Palette Knives.

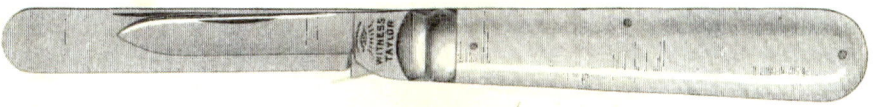

No. F765.

No. A766. NICKEL BOLSTER.

SECTION B
PAGE 23

Taylor's WITNESS SHEFFIELD.

Desk and Erasing Knives.

ILLUSTRATIONS ARE ACTUAL SIZE OF ARTICLES.

When ordering, prefix the LETTER to the Pattern Number to denote the kind of Handle required, viz:—
A—Black. **B**—White Bone. **C**—Coco.

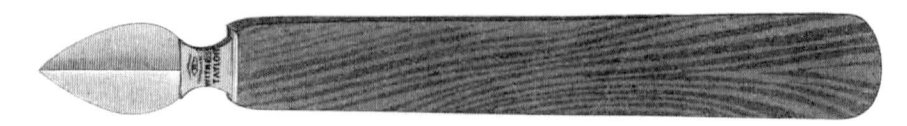

No. C783.

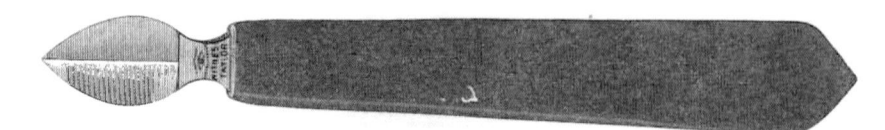

No. A784.

No. C787.

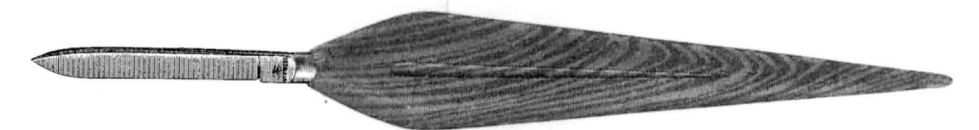

No. C785.

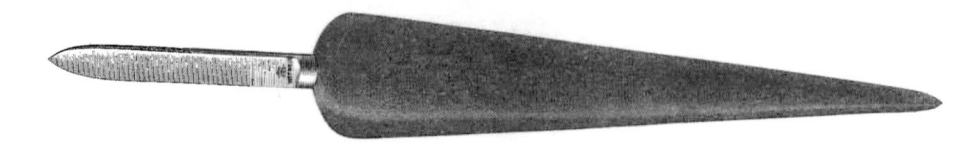

No. A786.

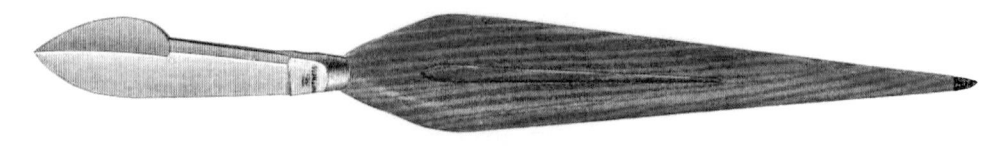

No. C788.

No. A782.

SECTION B
PAGE 24

Taylor's Ladies' Small Pen Knives.
WITNESS SHEFFIELD
ONE & TWO BLADES.
ILLUSTRATIONS ARE ACTUAL SIZE OF ARTICLES.

When ordering, prefix the LETTER to the Pattern Number to denote the kind of handle required, viz.:—
Plain **No.** is Stag. **A**—Black. **C**—Coco. **D**—Black Diamond Chequered. **F**—Ivory.
G—Tortoiseshell. **H**—Pearl. **M**—Nickel. **WH**—White Xylonite.

No. F901

No. F1166

No. F2263. With Bolsters, as **No. 2245** (p. 25) and with Shackle is **No. F2263½**

No. A1109

No. G1169

No. F1197

No. C978

No. F1200

No. A2249

No. H2253

SECTION B
PAGE 25

Taylor's Ladies' Small Pen Knives.

WITNESS SHEFFIELD

TWO & THREE BLADES.
ILLUSTRATIONS ARE ACTUAL SIZE OF ARTICLES.

When ordering, prefix the LETTER to the Pattern Number to denote the kind of handle required, viz.:—
PLAIN **No.** IS STAG. **A**—BLACK. **C**—COCO. **D**—BLACK DIAMOND CHEQUERED. **F**—IVORY.
G—TORTOISESHELL. **H**—PEARL. **M**—NICKEL. **WH**—WHITE XYLONITE.

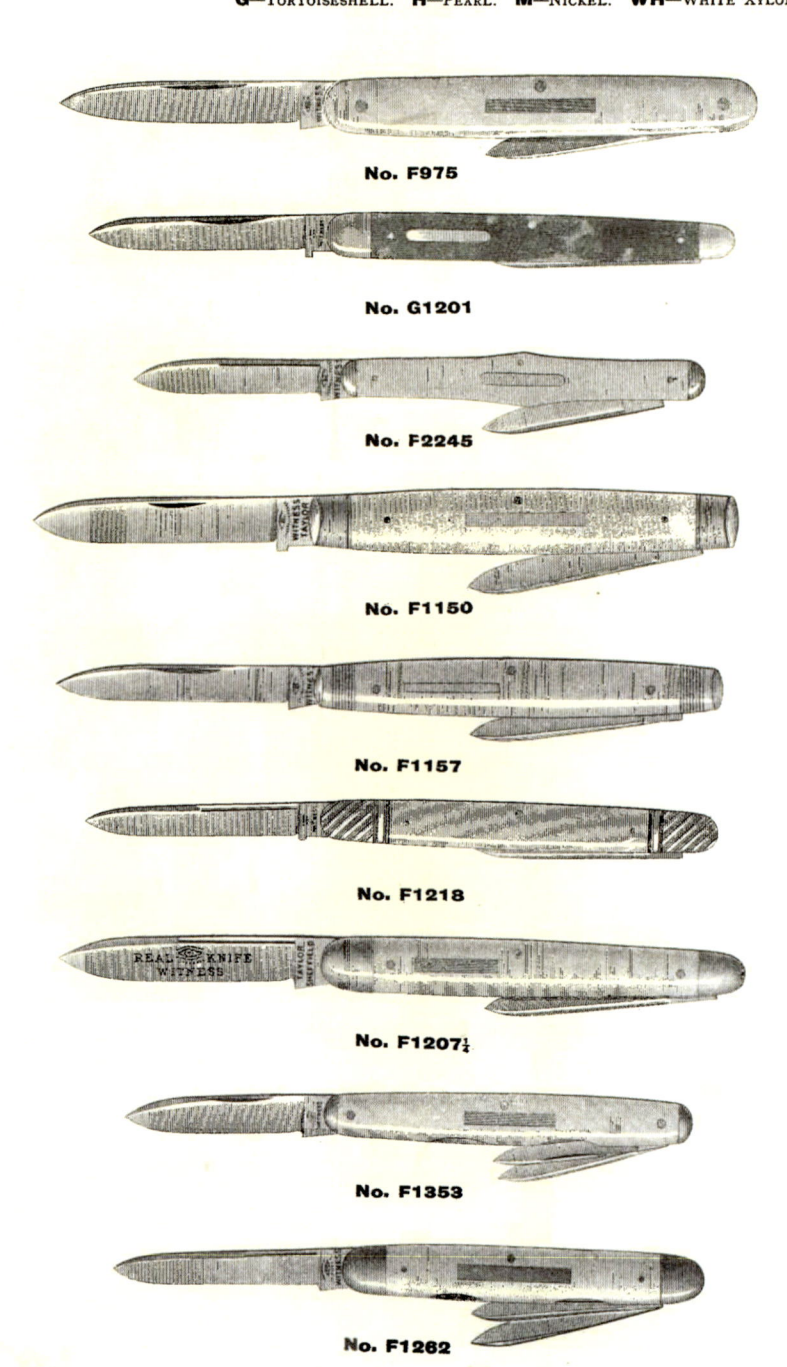

No. F975

No. G1201

No. F2245

No. F1150

No. F1157

No. F1218

No. F1207½

No. F1353

No. F1262

SECTION B
PAGE 26

Taylor's Witness
SHEFFIELD

Pen Knives.

TWO BLADES.
ILLUSTRATIONS ARE ACTUAL SIZE OF ARTICLES.

When ordering, prefix the LETTER to the Pattern Number to denote the kind of handle required, viz.:—
PLAIN **No.** IS STAG. **A**—BLACK. **C**—COCO. **D**—BLACK DIAMOND CHEQUERED. **F**—IVORY.
G—TORTOISESHELL. **H**—PEARL. **M**—NICKEL. **WH**—WHITE XYLONITE.

No. M1001
,, M1001½ Easy Open Ring Knife.

No. WH971

No. C977

No. M1017
,, M1017½ is Flat.

No. F1199

No. F985
,, 983 has Glazed Blades.

No. F989

No. F1156

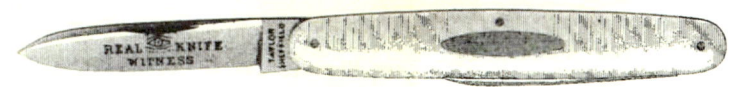

No. F1162

SECTION B
PAGE 27

Taylor's Witness Sheffield

Pen Knives.
TWO BLADES.
ILLUSTRATIONS ARE ACTUAL SIZE OF ARTICLES.

When ordering, prefix the LETTER to the Pattern Number to denote the kind of handle required, viz.:—
PLAIN **No.** IS STAG. **A**—BLACK. **C**—COCO. **D**—BLACK DIAMOND CHEQUERED. **F**—IVORY.
G—TORTOISESHELL. **H**—PEARL. **M**—NICKEL. **WH**—WHITE XYLONITE.

No. WH1195

No. F2173

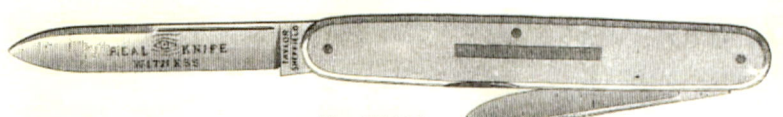

No. F1163

No. 1230. 2¾″ is No. 1226

No. A2246

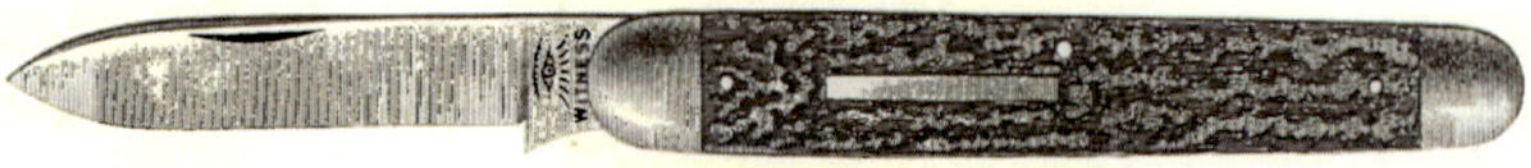

No. 2259

No. C1004

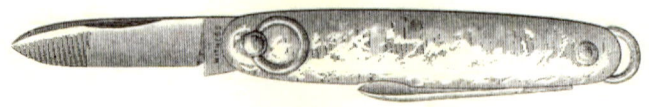

No. H998

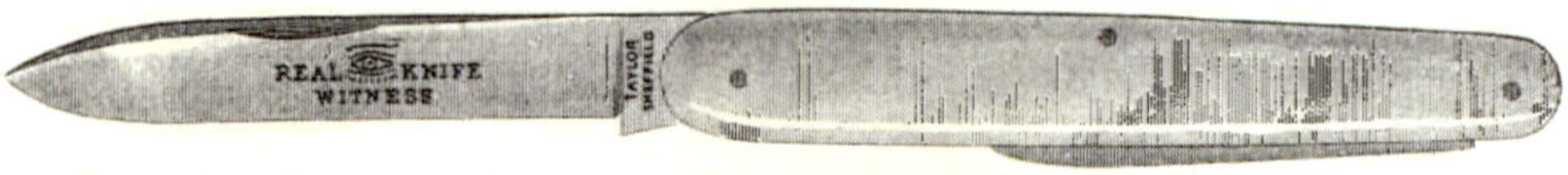

No. F1002. 3¼″ is No. 987

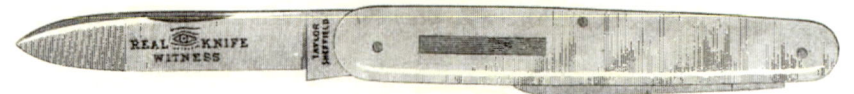

No. F1007

SECTION B
PAGE 28

TAYLOR'S WITNESS SHEFFIELD.

Pen Knives.

TWO BLADES.

ILLUSTRATIONS ARE ACTUAL SIZE OF ARTICLES.

When ordering, prefix the LETTER to the Pattern Number to denote the kind of handle required, viz.:—

PLAIN **No.** IS STAG. **A**—BLACK. **C**—COCO. **D**—BLACK DIAMOND CHEQUERED. **F**—IVORY
G—TORTOISESHELL. **H**—PEARL. **M**—NICKEL. **WH**—WHITE XYLONITE.

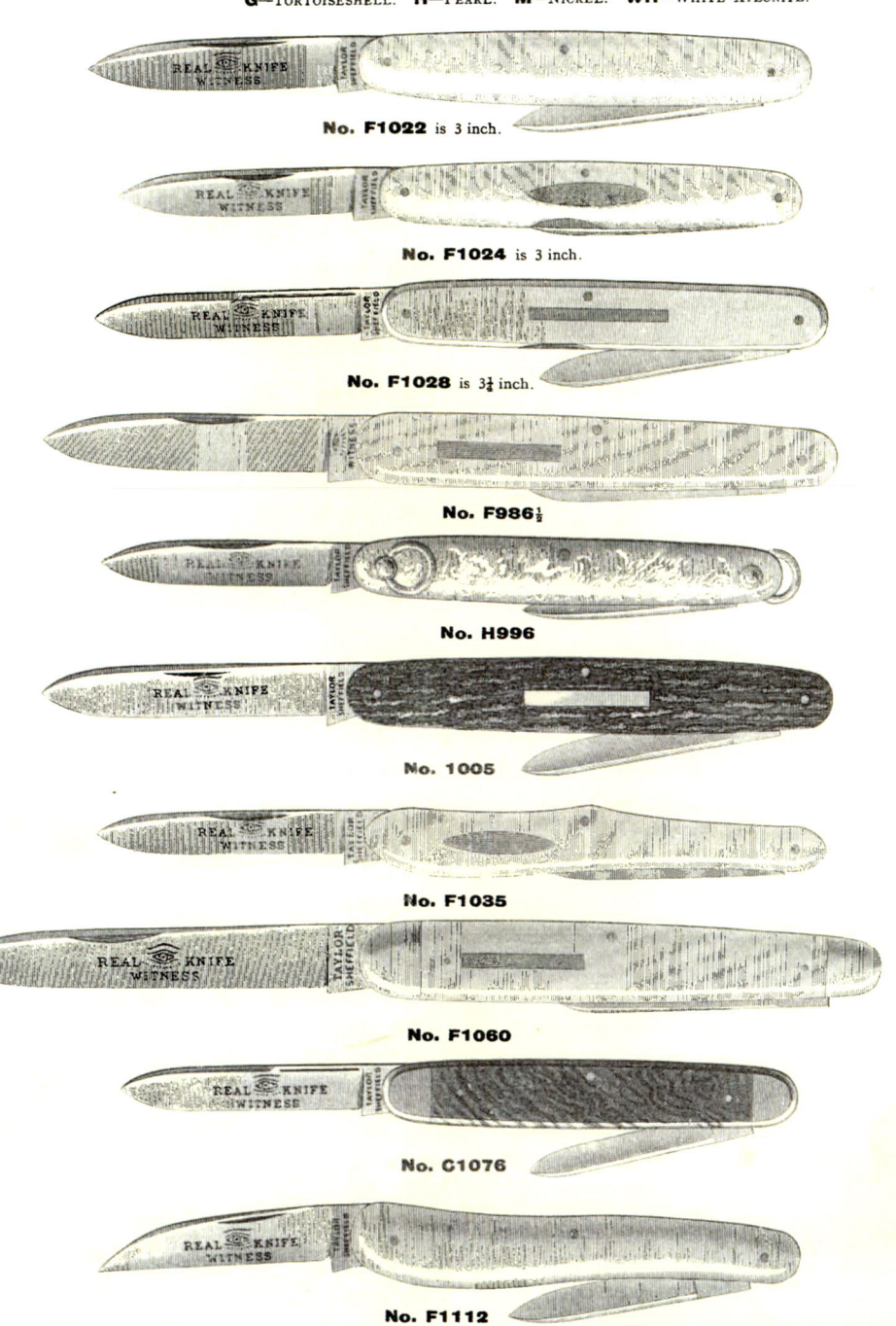

No. F1022 is 3 inch.

No. F1024 is 3 inch.

No. F1028 is 3¼ inch.

No. F986½

No. H996

No. 1005

No. F1035

No. F1060

No. C1076

No. F1112

SECTION B PAGE 29

Taylor's Witness Sheffield

Pen Knives.

TWO BLADES.

ILLUSTRATIONS ARE ACTUAL SIZE OF ARTICLES.

When ordering, prefix the LETTER to the Pattern Number to denote the kind of handle required, viz.:—

PLAIN **No.** IS STAG. **A**—BLACK. **C**—COCO. **D**—BLACK DIAMOND CHEQUERED. **F**—IVORY.
G—TORTOISESHELL. **H**—PEARL. **M**—NICKEL. **WH**—WHITE XYLONITE.

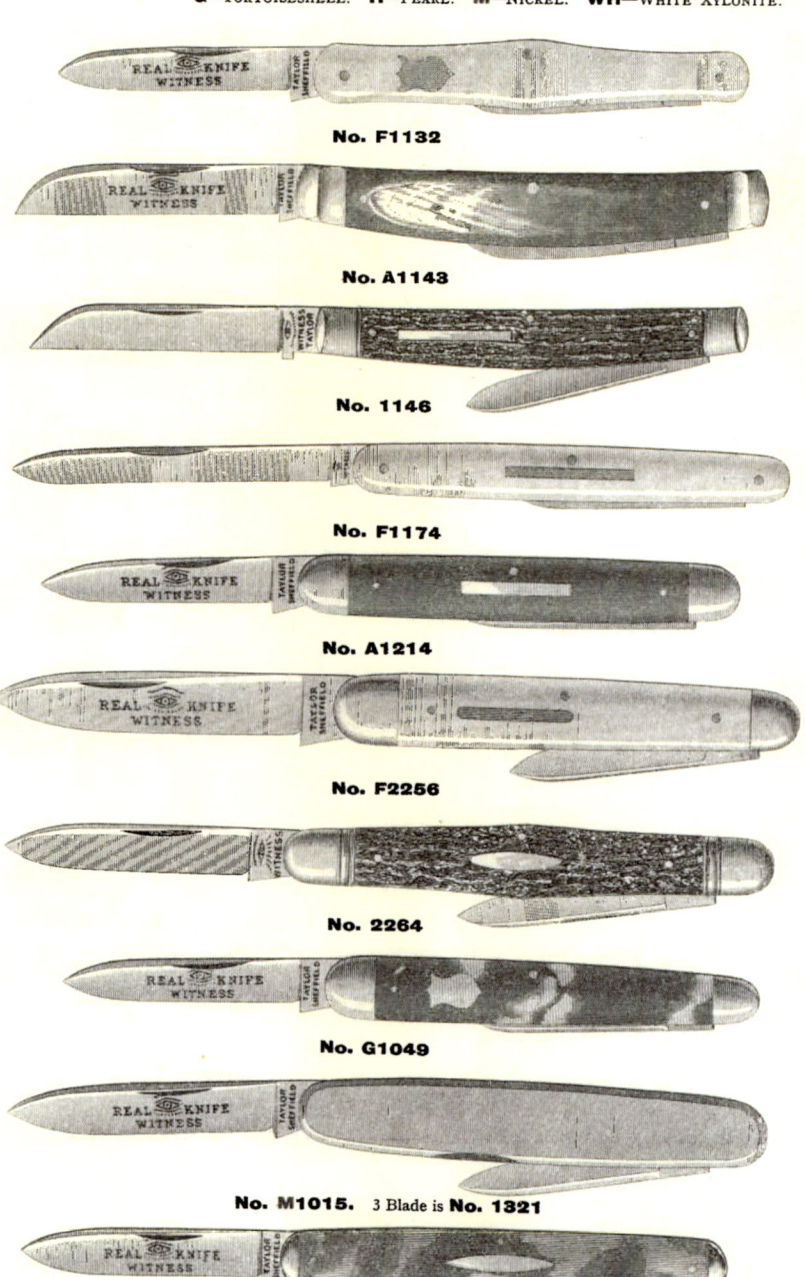

No. F1132

No. A1143

No. 1146

No. F1174

No. A1214

No. F2256

No. 2264

No. G1049

No. M1015.   3 Blade is No. 1321

No. G1039

TAYLOR'S WITNESS SHEFFIELD

Pen Knives.

TWO BLADES.

ILLUSTRATIONS ARE ACTUAL SIZE OF ARTICLES.

When ordering, prefix the LETTER to the Pattern Number to denote the kind of handle required, viz.:—
PLAIN **No.** IS STAG. **A**—BLACK. **C**—COCO. **D**—BLACK DIAMOND CHEQUERED. **F**—IVORY.
G—TORTOISESHELL. **H**—PEARL. **M**—NICKEL. **WH**—WHITE XYLONITE.

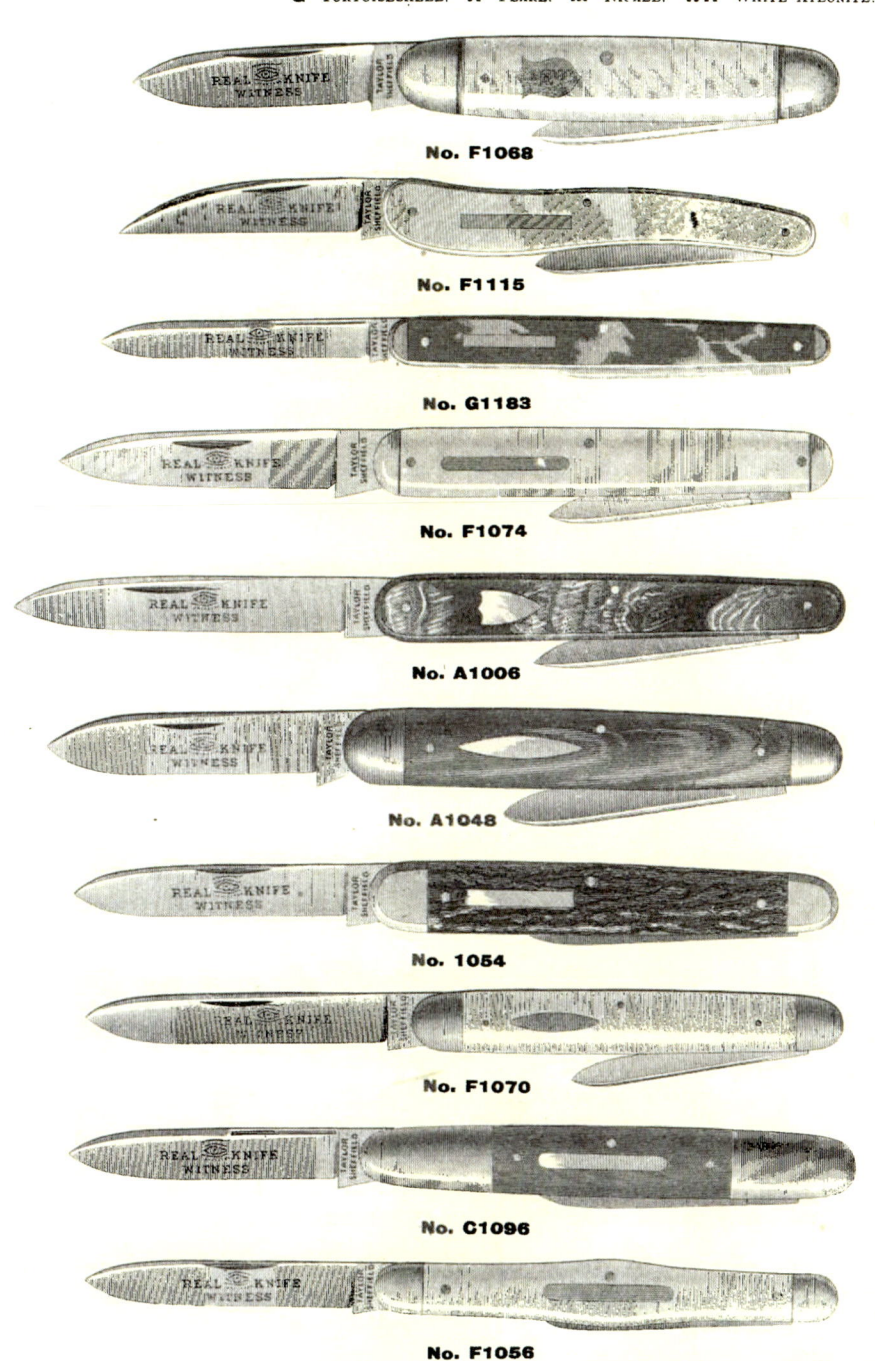

SECTION B
PAGE 30

No. F1068

No. F1115

No. G1183

No. F1074

No. A1006

No. A1048

No. 1054

No. F1070

No. C1096

No. F1056

SECTION B
PAGE 31

TAYLOR'S WITNESS SHEFFIELD

Pen Knives.
TWO BLADES.
ILLUSTRATIONS ARE ACTUAL SIZE OF ARTICLES.

When ordering, prefix the LETTER to the Pattern Number to denote the kind of handle required, viz.:—
PLAIN **No.** IS STAG. **A**—BLACK. **C**—COCO. **D**—BLACK DIAMOND CHEQUERED. **F**—IVORY.
G—TORTOISESHELL. **H**—PEARL. **M**—NICKEL. **WH**—WHITE XYLONITE.

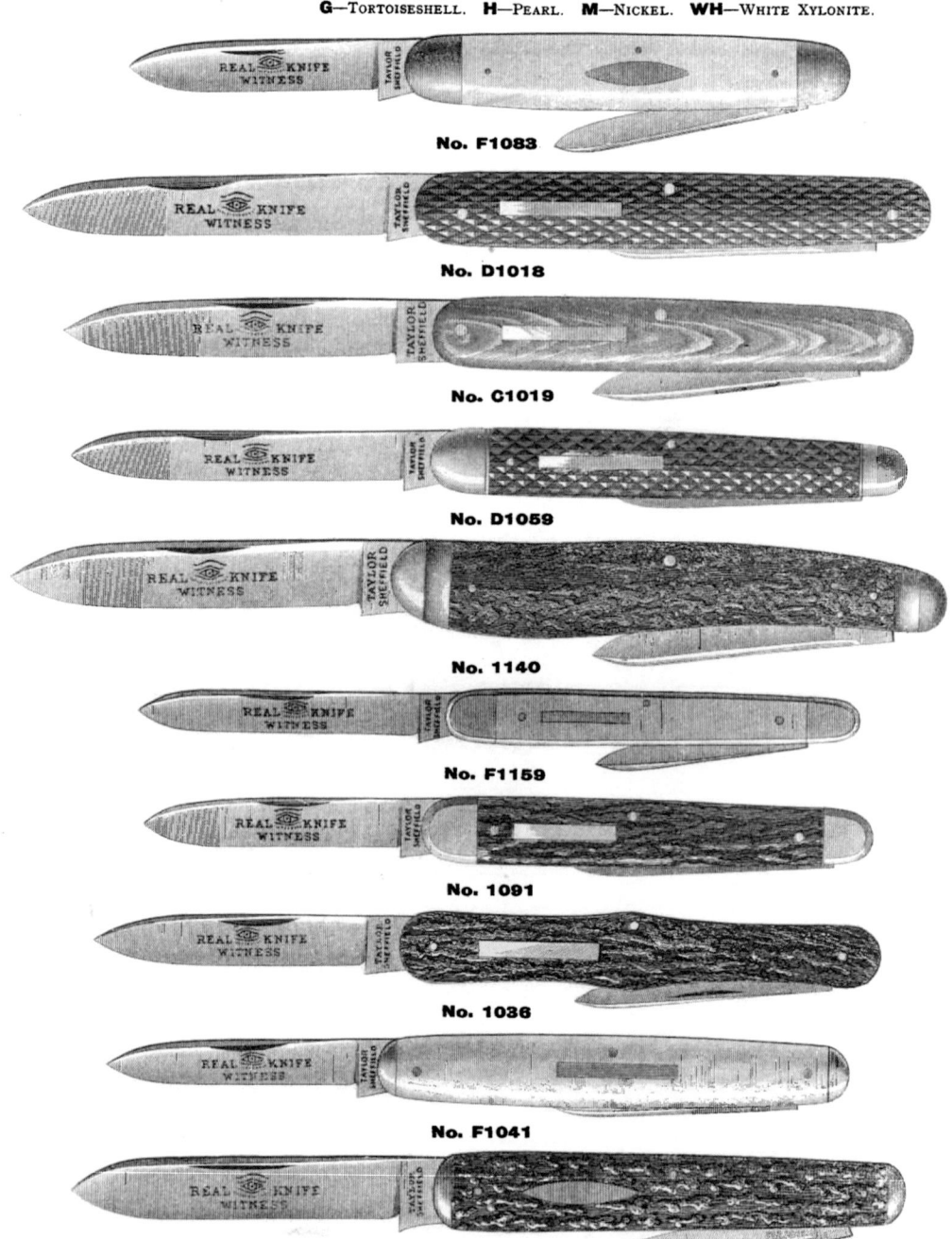

No. F1083

No. D1018

No. C1019

No. D1059

No. 1140

No. F1159

No. 1091

No. 1036

No. F1041

No. 1046

SECTION B
PAGE 32

Taylor's WITNESS SHEFFIELD

Pen Knives.

TWO BLADES.

ILLUSTRATIONS ARE ACTUAL SIZE OF ARTICLES.

When ordering, prefix the LETTER to the Pattern Number to denote the kind of handle required, viz.:—
PLAIN **No.** IS STAG. **A**—BLACK. **C**—COCO. **D**—BLACK DIAMOND CHEQUERED. **F**—IVORY.
G—TORTOISESHELL. **H**—PEARL. **M**—NICKEL. **WH**—WHITE XYLONITE.

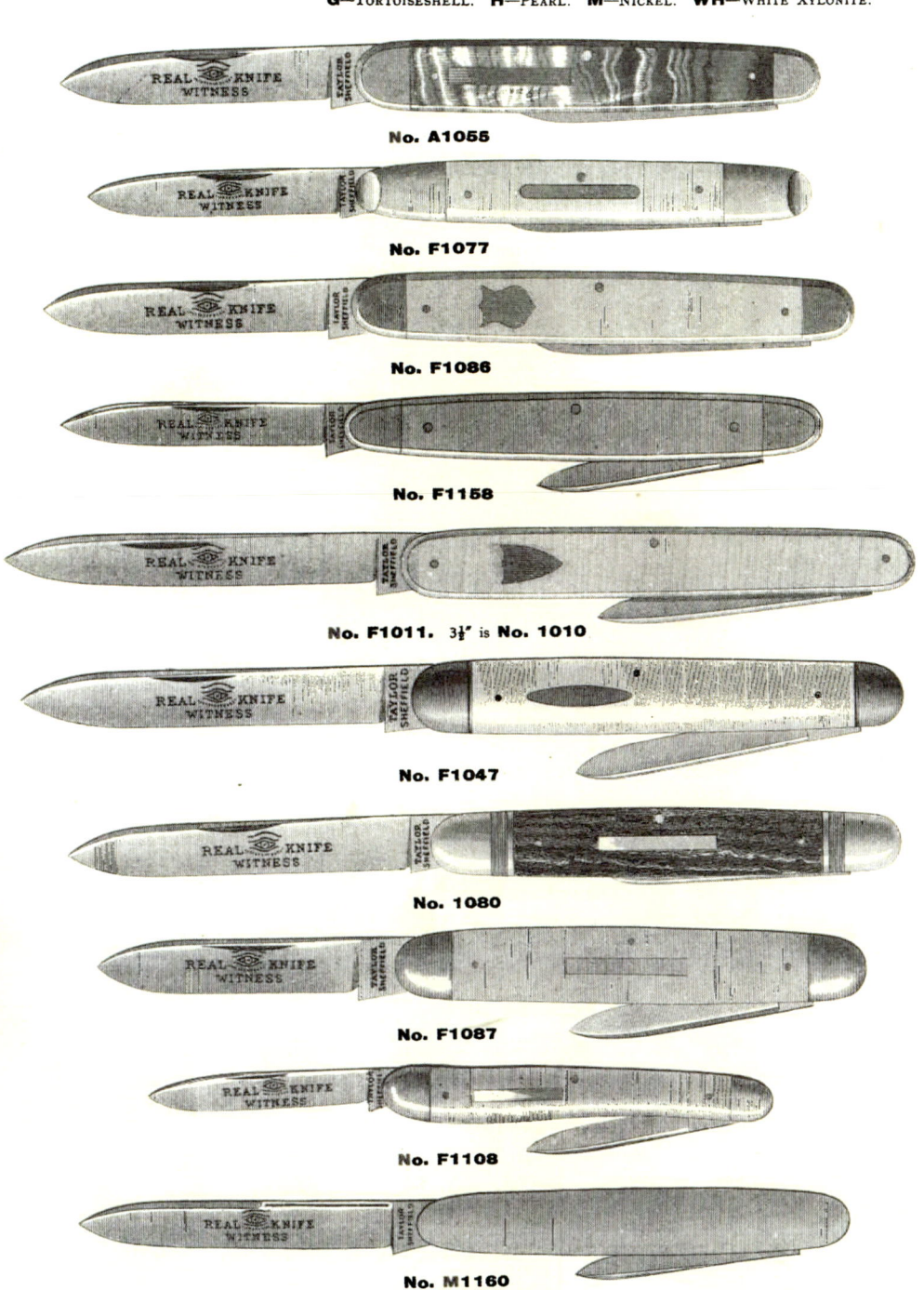

No. A1055

No. F1077

No. F1086

No. F1158

No. F1011.   3¼″ is No. 1010

No. F1047

No. 1080

No. F1087

No. F1108

No. M1160

SECTION B
PAGE 33

Taylor's Witness Sheffield

Pen Knives.

TWO BLADES.

ILLUSTRATIONS ARE ACTUAL SIZE OF ARTICLES.

When ordering, prefix the LETTER to the Pattern Number to denote the kind of handle required, viz.:—

Plain **No.** is Stag. **A**—Black. **C**—Coco. **D**—Black Diamond Chequered. **F**—Ivory. **G**—Tortoiseshell. **H**—Pearl. **M**—Nickel. **WH**—White Xylonite.

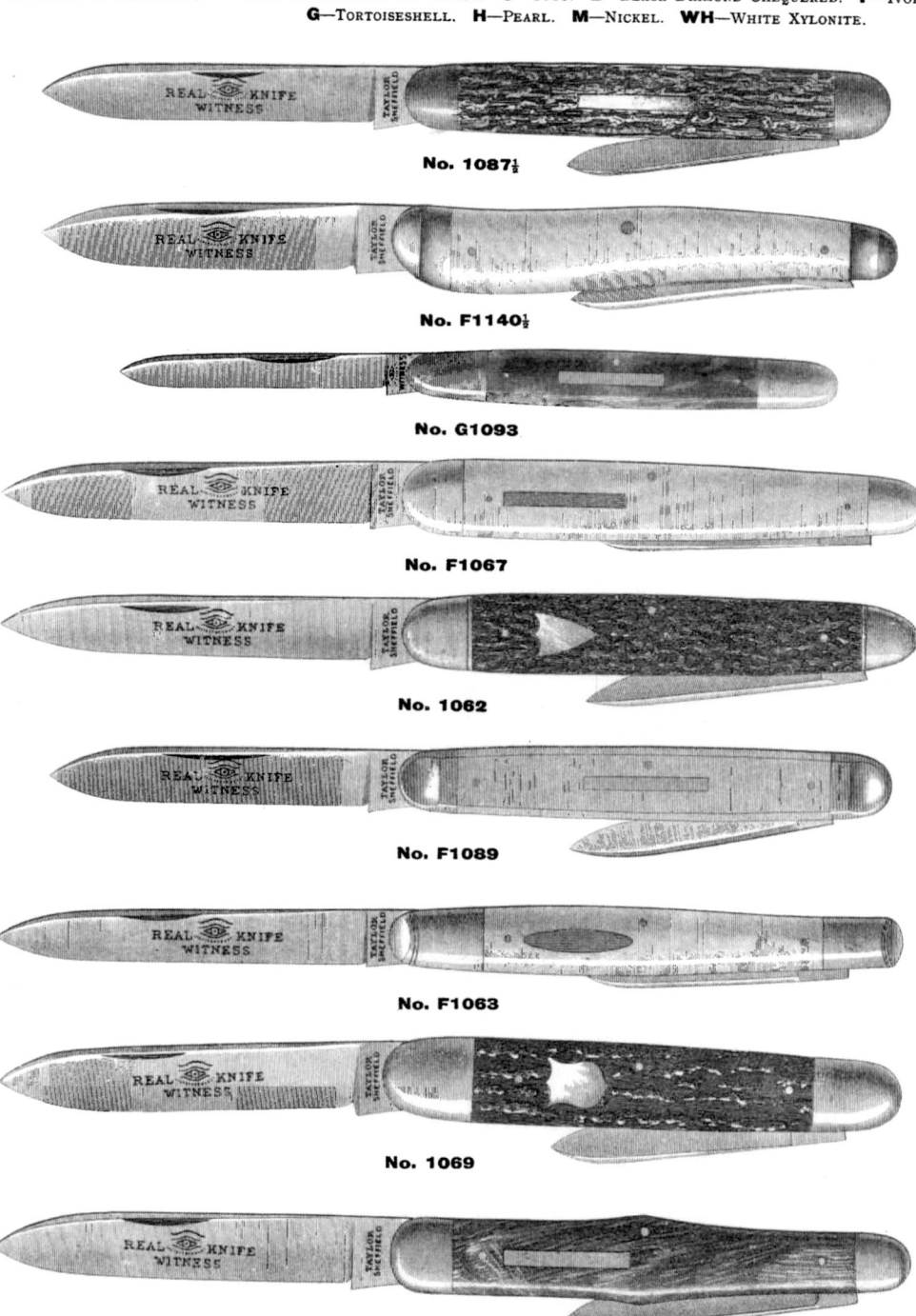

No. 1087½

No. F1140½

No. G1093

No. F1067

No. 1062

No. F1089

No. F1063

No. 1069

No. A1138

SECTION B
PAGE 34

Taylor's Witness Sheffield

Pen Knives.

TWO BLADES.

ILLUSTRATIONS ARE ACTUAL SIZE OF ARTICLES.

When ordering, prefix the LETTER to the Pattern Number to denote the kind of handle required, viz.:—

PLAIN **No.** IS STAG. **A**—BLACK. **C**—COCO. **D**—BLACK DIAMOND CHEQUERED. **F**—IVORY.
G—TORTOISESHELL. **H**—PEARL. **M**—NICKEL. **WH**—WHITE XYLONITE.

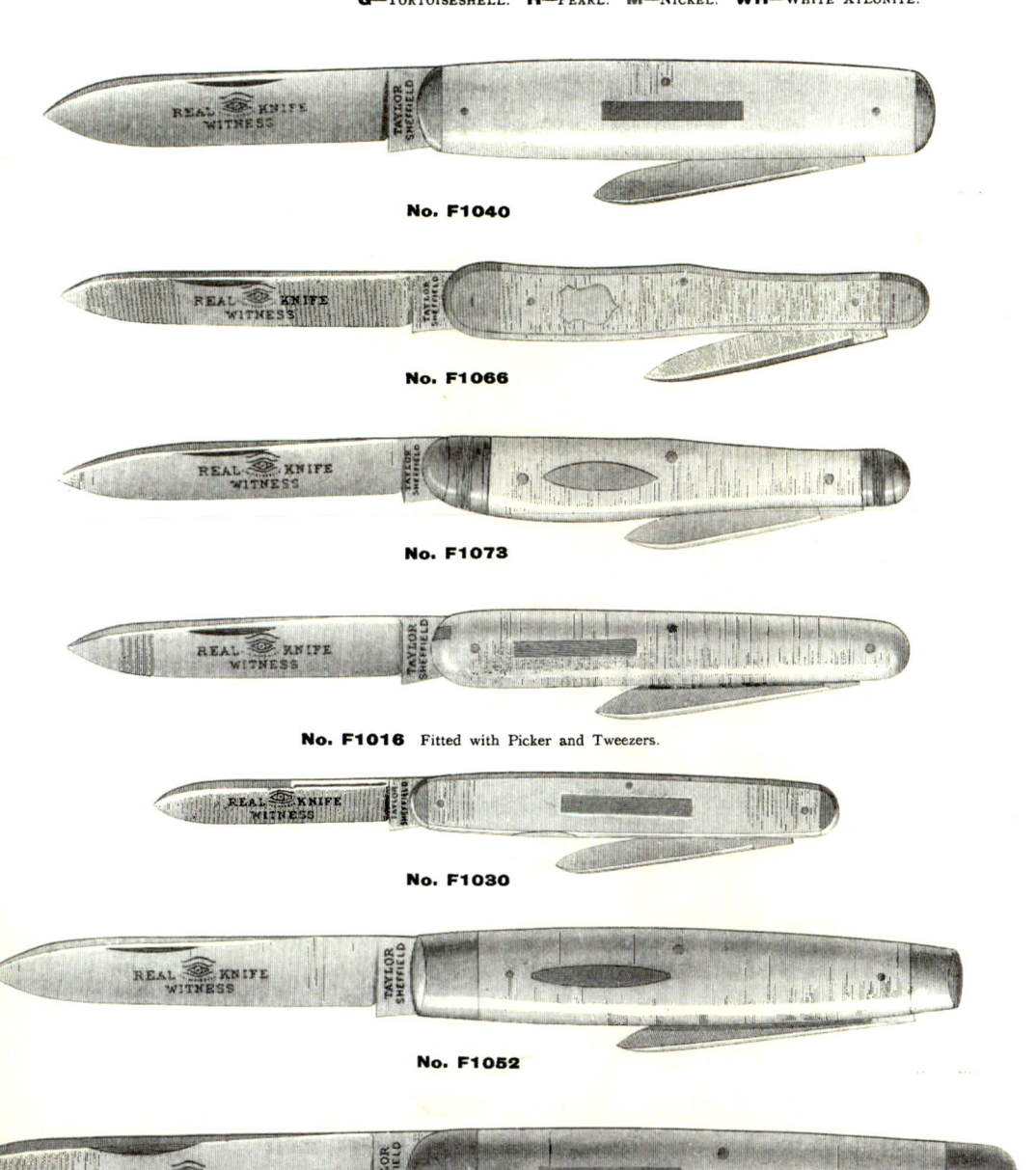

No. F1040

No. F1066

No. F1073

No. F1016 Fitted with Picker and Tweezers.

No. F1030

No. F1052

No. F1061

SECTION B
PAGE 35

Taylor's Witness Sheffield

Pen Knives.

THREE BLADES.

ILLUSTRATIONS ARE ACTUAL SIZE OF ARTICLES.

When ordering, prefix the LETTER to the Pattern Number to denote the kind of handle required, viz.:—
Plain **No.** is Stag. **A**—Black. **C**—Coco. **D**—Black Diamond Chequered. **F**—Ivory.
G—Tortoiseshell. **H**—Pearl. **M**—Nickel. **WH**—White Xylonite.

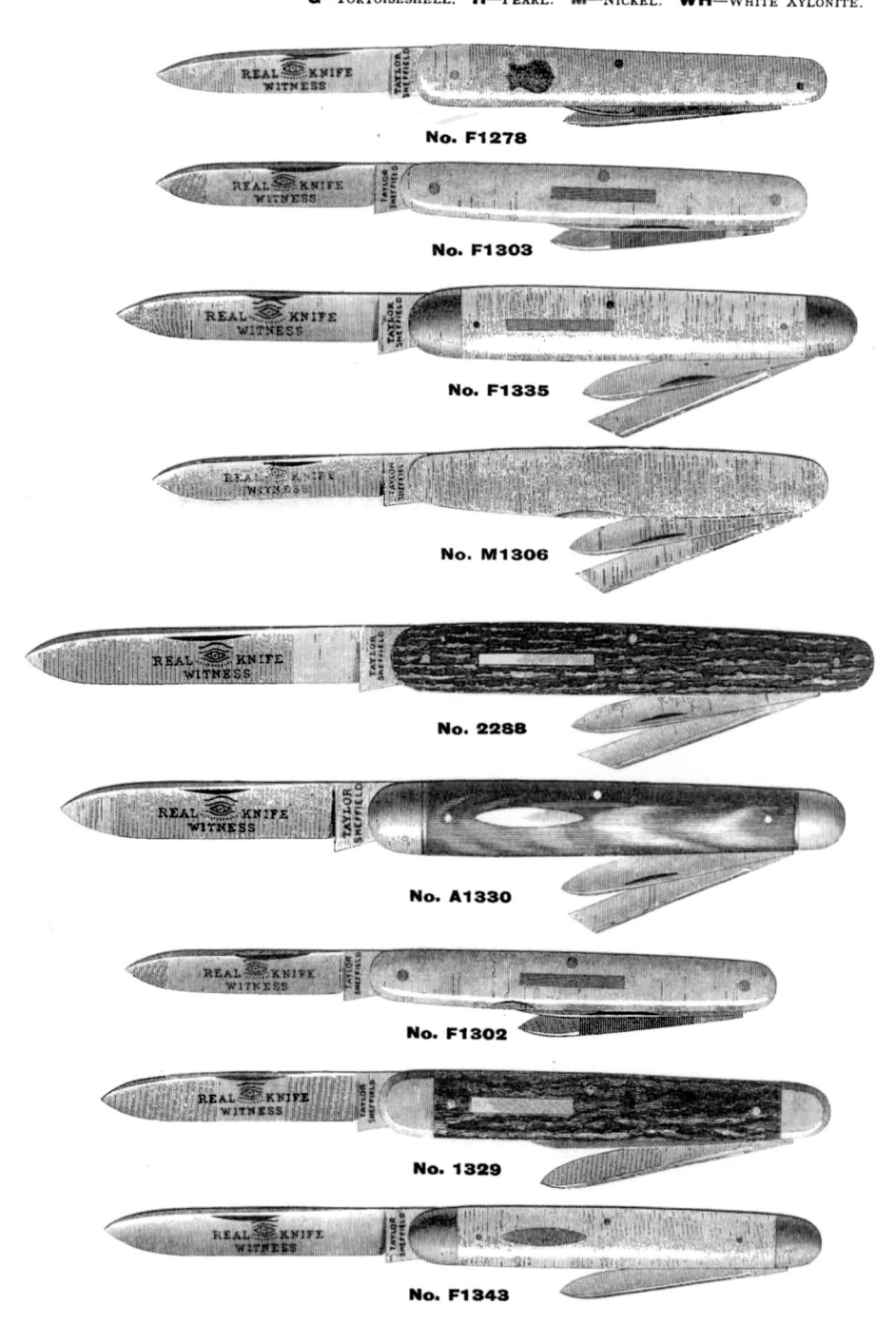

No. F1278

No. F1303

No. F1335

No. M1306

No. 2288

No. A1330

No. F1302

No. 1329

No. F1343

SECTION B
PAGE 36

Pen Knives.

TAYLOR'S WITNESS SHEFFIELD.

THREE BLADES.

ILLUSTRATIONS ARE ACTUAL SIZE OF ARTICLES.

When ordering, prefix the LETTER to the Pattern Number to denote the kind of handle required, viz.:—

Plain **No.** is Stag. **A**—Black. **C**—Coco. **D**—Black Diamond Chequered. **F**—Ivory.
G—Tortoiseshell. **H**—Pearl. **M**—Nickel. **WH**—White Xylonite.

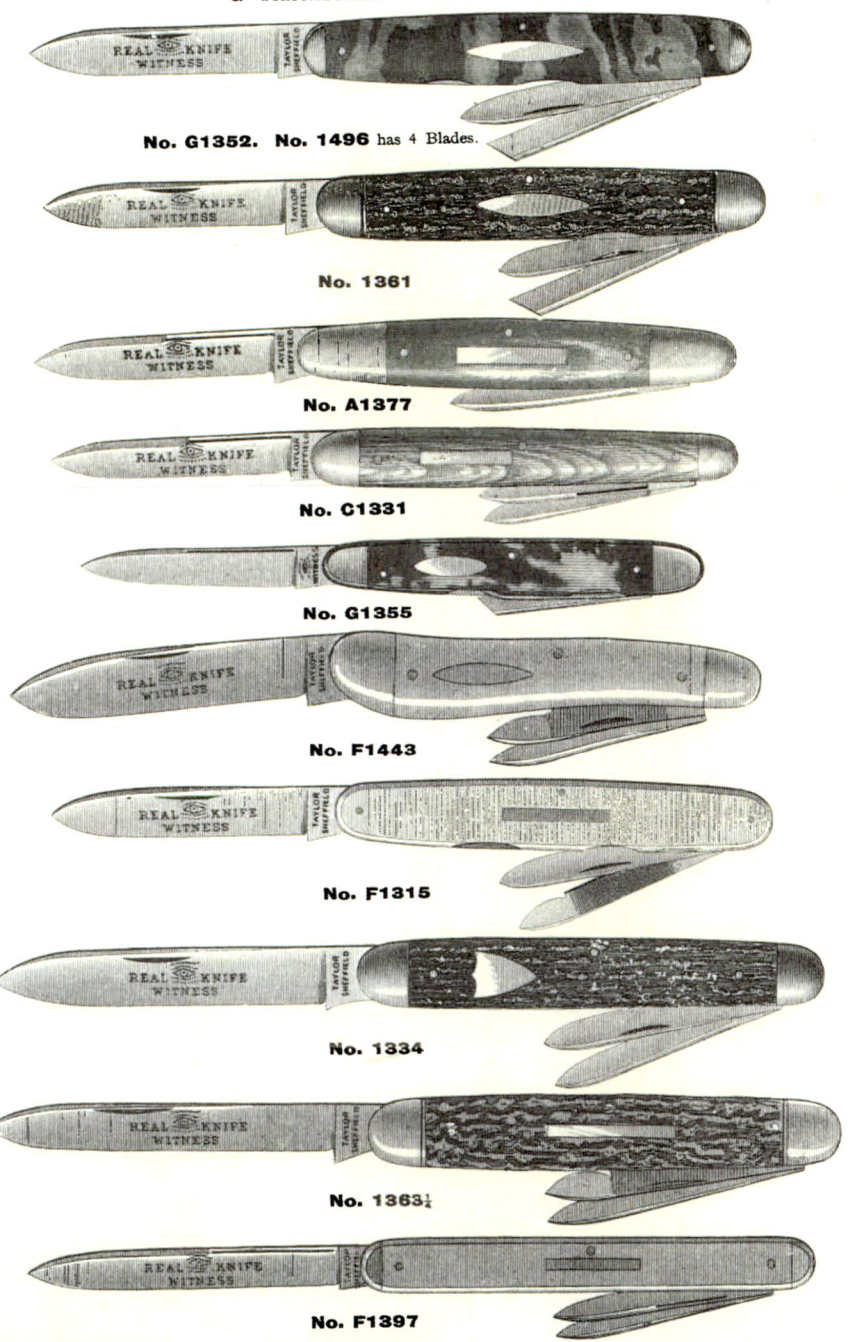

No. G1352. No. 1496 has 4 Blades.

No. 1361

No. A1377

No. C1331

No. G1355

No. F1443

No. F1315

No. 1334

No. 1363½

No. F1397

SECTION B
PAGE 37

Taylor's
WITNESS
SHEFFIELD.

Pen Knives.

THREE BLADES.
ILLUSTRATIONS ARE ACTUAL SIZE OF ARTICLES.

When ordering, prefix the LETTER to the Pattern Number to denote the kind of handle required, viz.:—
PLAIN **No.** IS STAG. **A**—BLACK. **C**—COCO. **D**—BLACK DIAMOND CHEQUERED. **F**—IVORY.
G—TORTOISESHELL. **H**—PEARL. **M**—NICKEL. **WH**—WHITE XYLONITE.

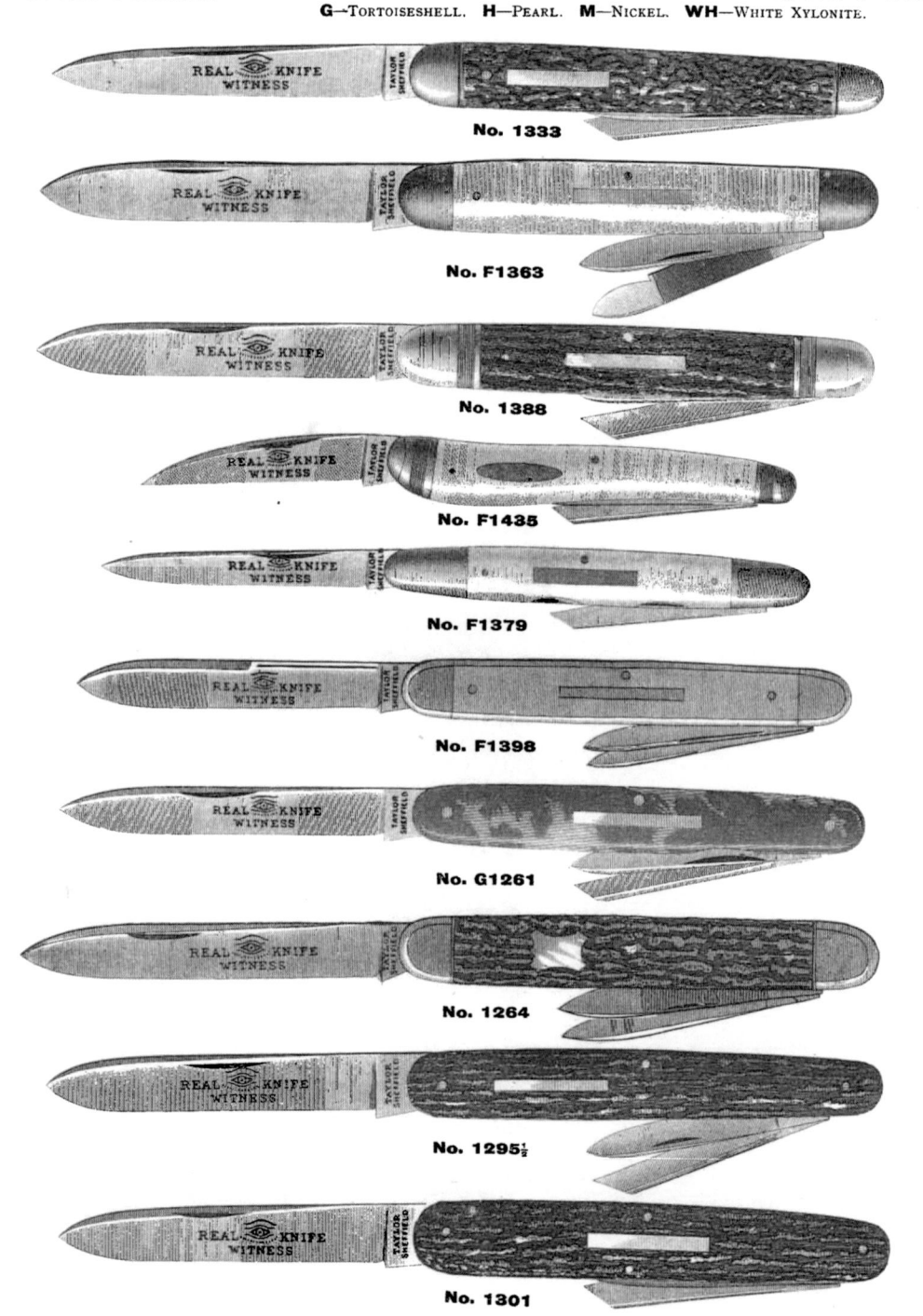

No. 1333

No. F1363

No. 1388

No. F1435

No. F1379

No. F1398

No. G1261

No. 1264

No. 1295½

No. 1301

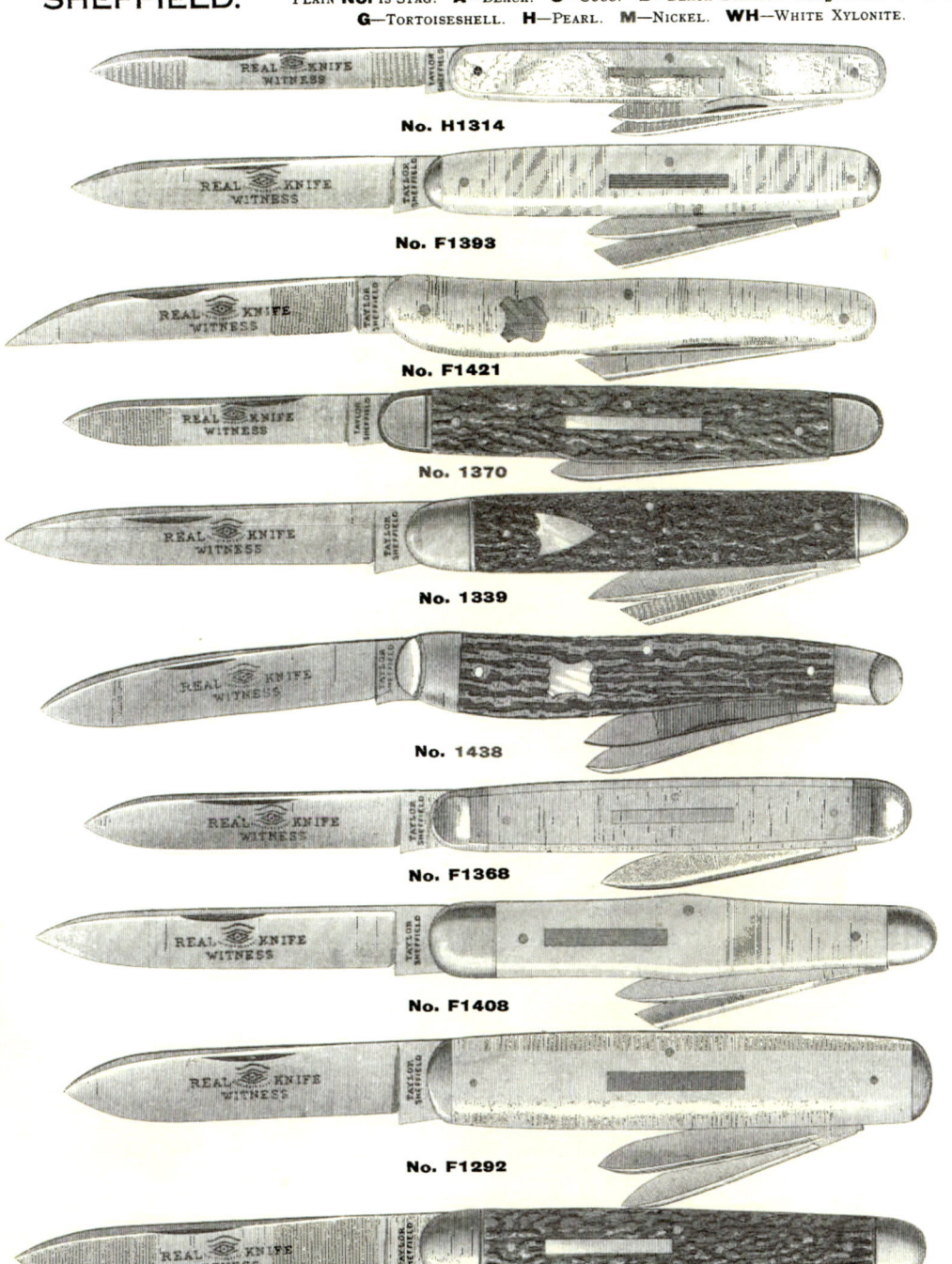

SECTION B
PAGE 38

Taylor's Witness Sheffield

Pen Knives.
THREE BLADES.
ILLUSTRATIONS ARE ACTUAL SIZE OF ARTICLES.

When ordering, prefix the LETTER to the Pattern Number to denote the kind of handle required, viz.:—

PLAIN **No.** IS STAG. **A**—BLACK. **C**—COCO. **D**—BLACK DIAMOND CHEQUERED. **F**—IVORY.
G—TORTOISESHELL. **H**—PEARL. **M**—NICKEL. **WH**—WHITE XYLONITE.

No. H1314

No. F1393

No. F1421

No. 1370

No. 1339

No. 1438

No. F1368

No. F1408

No. F1292

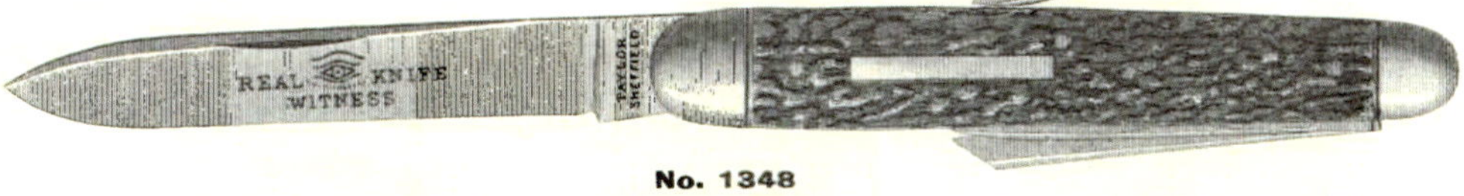

No. 1348

SECTION B
PAGE 39

Taylor's
WITNESS
SHEFFIELD.

Pen Knives.

FOUR BLADES.

ILLUSTRATIONS ARE ACTUAL SIZE OF ARTICLES.

When ordering, prefix the LETTER to the Pattern Number to denote the kind of handle required, viz.:—
Plain **No.** is Stag. **A**—Black. **C**—Coco. **D**—Black Diamond Chequered. **F**—Ivory.
G—Tortoiseshell. **H**—Pearl. **M**—Nickel. **WH**—White Xylonite.

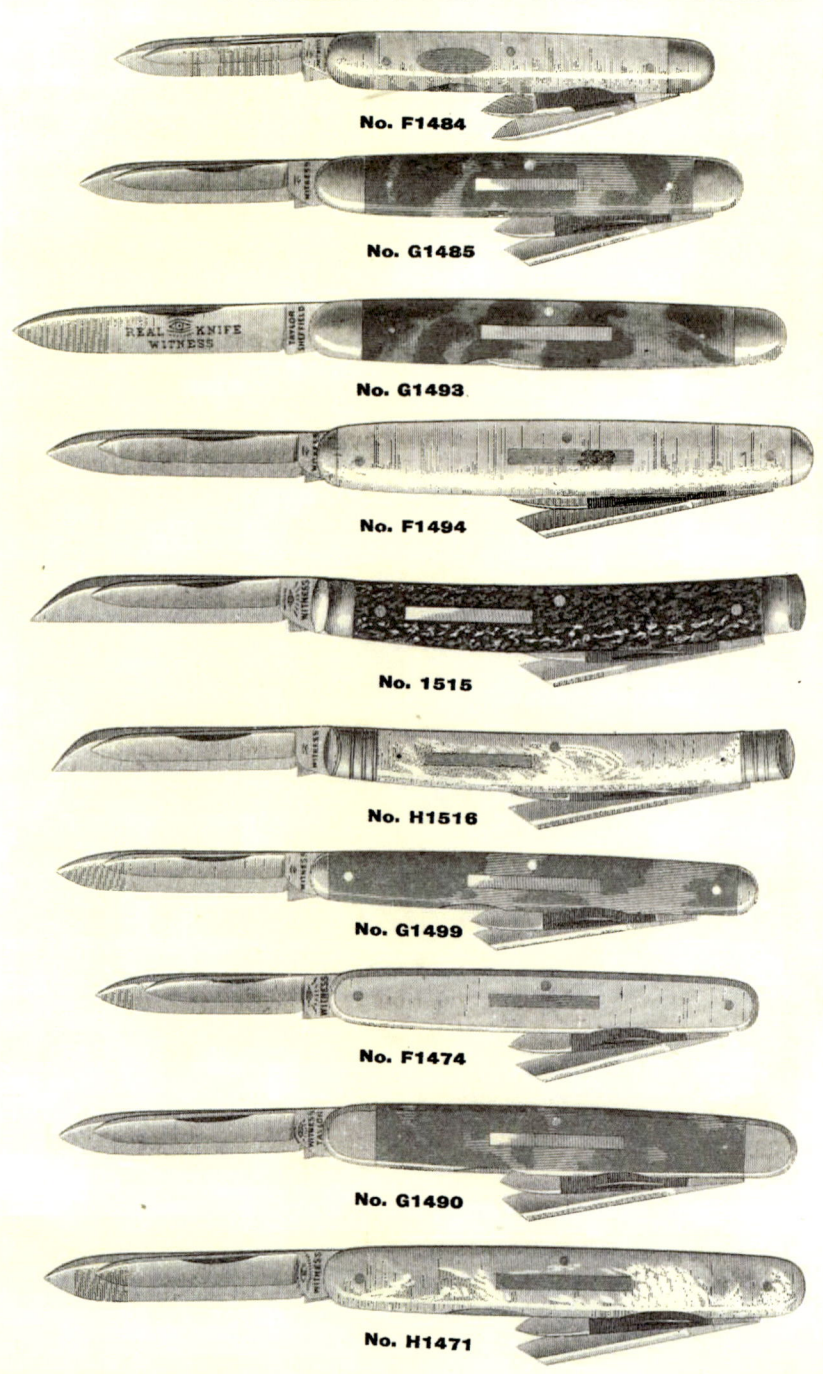

No. F1484

No. G1485

No. G1493

No. F1494

No. 1515

No. H1516

No. G1499

No. F1474

No. G1490

No. H1471

SECTION B
PAGE 40

Pen Knives.

TAYLOR'S WITNESS SHEFFIELD.

ILLUSTRATIONS ARE ACTUAL SIZE OF ARTICLES.

When ordering, prefix the LETTER to the Pattern Number to denote the kind of handle required, viz.:—
PLAIN **No.** IS STAG. **A**—BLACK. **C**—COCO. **D**—BLACK DIAMOND CHEQUERED. **F**—IVORY.
G—TORTOISESHELL. **H**—PEARL. **M**—NICKEL. **WH**—WHITE XYLONITE.

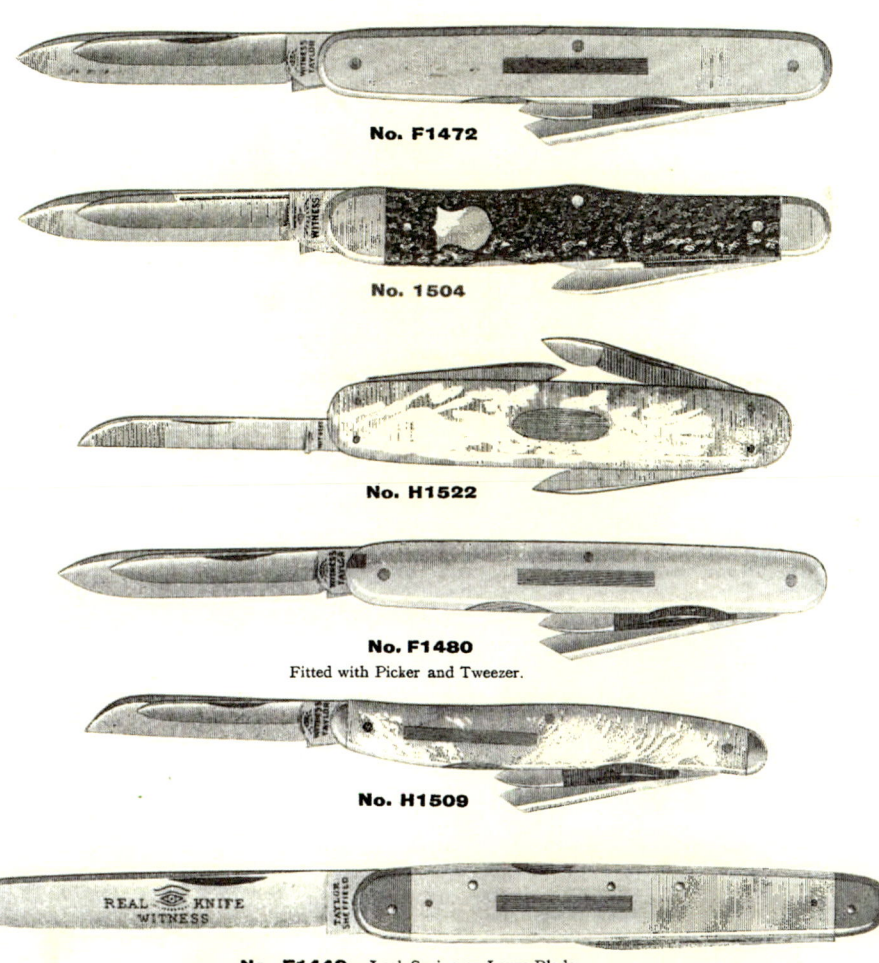

No. F1472

No. 1504

No. H1522

No. F1480
Fitted with Picker and Tweezer.

No. H1509

No. F1449. Lock Spring on Large Blade.

Shows Worked Back of **Nos. 1481** and **1032**.

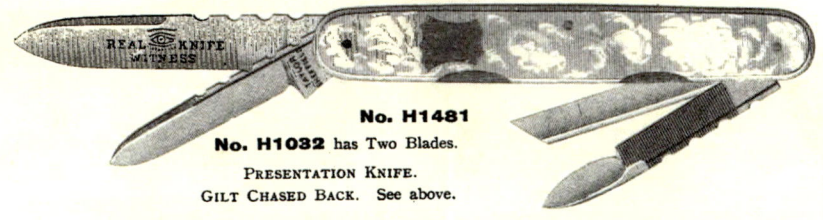

No. H1481
No. H1032 has Two Blades.
PRESENTATION KNIFE.
GILT CHASED BACK. See above.

No. H1033 Plain Back, Not Gilt, has Two Blades and is 3¼″

**SECTION B
PAGE 41**

Taylor's WITNESS SHEFFIELD.

Scissor Knives.

ILLUSTRATIONS ARE ACTUAL SIZE OF ARTICLES.

When ordering, prefix the LETTER to the Pattern Number to denote the kind of handle required, viz.:—
PLAIN **No.** IS STAG. **A**—BLACK. **C**—COCO. **D**—BLACK DIAMOND CHEQUERED. **F**—IVORY.
G—TORTOISESHELL. **H**—PEARL. **M**—NICKEL. **WH**—WHITE XYLONITE.

No. M1527

No. F1544

No. G1530
2¼″ is No. 1529

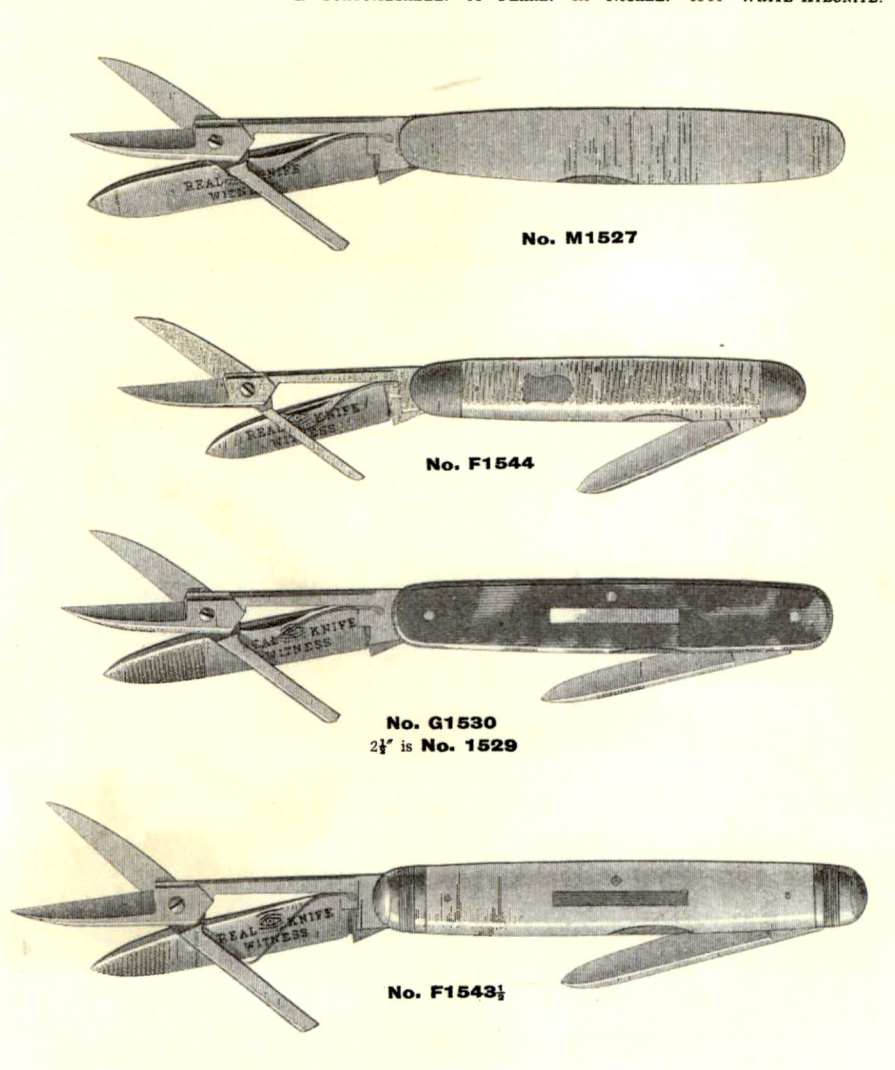

No. F1543½

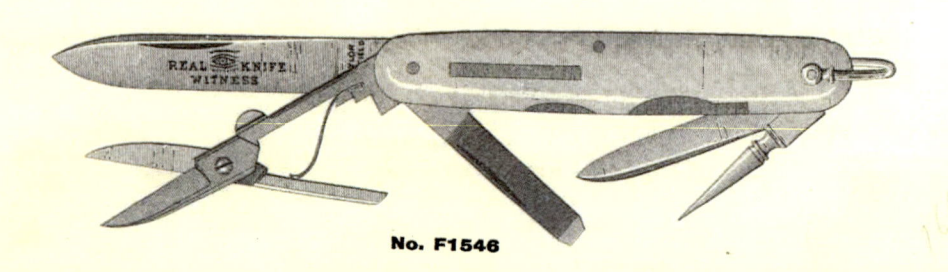

No. F1546

SECTION B
PAGE 42

Taylor's
WITNESS SHEFFIELD.

Smokers' Knives.

ILLUSTRATIONS ARE ACTUAL SIZE OF ARTICLES.

When ordering, prefix the LETTER to the Pattern Number to denote the kind of handle required, viz.:—
PLAIN **No.** IS STAG. **A**—BLACK. **C**—COCO. **D**—BLACK DIAMOND CHEQUERED. **F**—IVORY.
G—TORTOISESHELL. **H**—PEARL. **M**—NICKEL. **WH**—WHITE XYLONITE.

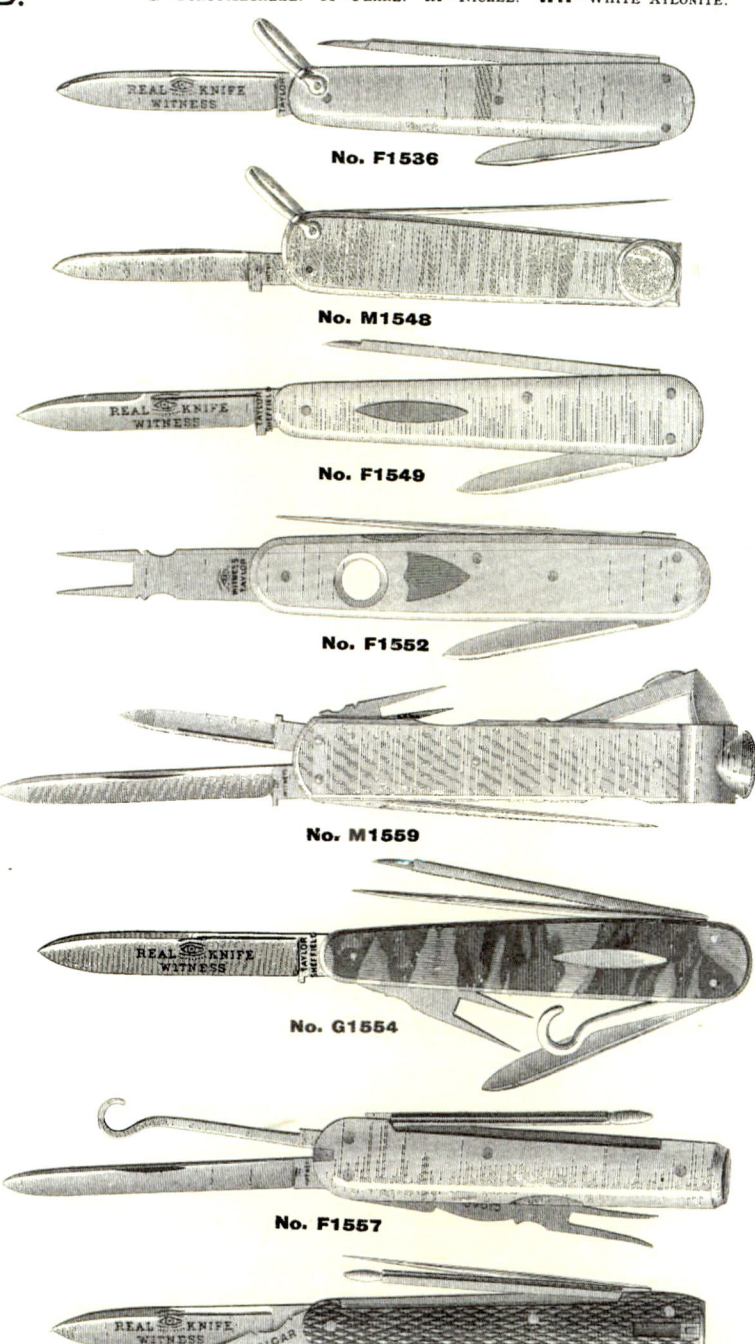

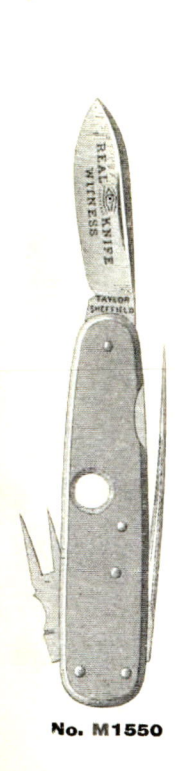

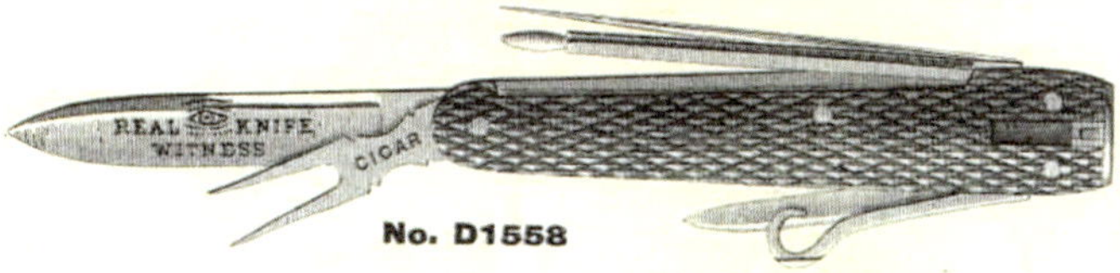

No. F1536

No. M1548

No. F1549

No. F1552

No. M1550

No. M1559

No. G1554

No. F1557

No. D1558

SECTION B
PAGE 43

Taylor's WITNESS SHEFFIELD.

Champagne Knives.

ILLUSTRATIONS ARE ACTUAL SIZE OF ARTICLES.

When ordering, prefix the LETTER to the Pattern Number to denote the kind of handle required, viz.:—
PLAIN **No.** IS STAG.   **A**—BLACK.   **C**—COCO.   **D**—BLACK DIAMOND CHEQUERED.   **F**—IVORY.
G—TORTOISESHELL.   **H**—PEARL.   **M**—NICKEL.   **WH**—WHITE XYLONITE.

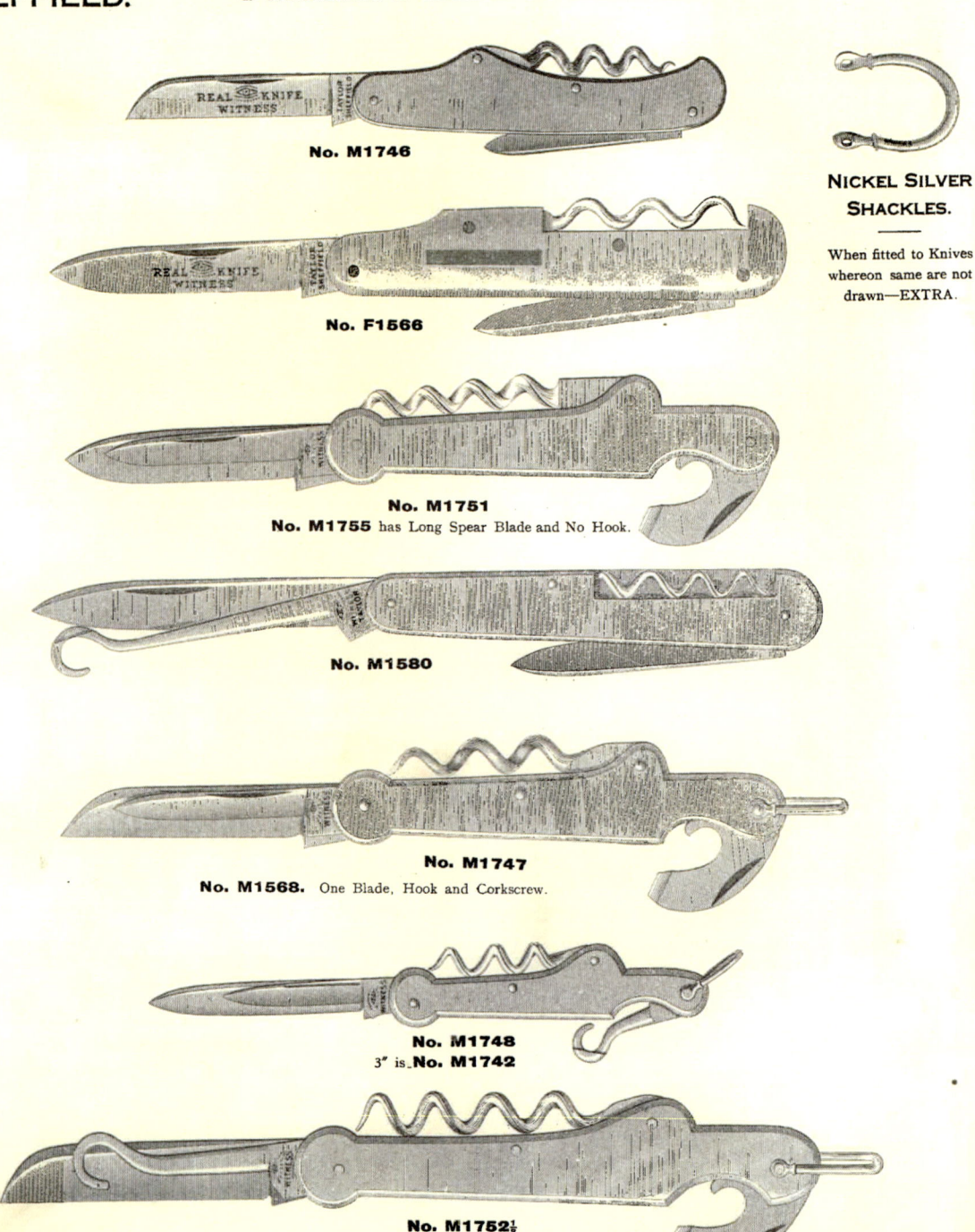

No. M1746

No. F1566

NICKEL SILVER SHACKLES.

When fitted to Knives whereon same are not drawn—EXTRA.

No. M1751
No. M1755 has Long Spear Blade and No Hook.

No. M1580

No. M1747
No. M1568. One Blade, Hook and Corkscrew.

No. M1748
3″ is **No. M1742**

No. M1752½

No. M1752 has Pen Blade in place of Button Hook.

TAYLOR'S WITNESS SHEFFIELD.

Shooting & Fishing Knives.

ILLUSTRATIONS ARE ACTUAL SIZE OF ARTICLES.

When ordering, prefix the LETTER to the Pattern Number to denote the kind of handle required, viz.:—
PLAIN **No.** IS STAG. **A**—BLACK. **C**—COCO. **D**—BLACK DIAMOND CHEQUERED. **F**—IVORY.
G—TORTOISESHELL. **H**—PEARL. **M**—NICKEL. **WH**—WHITE XYLONITE.

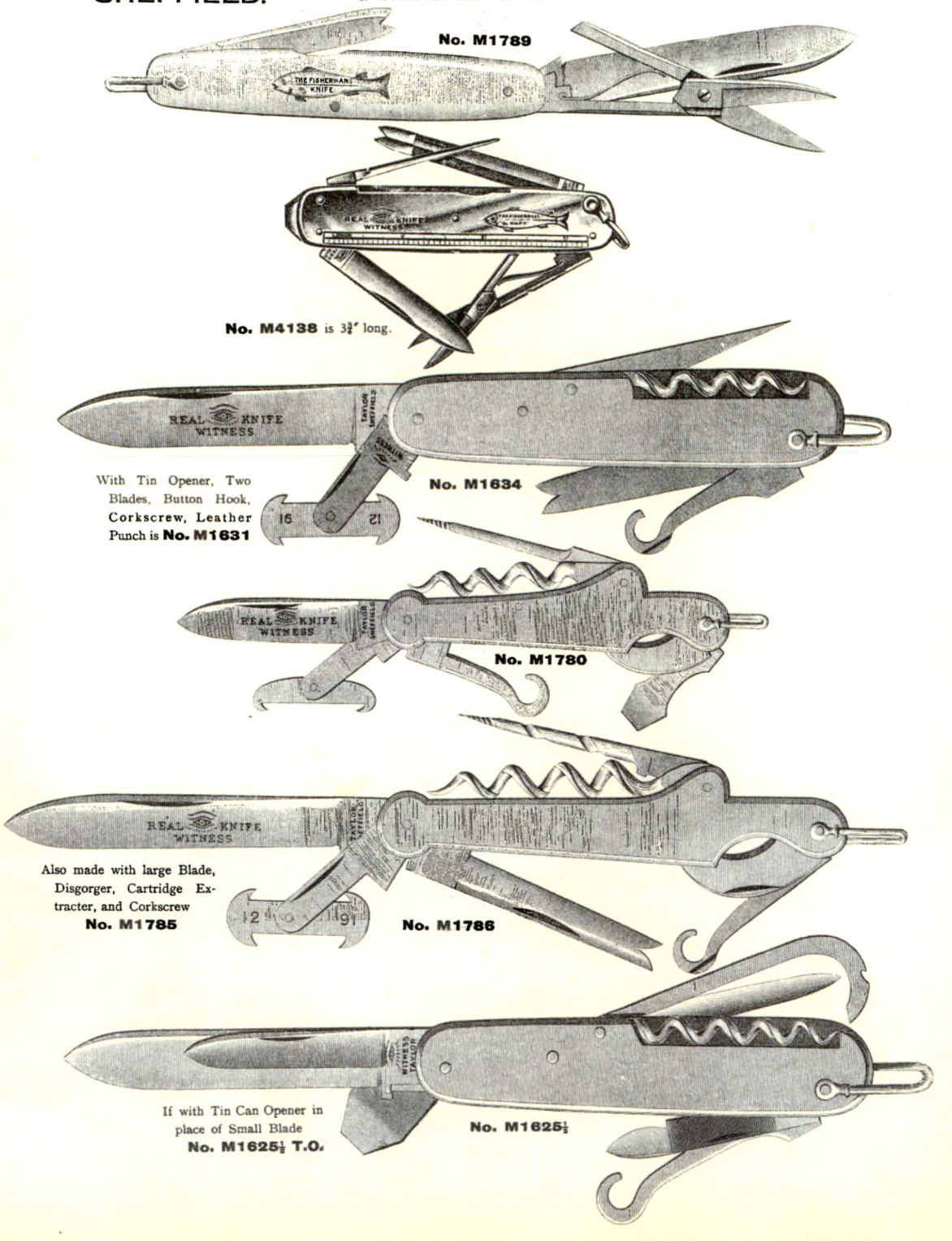

SECTION B
PAGE 44

No. M1789

No. M4138 is 3¾" long.

With Tin Opener, Two Blades, Button Hook, Corkscrew, Leather Punch is **No. M1631**

No. M1634

No. M1780

Also made with large Blade, Disgorger, Cartridge Extracter, and Corkscrew
No. M1785

No. M1786

If with Tin Can Opener in place of Small Blade
No. M1625½ T.O.

No. M1625½

SECTION B
PAGE 45

Taylor's Witness Sheffield.

Sportsmen's Knives.

ILLUSTRATIONS ARE ACTUAL SIZE OF ARTICLES.

When ordering, prefix the LETTER to the Pattern Number to denote the kind of handle required, viz.:—
Plain **No.** is Stag. **A**—Black. **C**—Coco. **D**—Black Diamond Chequered. **F**—Ivory.
G—Tortoiseshell. **H**—Pearl. **M**—Nickel. **WH**—White Xylonite.

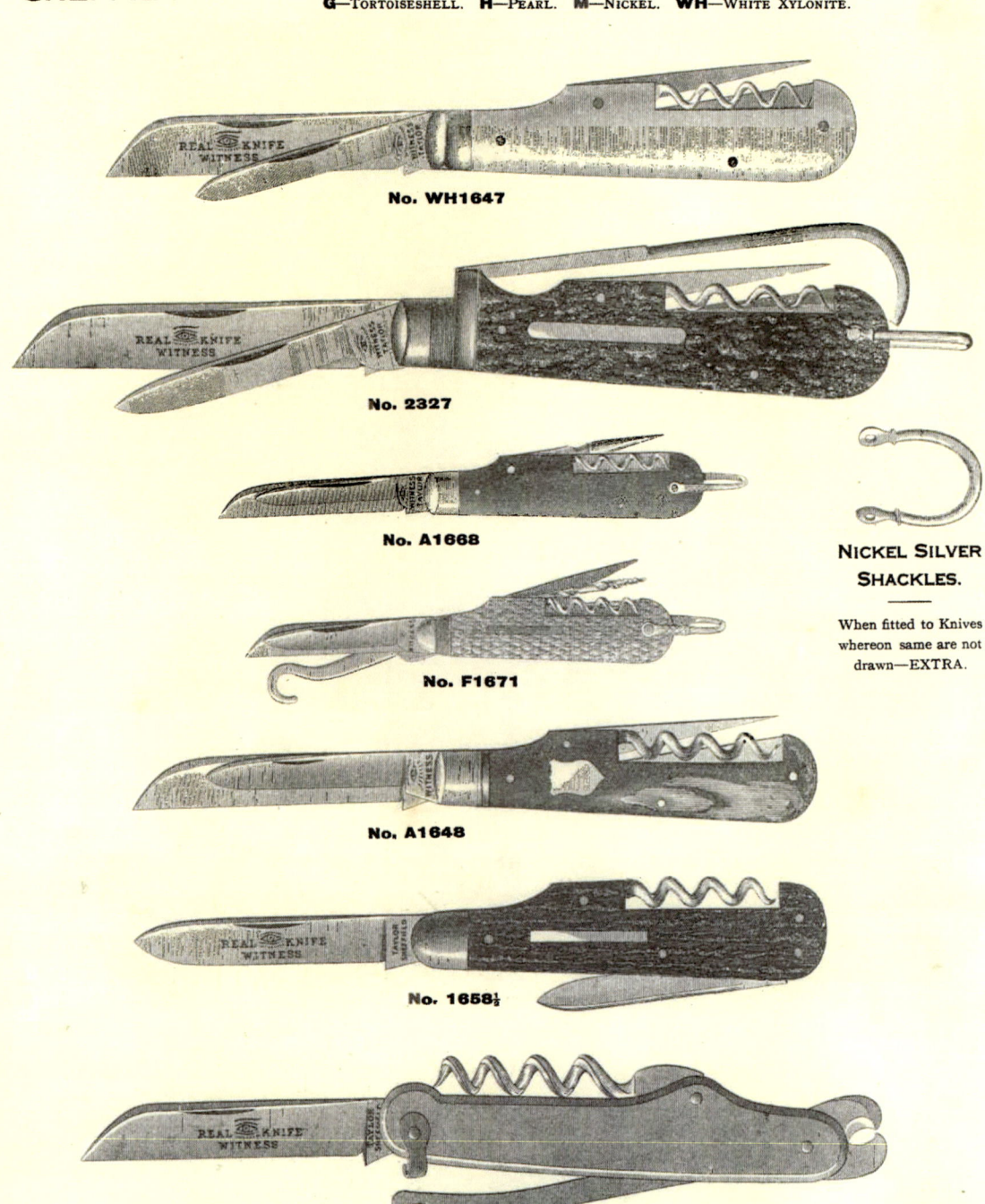

No. WH1647

No. 2327

No. A1668

No. F1671

NICKEL SILVER SHACKLES.

When fitted to Knives whereon same are not drawn—EXTRA.

No. A1648

No. 1658½

No. M1788

Taylor's Witness Sheffield

Sportsmen's Knives.

SECTION B
PAGE 46

ILLUSTRATIONS ARE ACTUAL SIZE OF ARTICLES.

When ordering, prefix the LETTER to the Pattern Number to denote the kind of handle required, viz.:—
Plain **No.** is Stag. **A**—Black. **C**—Coco. **D**—Black Diamond Chequered. **F**—Ivory.
G—Tortoiseshell. **H**—Pearl. **M**—Nickel. **WH**—White Xylonite.

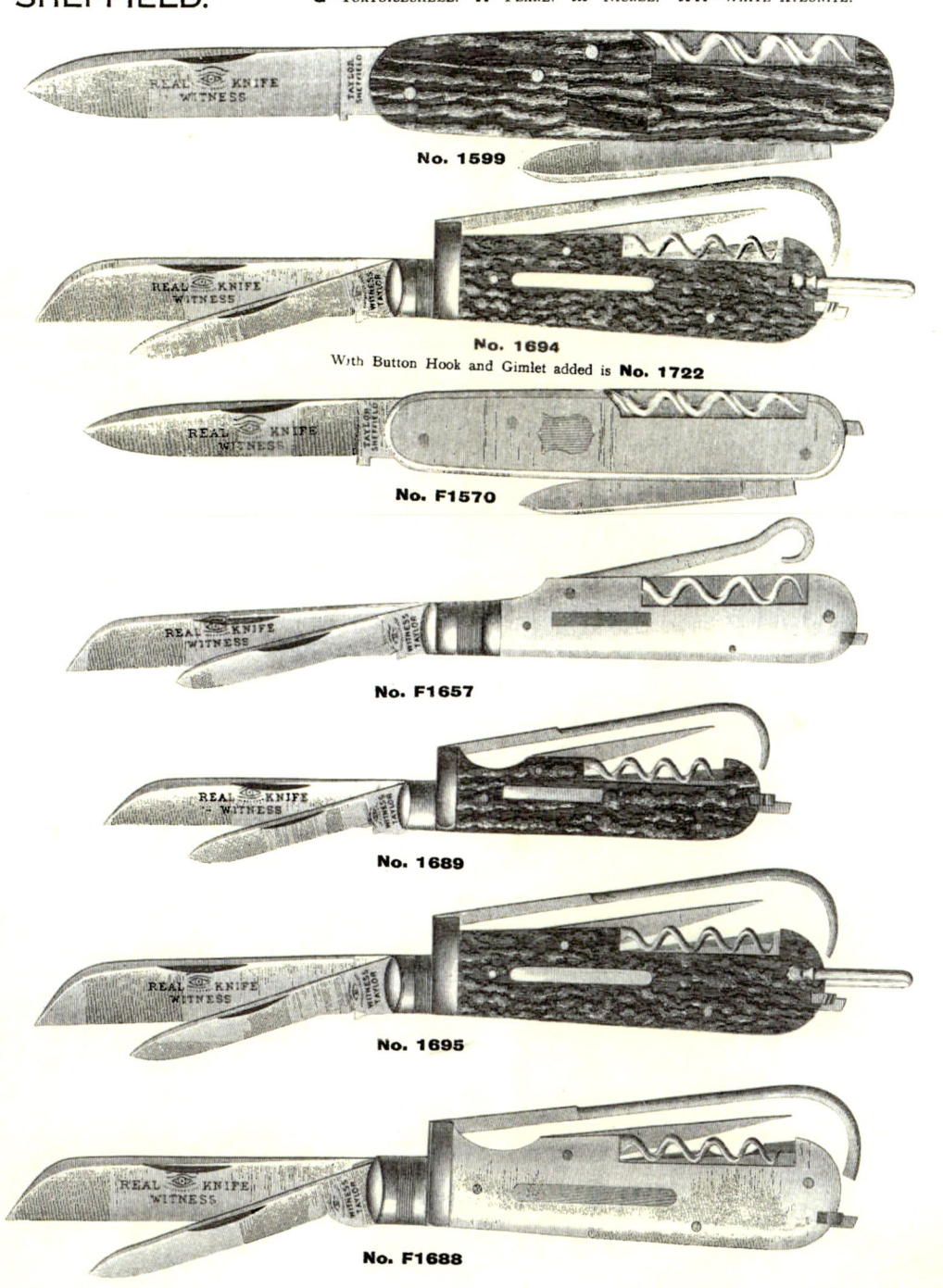

No. 1599

No. 1694
With Button Hook and Gimlet added is **No. 1722**

No. F1570

No. F1657

No. 1689

No. 1695

No. F1688

SECTION B
PAGE 47

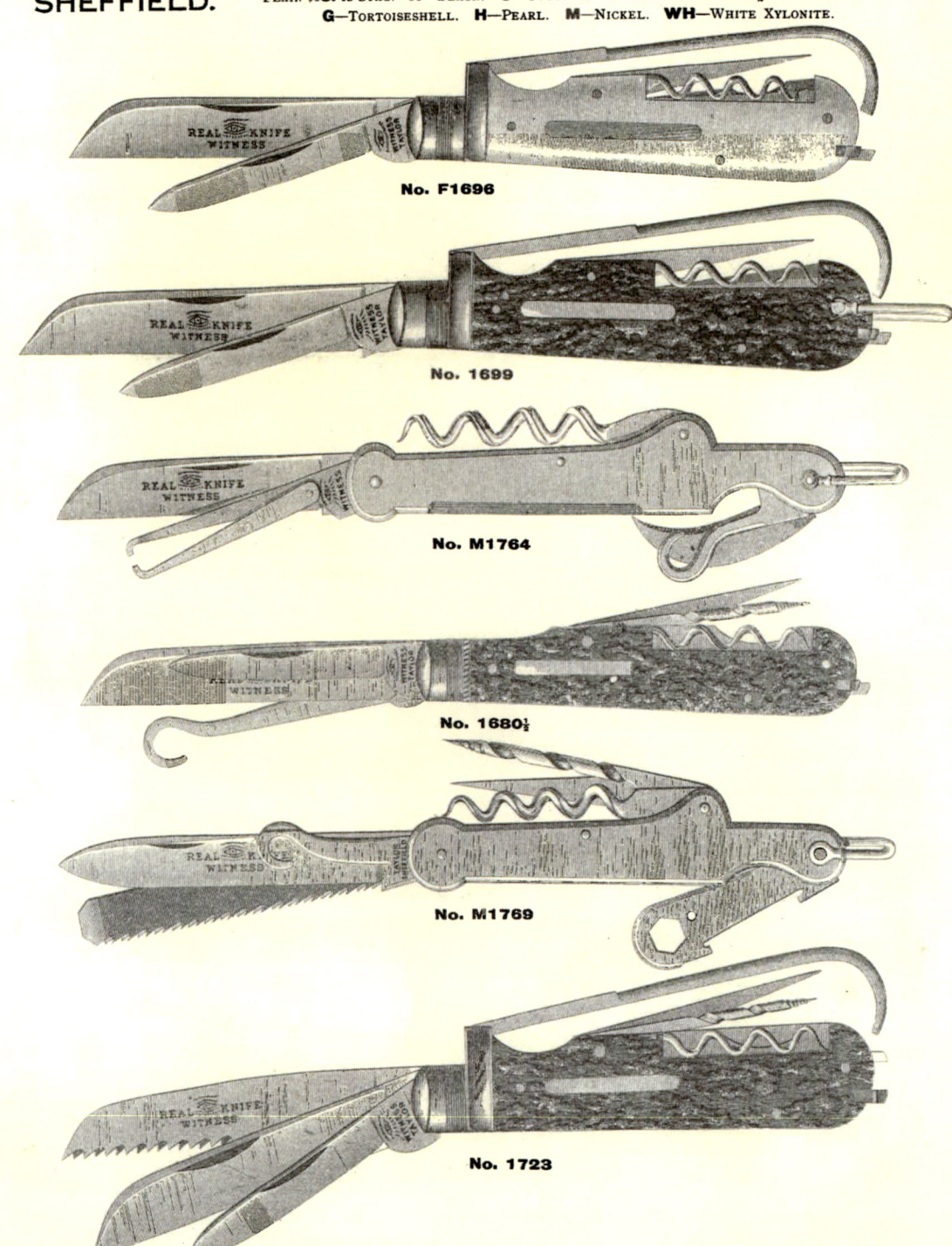

Taylor's Witness Sheffield.

Sportsmen's Knives.

ILLUSTRATIONS ARE ACTUAL SIZE OF ARTICLES.

When ordering, prefix the LETTER to the Pattern Number to denote the kind of handle required, viz.:—
PLAIN **No.** IS STAG. **A**—BLACK. **C**—COCO. **D**—BLACK DIAMOND CHEQUERED. **F**—IVORY.
G—TORTOISESHELL. **H**—PEARL. **M**—NICKEL. **WH**—WHITE XYLONITE.

No. F1696

No. 1699

No. M1764

No. 1680½

No. M1769

No. 1723

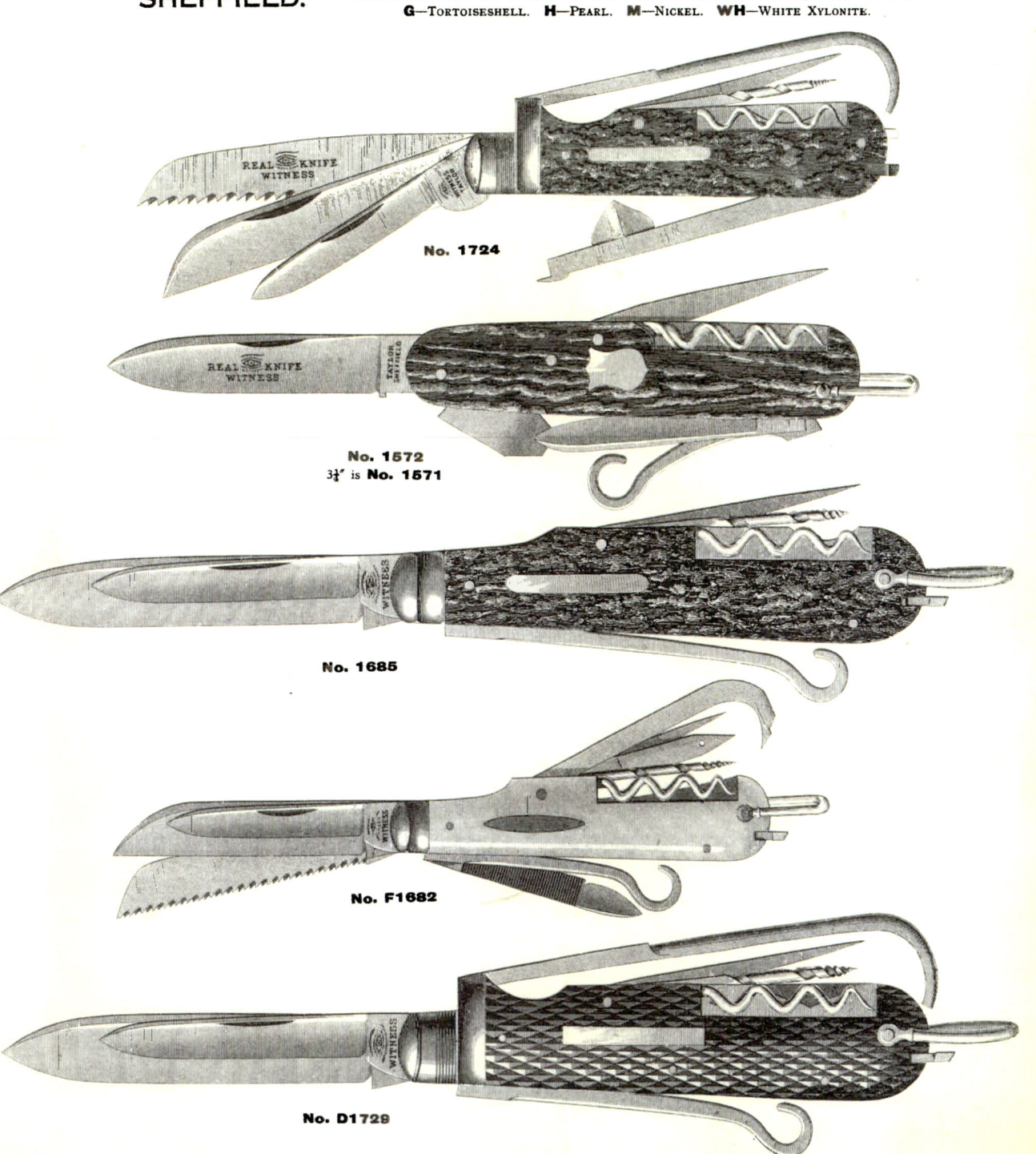

SECTION B
PAGE 48

Taylor's Witness Sheffield — Sportsmen's Knives.

ILLUSTRATIONS ARE ACTUAL SIZE OF ARTICLES.

When ordering, prefix the LETTER to the Pattern Number to denote the kind of handle required, viz.:—
PLAIN **No.** IS STAG. **A**—BLACK. **C**—COCO. **D**—BLACK DIAMOND CHEQUERED. **F**—IVORY.
G—TORTOISESHELL. **H**—PEARL. **M**—NICKEL. **WH**—WHITE XYLONITE.

No. 1724

No. 1572
3¼″ is No. 1571

No. 1685

No. F1682

No. D1729

SECTION B
PAGE 49

Taylor's Witness Sheffield.

Pen Knives

With Stainless Steel Blades.
Illustrations are actual size of articles.

When ordering, prefix the LETTER to the Pattern Number to denote the kind of handle required, viz.:—

Plain **No.** is Stag. **A**—Black. **C**—Coco. **D**—Black Diamond Chequered. **F**—Ivory.
G—Tortoiseshell. **H**—Pearl. **M**—Nickel. **WH**—White Xylonite.

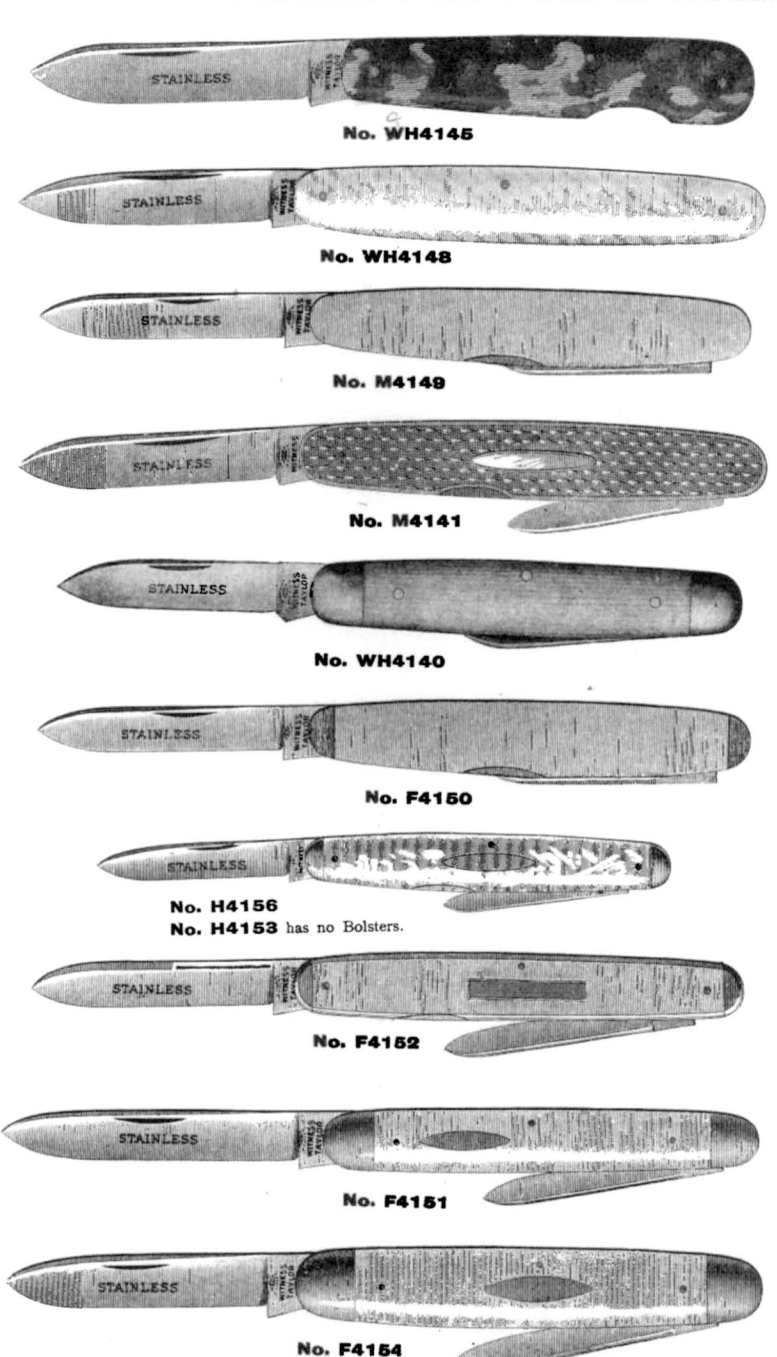

No. WH4145

No. WH4148

No. M4149

No. M4141

No. WH4140

No. F4150

No. H4156
No. H4153 has no Bolsters.

No. F4152

No. F4151

No. F4154

Taylor's Witness

SCISSORS & SHEARS

LONDON OFFICE & SHOWROOMS:
BATH HOUSE
57 HOLBORN VIADUCT E.C.1
Telephone: City 7982

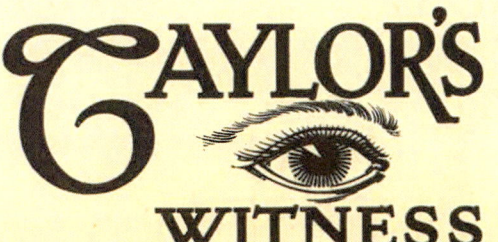

Offices & Showrooms:
DUBLIN MELBOURNE SYDNEY
GEORGETOWN CAPETOWN
JOHANNESBURG NAIROBI
CALGARY MONTREAL PARIS

QUALITY and SERVICE are the dominant features of this outstanding range of fine Scissors. Each pair of Scissors and Shears is stamped with our registered Trade Mark "EYE WITNESS," and is guaranteed.

"EYE WITNESS" the world around, is a name which has stood for ninety years as a symbol of quality and elegance in Scissors and Shears.

The illustrations are actual photographs. All our patterns are of best quality Sheffield Steel, produced under modern conditions and careful supervision, ensuring excellence of workmanship.

Solid construction and superior finish make "EYE WITNESS" Scissors and Shears a profitable and easy-selling stock line.

Shears and Scissors for special Trade purposes are produced according to customers' requirements, for which we shall be pleased to quote you on application.

To ensure prompt despatch of orders entrusted to us large stocks are held ready for immediate delivery.

For prices of patterns see price list

NEEDHAM, VEALL & TYZACK, LTD.

CUTLERS & SILVERSMITHS

Telegrams:
EYEWITNESS
SHEFFIELD

Telephone:
CENTRAL
4428 & 4429

Manufacturers of
TAYLOR'S "EYE WITNESS"
TABLE CUTLERY POCKET CUTLERY
BUTCHERS' KNIVES AND STEELS
SCISSORS RAZORS
SILVER AND ELECTRO-PLATED WARE
IN DESIGNS TO SUIT ALL MARKETS

Codes:
A B C 4th 5th & 6th Eds.
MARCONI INTERNATIONAL
WESTERN UNION 5 LETTER
BENTLEY'S
LIEBER'S 1896

EYE WITNESS WORKS, SHEFFIELD, ENG.

SECTION D
PAGE 2

Taylor's Witness

Miscellaneous Shears

FOR SPECIAL PURPOSES

*All scissors bear the mark on the top side TAYLOR'S WITNESS
and on the under side* SHEFFIELD ENGLAND

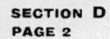

BANKERS' CHEQUE SCISSORS

No. 795. Nickel Plated
Sizes: 9" and 10"

POULTRY SCISSORS
No. 6.
Sizes: 9", 10" and 11"

Any of these patterns can be supplied with serrated blades, to prevent slipping

No. 10. Bent

No. 7 Bent Shank

No. 9. Japanned Handles
Sizes: 7", 7½" and 8"

RUBBER or LEATHER SHEARS
No. 10
Size: 9"

No. 11 Japanned Handles.
Size: 8"

MAT SHEARS
No. 7. Bright.
These Shears are expressly made for the manufacture of Mats, etc.
Sizes: 10", 11" and 12"

These shears are specially made for cutting leather, cotton belting, rubber, or similar substances.

TAYLOR'S WITNESS

Horticulture Scissors and Shears and Metal Workers' Shears

SECTION D
PAGE 3

PRUNING SHEARS
Forged Steel throughout, superior finish

METAL WORKERS' or TINSMITHS' SHEARS
Solid Steel throughout

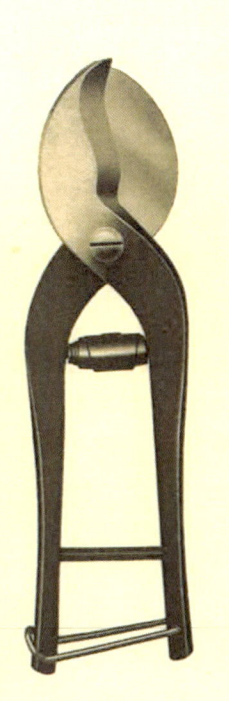

No. 1
Sizes: 7" and 8"

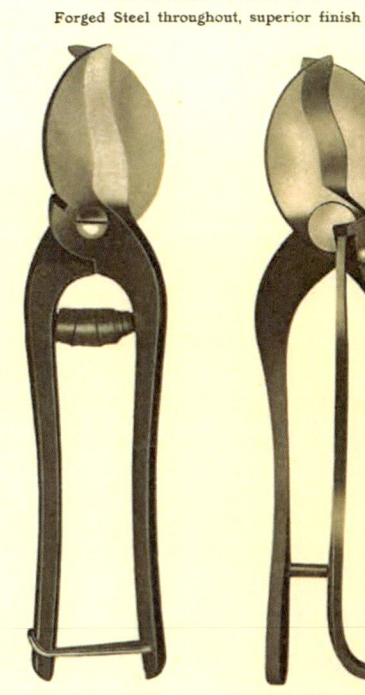

No. 2
Sizes: 7" and 8"

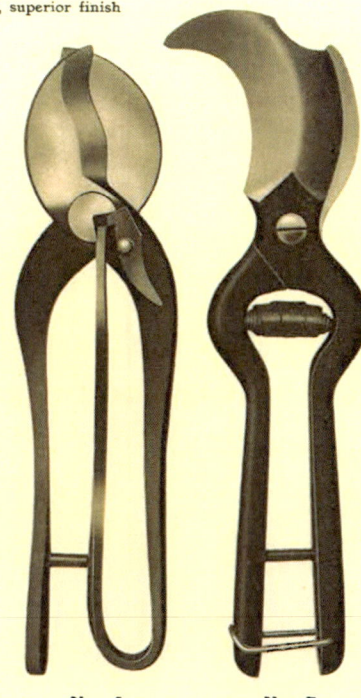

No. 4
Sizes: 7" and 8"

No. 5
Size: 9"

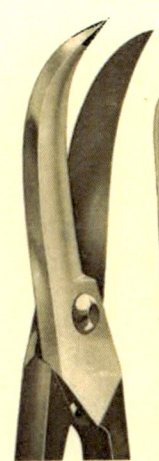

No. 12
Curved Blades
Sizes: 6" to 16"

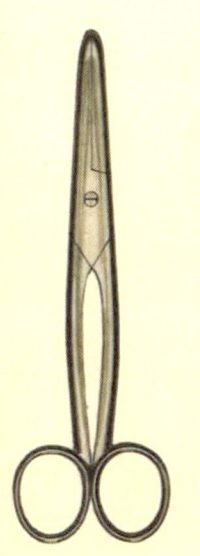

No. 12
Sizes: 6" to 16"

FLOWER GATHERER
No. 640. Bright
No. 645. Nickel Plated
No. 649. Stainless
Sizes from 5" to 9"

VINE SCISSORS
No. 660. Bright
No. 665. Nickel Plated
No. 669. Stainless
Sizes from 5½" to 7"

No. 670. Bright
No. 675. Nickel Plated
Sizes from 4½" to 6"

PRUNING SCISSORS
No. 610. Bright
No. 612. Bright and Japanned
No. 615. Nickel Plated
Sizes from 5" to 6½"

(Pocket Size)
No. 600. Bright
No. 605. Nickel Plated
No. 609. Stainless
Size: 4"

SECTION D
PAGE 4

Taylor's Witness — Tradesmen's Scissors

DOG TOE-NAIL SCISSOR
No. 720. Bright
Size: 3½″

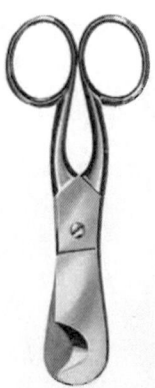

CIGARETTE SCISSOR
No. 620. Bright
Size: 4¼″

Vigo Point

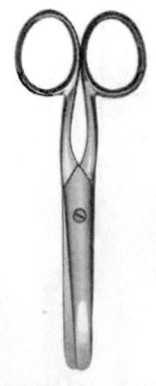

If Vigo points required delete letter "S" from number.

LACE-MAKER'S SCISSOR
No. 870. Bright
Sizes: 4½″ and 5″

Sheaths can be supplied. See Price List.

LAMP-WICK TRIMMERS
No. 880. Bright
No. 882. Bright with Black Japanned Handles
Sizes: 6″ and 7″

Bent Blade

Bent Shank

Bent Shank

PAPERHANGERS' SHEARS
No. 800S. Bright
No. 805S. Nickel Plated
No. 806S. Nickel Plated Blade with Japanned Handle
Sizes: 8″ to 12″

No. 810S. Bright
No. 815S. Nickel Plated
No. 816S. Nickel Plated Blade with Japanned Handles
Sizes: 10″ to 12″

CATTLE-MARKING SCISSORS
No. 820. Bright
Sizes: 6″ to 9″

HORSE TRIMMERS
With Curved Blades as illustrated
No. 830B. Bright
No. 832B. Bright with Black Japanned Handles
No. 834B. Bright with Leather covered Handles (as shown)
Sizes from 6½″ to 8″

With Straight Blades
No. 830. Bright
No. 832. Bright with Black Japanned Handles
No. 834. Bright with Leather Covered Handles
Sizes from 6½″ to 8½″

Taylor's Witness — Surgical and Dressing Scissors

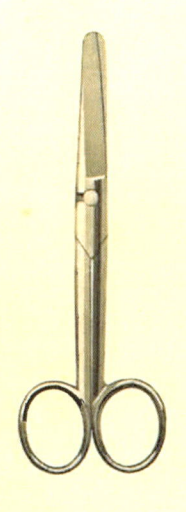

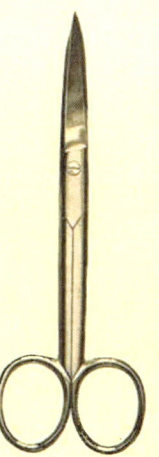

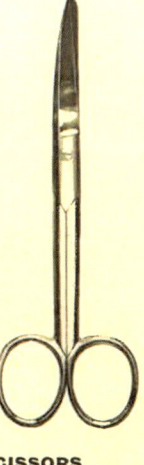

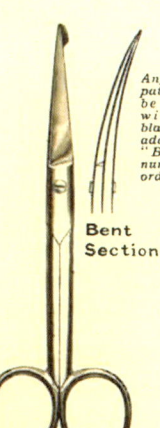

SECTION D
PAGE 5

Any of these patterns can be supplied with bent blades. Please add the letter "B" to the number when ordering.

Bent Section

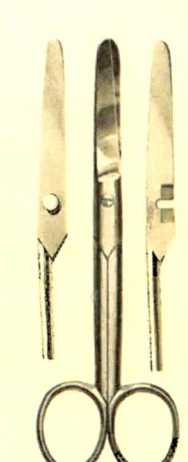

Any of these patterns can be supplied with Aseptic Joints at an extra cost of 12/- per dozen. Please add the word Aseptic to number when ordering. Sizes 4" to 6"

No. 910. Bright
No. 915. Nickel Plated
No. 919. Stainless
Sizes : 4" to 6"

DRESSING SCISSORS

No. 910. Spear, Bright
No. 915. Spear, Nickel Plated
No. 919. Spear, Stainless
Sizes : 4" to 6"

No. 910. Vigo, Bright
No. 915. Vigo, Nickel Plated
No. 919. Vigo, Stainless
Sizes : 4" to 6"

No. 910. Probe, Bright
No. 915. Probe, Nickel Plated
No. 919. Probe, Stainless
Sizes : 4" to 6"

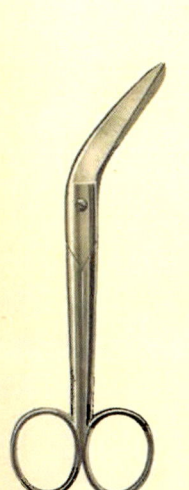

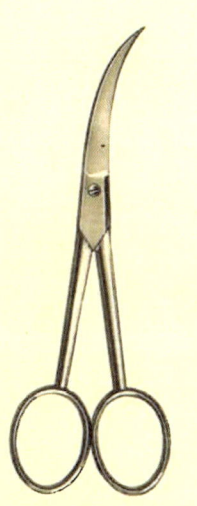

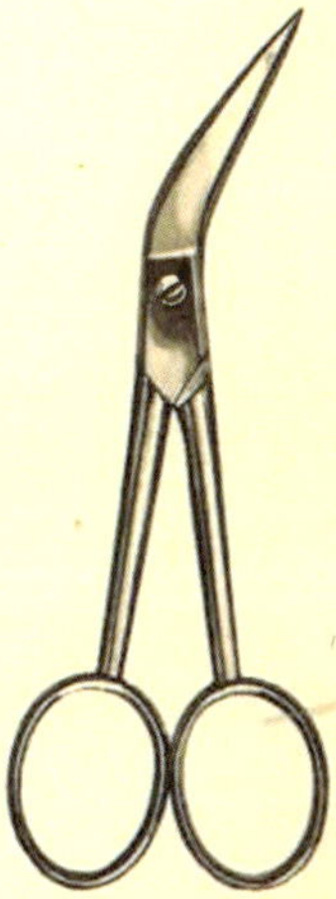

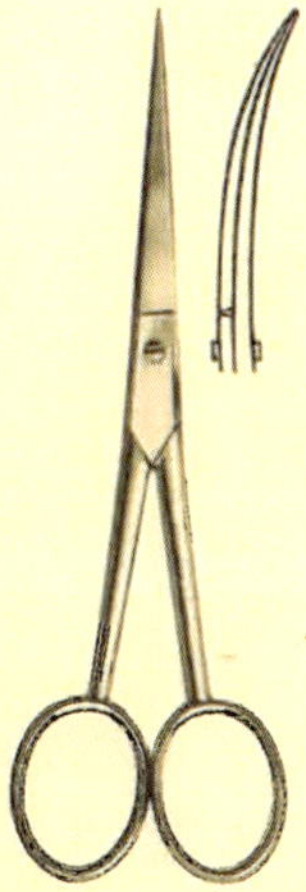

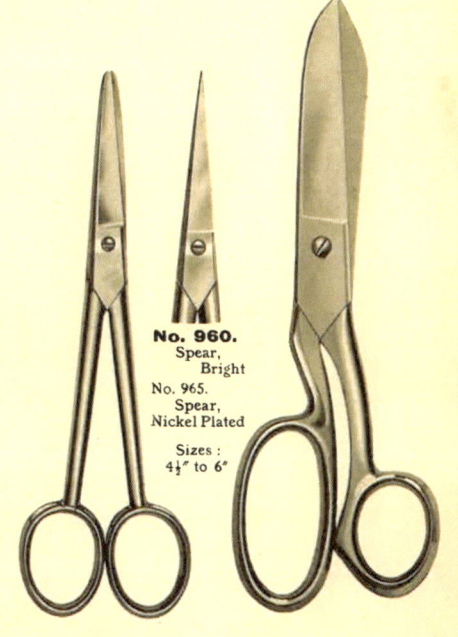

No. 960. Spear, Bright
No. 965. Spear, Nickel Plated
Sizes : 4½" to 6"

DRESSING SCISSOR
No. 910. Elbow, Bright
No. 915. Elbow, Nickel Plated
Sizes : 4" to 6"

DISSECTING SCISSORS

No. 940. Siclon, Bright
No. 945. Siclon, Nickel Plated
Sizes : 4" and 5"

No. 940. Elbow, Bright
No. 945. Elbow, Nickel Plated
Sizes : 4" and 5"

No. 940. Bright
No. 945. Nickel Plated
No. 949. Stainless
Sizes : 4" and 5"

GUM SCISSORS

sharp point, straight.
sharp point, curved.
blunt point, straight.
blunt point, curved.
No. 960. Bright
No. 965. Nickel Plated
Sizes : 4½" to 6"

BANDAGE SHEARS

No. 950. Bright
No. 955. Nickel Plated
Size : 7"

SECTION D PAGE 6

Taylor's Witness

General Household Scissors

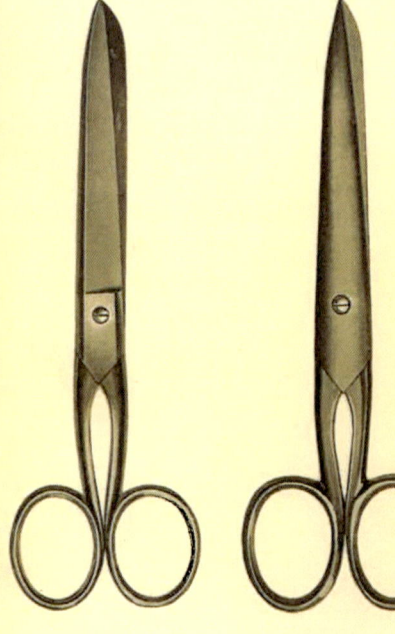

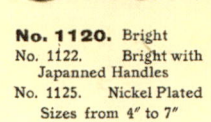

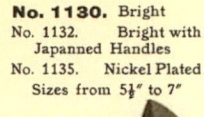

No. 1100. Bright
No. 1102.   Bright with Japanned Handles
No. 1103.   Bright with Bronzed Handles
No. 1105.   Nickel Plated
No. 1109.   Stainless
Sizes from 4″ to 8″

No. 1120. Bright
No. 1122.   Bright with Japanned Handles
No. 1125.   Nickel Plated
Sizes from 4″ to 7″

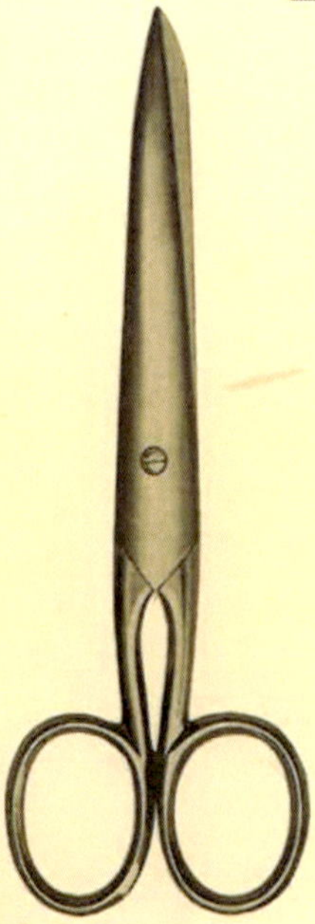

No. 1130. Bright
No. 1132.   Bright with Japanned Handles
No. 1135.   Nickel Plated
Sizes from 5½″ to 7″

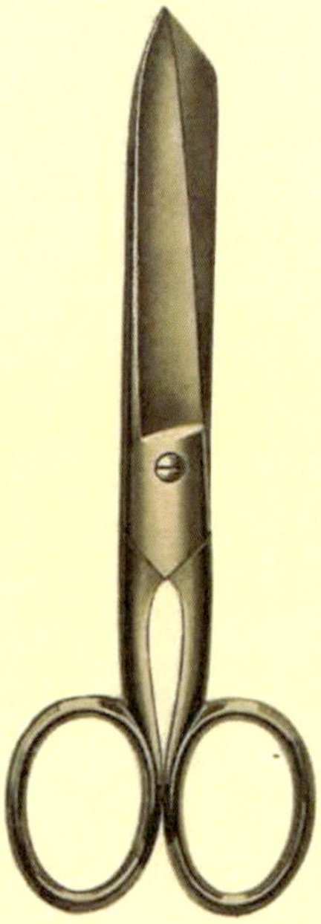

No. 1150. Bright
No. 1152.   Bright with Japanned Handles
No. 1153.   Bright with Bronzed Handles
No. 1155.   Nickel Plated
Sizes from 5½″ to 8″

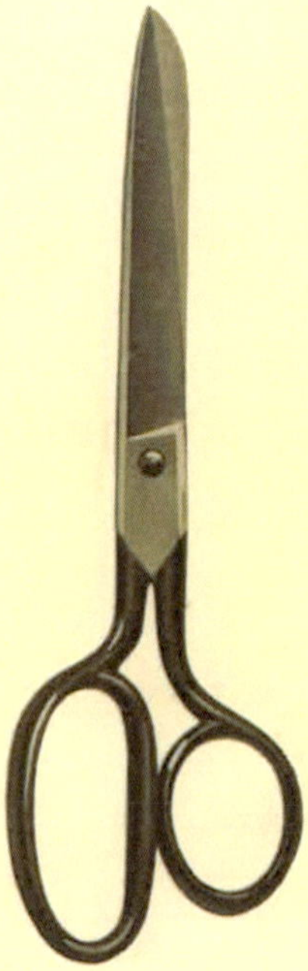

No. 1350. Bright
No. 1352.   Bright with Japanned Handles
Sizes from 4½″ to 9″

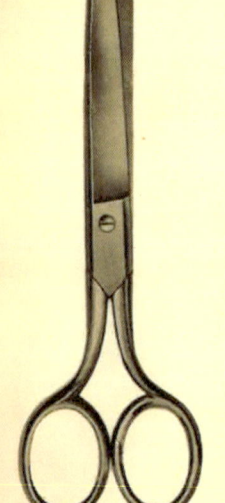

No. 1170. Bright
No. 1175.   Nickel Plated
Sizes from 4½″ to 7″

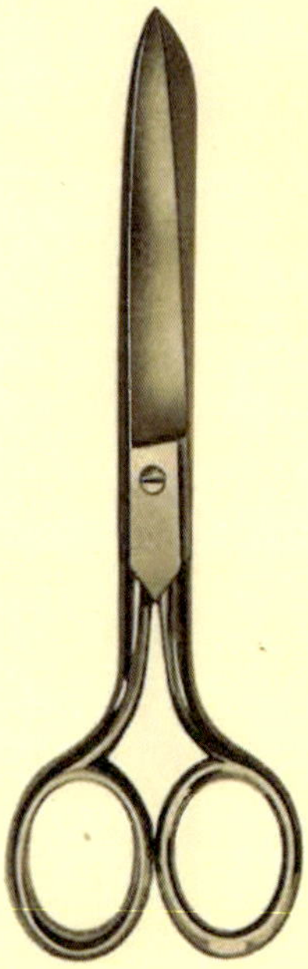

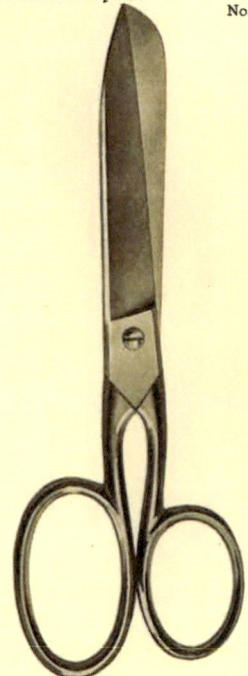

No. 1180. Bright
No. 1182.   Bright with Japanned Handles
No. 1183.   Bright with Bronzed Handles
No. 1185.   Nickel Plated
No. 1187.   Nickel Plated Blades and Gilt Handles
Sizes from 4½″ to 7″

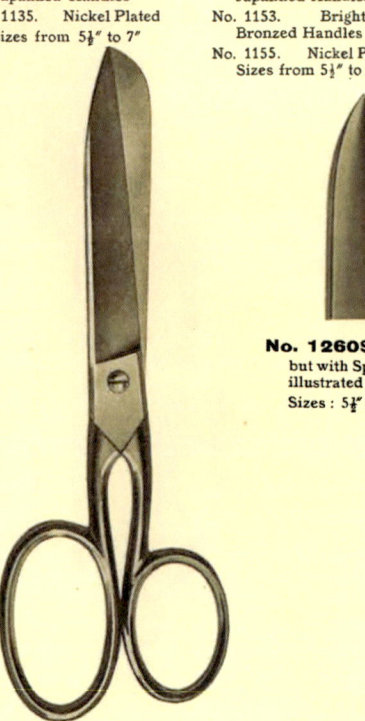

No. 1200. Bright
No. 1202.   Bright with Japanned Handles
No. 1203.   Bright with Bronzed Handles
No. 1205.   Nickel Plated
No. 1205½.   Bright with Plated Handles
No. 1209.   Stainless
Sizes from 5½″ to 10″

No. 1260S. As 1260 but with Spear Point as illustrated
Sizes : 5½″ to 12″

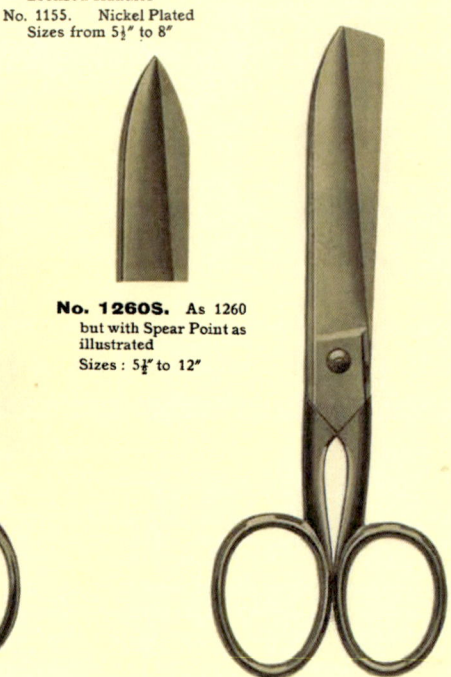

No. 1260. Bright
Sizes from 5½″ to 12″

***Taylor's* WITNESS**

Ladies' Cutting-out Scissors

SECTION D
PAGE 7

No. 1200. E.G. Bright
No. 1202. E.G. Bright with Japanned Handle
No. 1205. E.G. Nickel Plated
No. 1205½. E.G. Nickel Plated Bows and Shanks with Bright Blades
Sizes: 5½" to 9"

No. 1421. Nickel Plated Blades and Celluloid Handles
No. 1425. Nickel Plated
Sizes: 6" to 9"

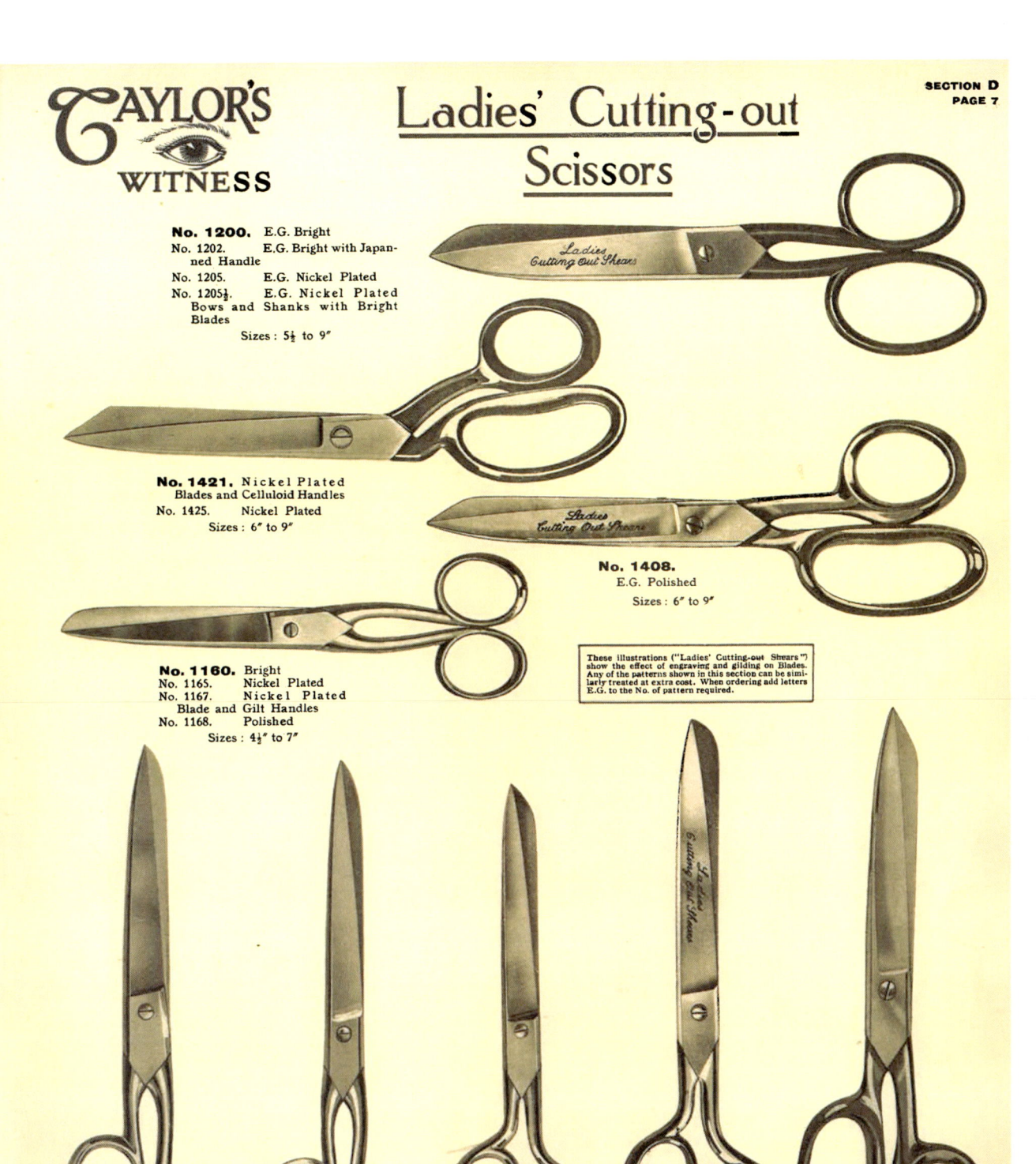

No. 1408. E.G. Polished
Sizes: 6" to 9"

No. 1160. Bright
No. 1165. Nickel Plated
No. 1167. Nickel Plated Blade and Gilt Handles
No. 1168. Polished
Sizes: 4½" to 7"

These illustrations ("Ladies' Cutting-out Shears") show the effect of engraving and gilding on Blades. Any of the patterns shown in this section can be similarly treated at extra cost. When ordering add letters E.G. to the No. of pattern required.

No. 1305. Nickel Plated
Sizes: 4½" to 8"

No. 1310. Bright
No. 1315. Nickel Plated
Sizes: 6" to 8"

No. 1340. Bright
No. 1342. Bright with Japanned Handles
No. 1345. Nickel Plated
No. 1346. Nickel Plated Blades and Japanned Handles
Sizes: 4½" to 9"

No. 1345. E.G. Nickel Plated
Sizes: 4½" to 9"

No. 1401. Nickel Plated Blades and Celluloid Handles
No. 1405. Nickel Plated
Sizes: 6" to 9"

Taylor's Witness — Tailors' Trimmers and Shears

SECTION D, PAGE 8

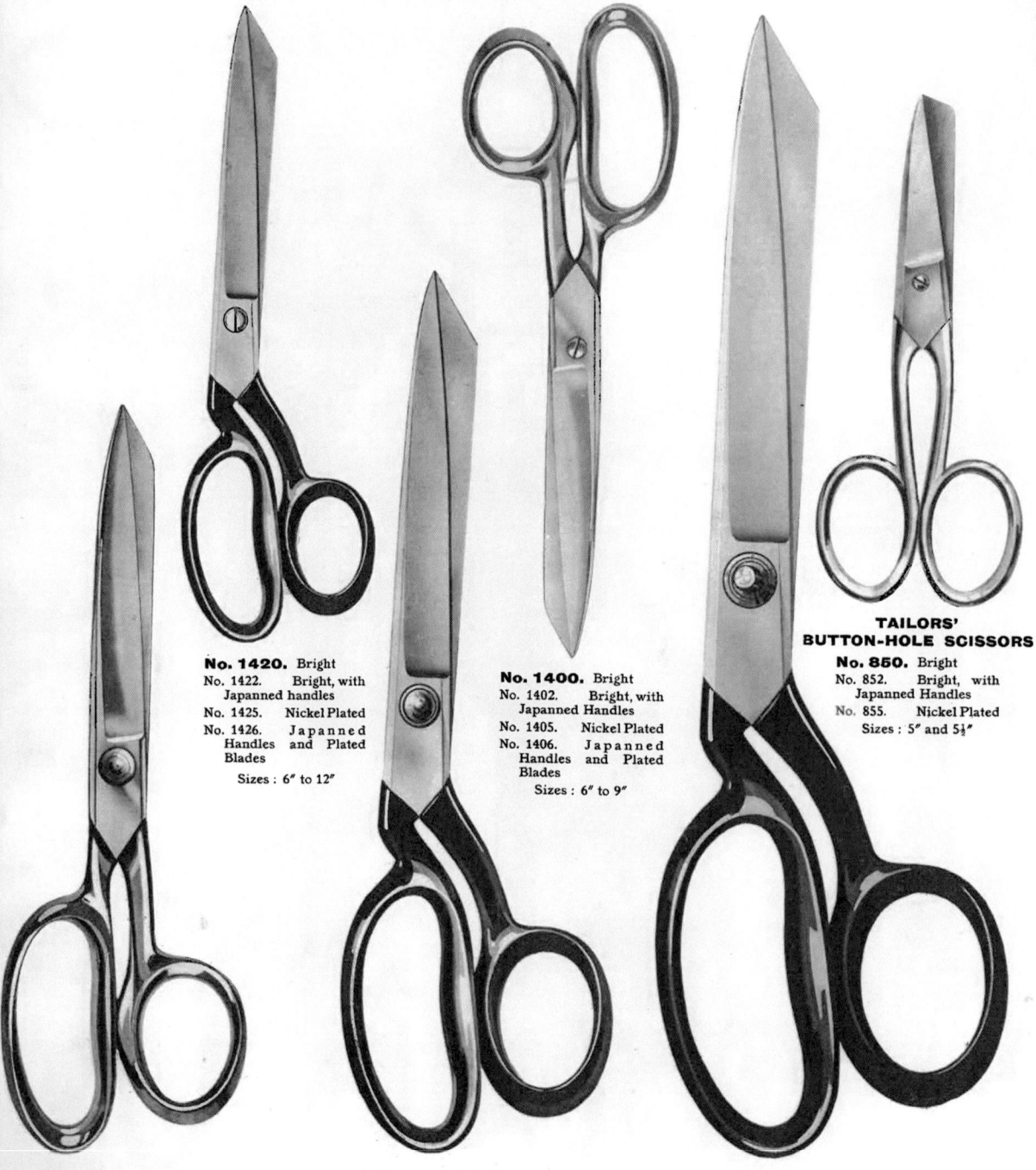

No. 1420. Bright
No. 1422. Bright, with Japanned handles
No. 1425. Nickel Plated
No. 1426. Japanned Handles and Plated Blades
Sizes: 6" to 12"

No. 1400. Bright
No. 1402. Bright, with Japanned Handles
No. 1405. Nickel Plated
No. 1406. Japanned Handles and Plated Blades
Sizes: 6" to 9"

TAILORS' BUTTON-HOLE SCISSORS
No. 850. Bright
No. 852. Bright, with Japanned Handles
No. 855. Nickel Plated
Sizes: 5" and 5½"

No. 1412. Bright, with Japanned Handles
No. 1416. Japanned Handles and Plated Blades
Sizes: 9" to 12"

No. 1432. Bright, with Japanned Handles
No. 1436. Japanned Handles and Plated Blades
Sizes: 9" to 13"

No. 1442. Bright, with Japanned Handles
No. 1446. Japanned Handles and Plated Blades
Sizes: 9" to 13"
This pattern is fitted with long Brass Screw which acts as a Rest

Taylor's Witness

Stainless

SECTION D — PAGE 9

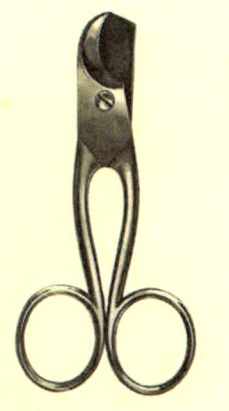

PRUNERS
Pocket Size
No. 609. Stainless
Size : 4″

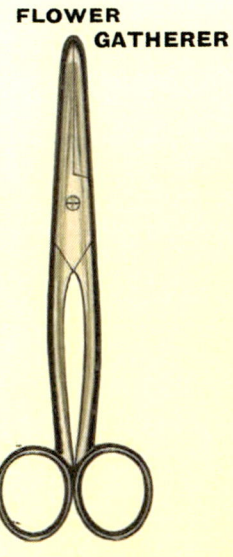

FLOWER GATHERER
No. 649. Stainless
Size : 6″

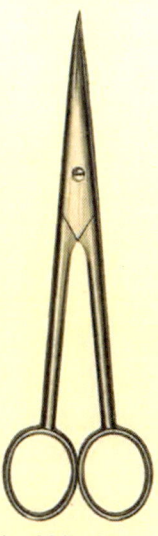

VINE SCISSORS
No. 669. Stainless
Sizes : 6″, 6½″ and 7″

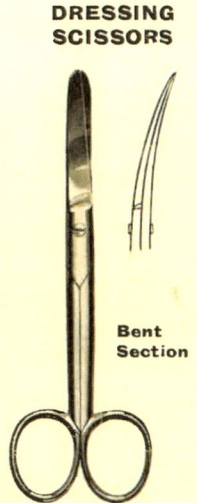

DRESSING SCISSORS
Bent Section
No. 919. Stainless
Sizes : 5″ and 6″

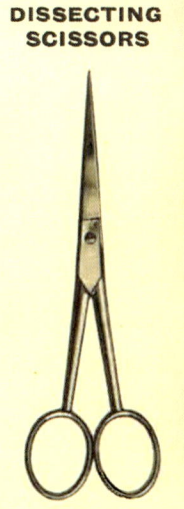

DISSECTING SCISSORS
No. 949. Stainless
Sizes : 4½″ and 5″

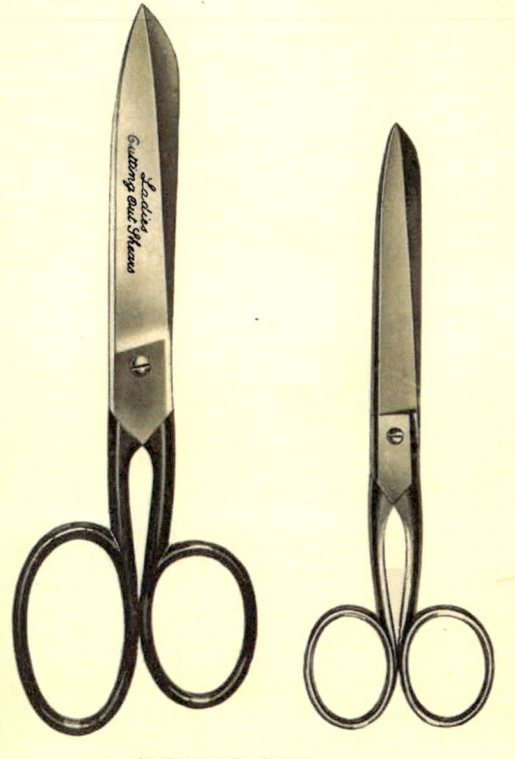

CUTTING OUT
Ladies Cutting Out Shears
No. 1209. Stainless
Sizes : 6″, 6½″ and 7″

No. 1109. Stainless
Sizes : 4½″ to 7″

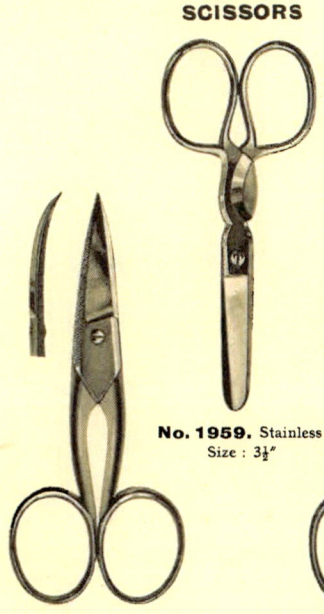

NAIL
No. 2109. Stainless
Size : 3½″

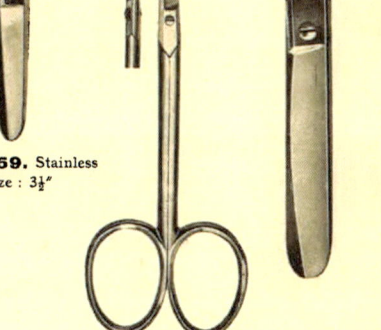

CIGAR SCISSORS
No. 1959. Stainless
Size : 3½″

MANICURE
No. 2999. Stainless
Size : 4″

DRAPERS'
No. 1989. Stainless
Sizes : 4½″ and 5″

SECTION D
PAGE 10

Taylor's WITNESS

Sewing Scissors

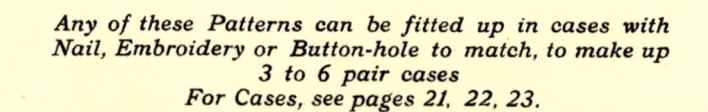

Any of these Patterns can be fitted up in cases with Nail, Embroidery or Button-hole to match, to make up 3 to 6 pair cases
For Cases, see pages 21, 22, 23.

No. 1535. Nickel Plated
No. 1537. Nickel Plated Blade and Gilt Handles
Sizes: 4½" to 6½"

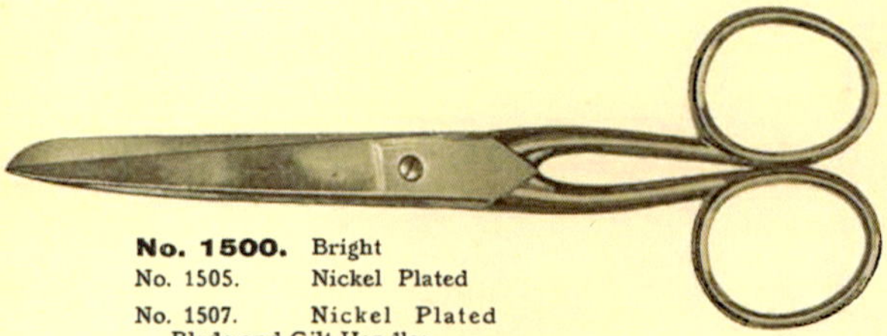

No. 1500. Bright
No. 1505. Nickel Plated
No. 1507. Nickel Plated Blade and Gilt Handles
No. 1508. Polished
Sizes: 4½" to 7"

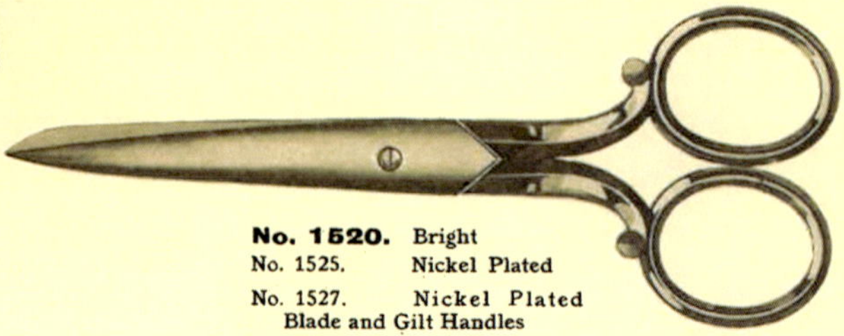

No. 1520. Bright
No. 1525. Nickel Plated
No. 1527. Nickel Plated Blade and Gilt Handles
Sizes: 4½" and 5½"

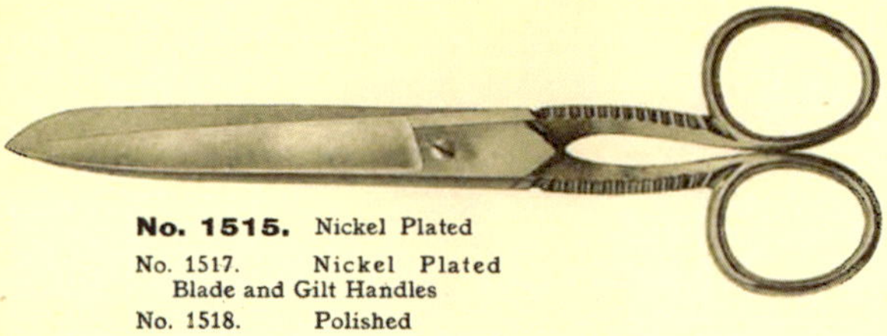

No. 1515. Nickel Plated
No. 1517. Nickel Plated Blade and Gilt Handles
No. 1518. Polished
Sizes: 4½" to 7"

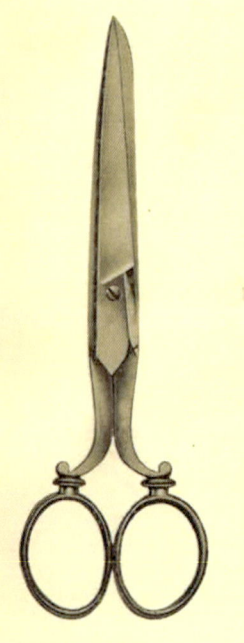

No. 1595. Nickel Plated
No. 1597. Nickel Plated Blade and Gilt Handles
No. 1598. Polished
Sizes: 4½" to 7"

No. 1600. Bright
No. 1605. Nickel Plated
Sizes: 4½" to 7"

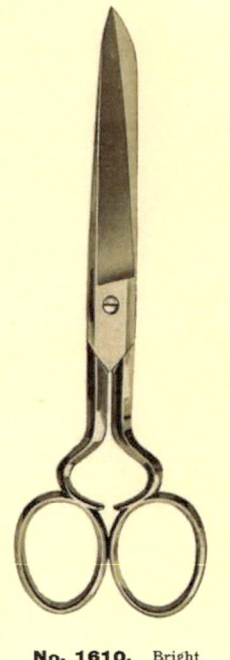

No. 1610. Bright
No. 1615. Nickel Plated
No. 1617. Nickel Plated Blade and Gilt Handles
No. 1618. Polished
Sizes: 4½" to 7"

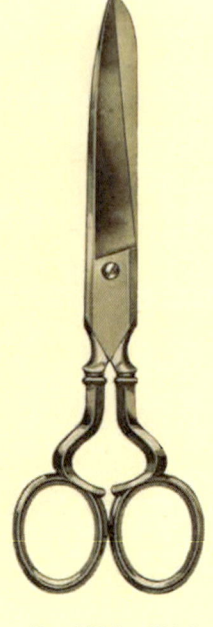

No. 1625. Nickel Plated
No. 1627. Nickel Plated Blade and Gilt Handles
Sizes: 4½" and 5½"

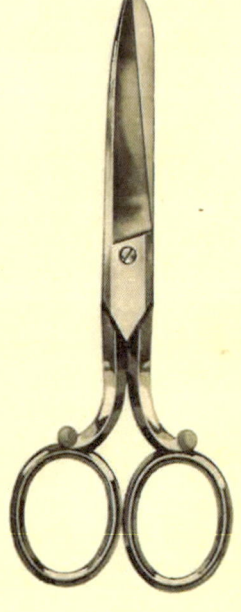

No. 1640. Bright
No. 1645. Nickel Plated
No. 1647. Nickel Plated Blade and Gilt Handles
No. 1648. Polished
Sizes: 4½" to 7"

Taylor's Witness — Sewing Scissors

SECTION D
PAGE 11

Any of these Patterns can be fitted up in cases with Nail, Embroidery, or Button-hole to match, to make up 3 to 6 pair cases.
For Cases, see pages 21, 22, 23,

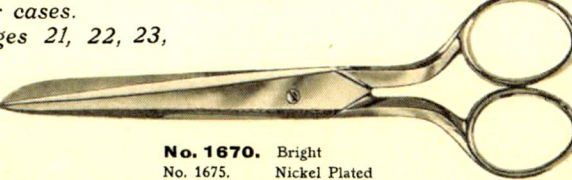

No. 1670. Bright
No. 1675. Nickel Plated
No. 1677. Nickel Plated Blades and Gilt Handles
No. 1678. Polished
Sizes: 4½″ to 7″

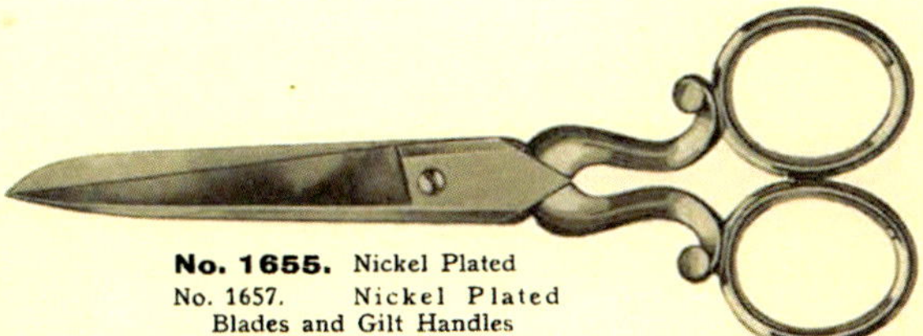

No. 1655. Nickel Plated
No. 1657. Nickel Plated Blades and Gilt Handles
Sizes: 4½″ and 5½″

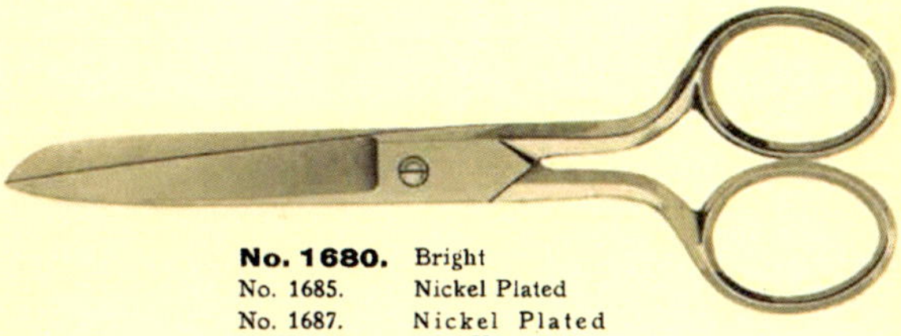

No. 1680. Bright
No. 1685. Nickel Plated
No. 1687. Nickel Plated Blades and Gilt Handles
No. 1688. Polished
Sizes: 4½″ to 7″

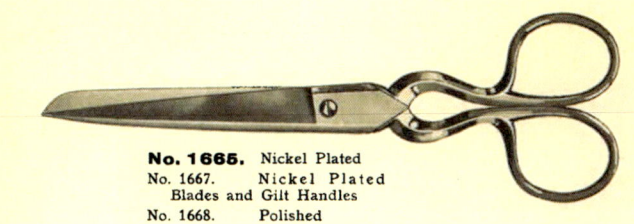

No. 1665. Nickel Plated
No. 1667. Nickel Plated Blades and Gilt Handles
No. 1668. Polished
Sizes: 4½″ to 6″

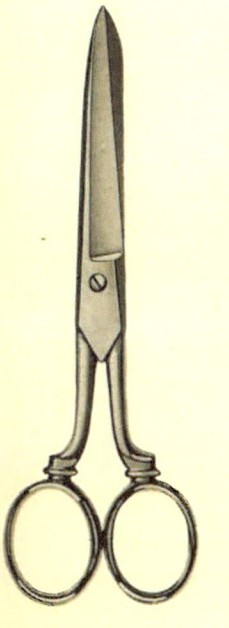

No. 1695. Nickel Plated
No. 1697. Nickel Plated Blades and Gilt Handles
Sizes: 4½″ to 7″

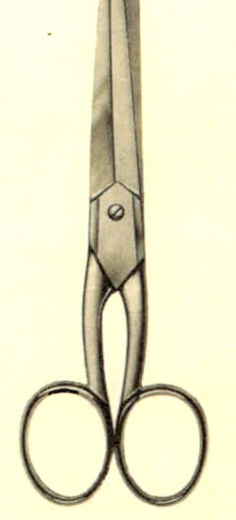

No. 1805. Nickel Plated
No. 1807. Nickel Plated Blades and Gilt Handles
No. 1808. Polished
Sizes: 4½″ to 7″

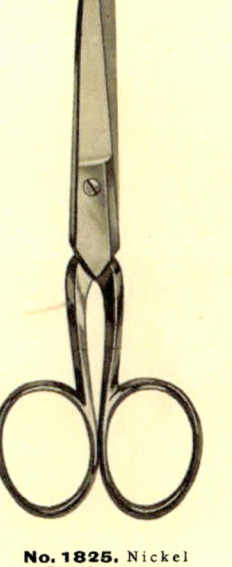

No. 1825. Nickel Plated
No. 1827. Nickel Plated Blades and Gilt Handles
No. 1828. Polished
Sizes: 4½″ to 7″

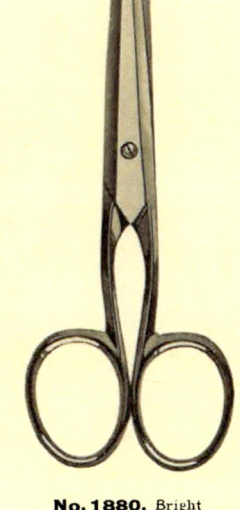

No. 1880. Bright
No. 1885. Nickel Plated
No. 1887. Nickel Plated Blades and Gilt Handles
No. 1888. Polished
Sizes: 4½″ to 7″

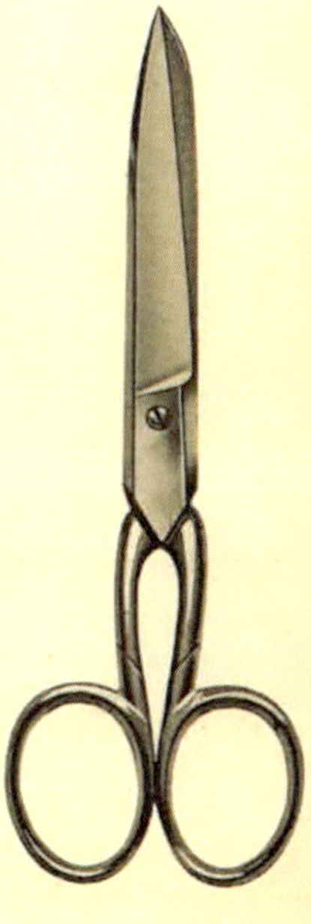

No. 1890. Bright
No. 1895. Nickel Plated
No. 1897. Nickel Plated Blades and Gilt Handles
No 1898. Polished
Sizes: 4½″ to 7″

SECTION D
PAGE 12

Taylor's Witness — Hairdressers' Scissors

Any pattern of hairdressers' scissors can be supplied with serrated blade to prevent hair slipping.

BLADES APART FOR CLEANING PURPOSES

Any pattern of Hairdressers' Scissors can be supplied with Hollow Ground Blades. When ordering add the words "Hollow Ground."

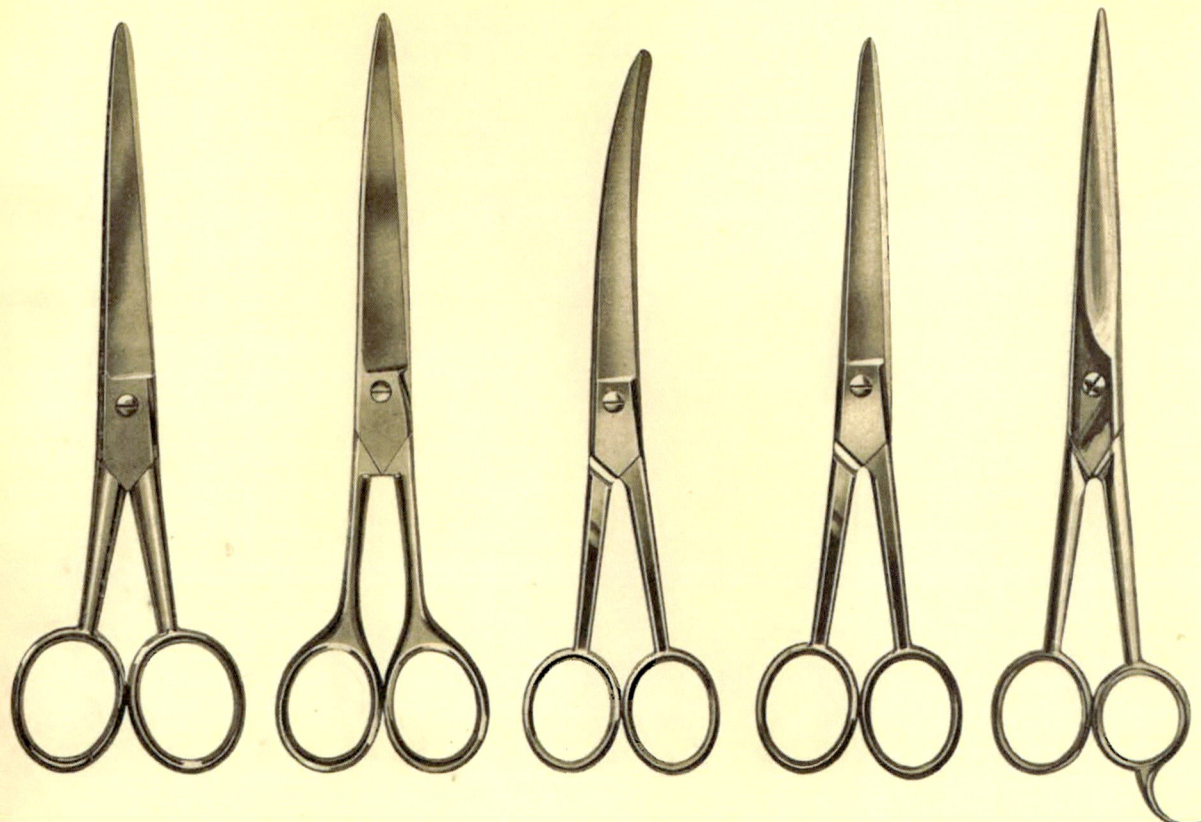

These illustrations are to show an Aseptic Joint. Any of the Hairdressers' Scissors can be supplied with Aseptic joint.

When ordering add the word "Aseptic" to number

No. 1700. Bright
No. 1702. Bright with Japanned Handles
No. 1705. Nickel Plated
Sizes: 6" to 7"

No. 1710. Bright
No. 1715. Nickel Plated
Sizes: 6" to 7"

No. 1720. Bright
No. 1725. Nickel Plated
Sizes: 6½" and 7"

No. 1730. Bright
No. 1735. Nickel Plated
Sizes: 6½" and 7"

No. 1740. Bright
No. 1745. Nickel Plated
Sizes: 6¼", 7" and 7½"

TAYLOR'S WITNESS

Hairdressers' Scissors

SECTION D
PAGE 13

Any pattern of hairdressers' scissors can be supplied with serrated blade, to prevent hair slipping.

No. 1860. Bright
No. 1865. Nickel Plated
Sizes: 6½″, 7″ and 7½″
Extra light with flat blades

No. 1810. Bright
No. 1815. Nickel Plated
Sizes: 6½″, 7″ and 7½″
Extra light pattern with one flat blade and one round blade, for close cutting

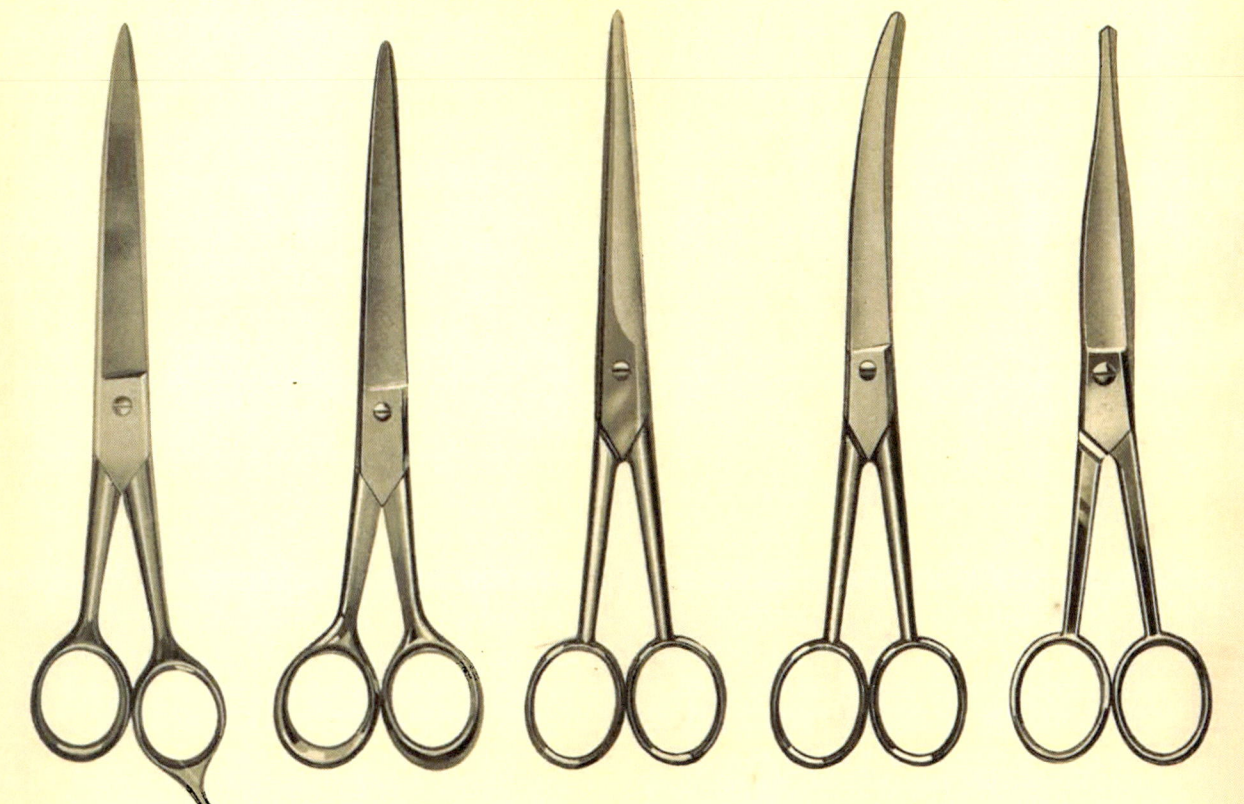

No. 1750.
Bright
No. 1752. Bright with Japanned Handles
No. 1755. Nickel Plated
Sizes: 6″ to 8″

No. 1760. Bright
No. 1762. Bright with Japanned Handles
No. 1765. Nickel Plated
Sizes: 6″ to 7½″

No. 1770. Bright
No. 1775. Nickel Plated
Sizes: 6½″, 7″ and 7½″

No. 1780. Bright
No. 1785. Nickel Plated
Sizes: 6½″, 7″ and 7½″

No. 1790. Bright
No. 1795. Nickel Plated
Size: 6½″ and 7″

SECTION D
PAGE 14

Taylor's Witness

Draper and Pocket Scissors

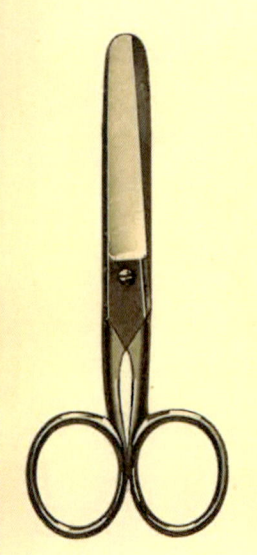

No. 1910. Bright
No. 1915. Nickel Plated
Sizes : 3½" to 6"

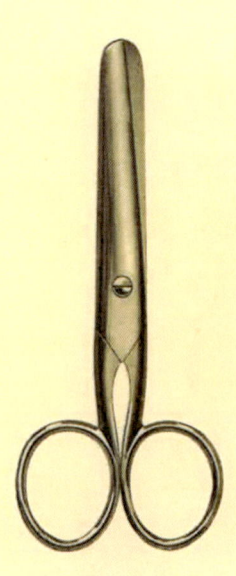

No. 1920. Bright
No. 1925. Nickel Plated
Sizes : 4" to 5½"

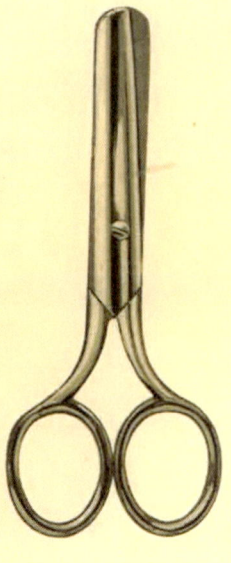

No. 1930. Bright
No. 1935. Nickel Plated
Sizes : 4" to 5"

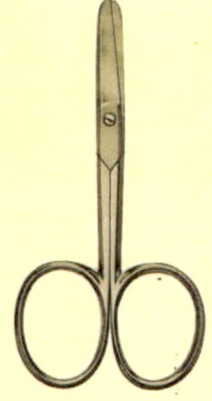

POCKET SCISSOR
No. 1900. Bright
No. 1905. Nickel Plated
No. 1909. Stainless
Size : 3"

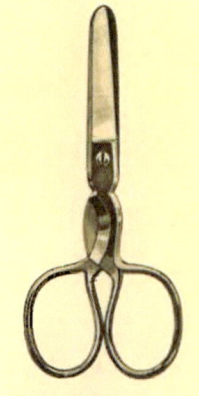

CIGAR SCISSOR
No. 1950. Bright
No. 1955. Nickel Plated
Sizes : 2¾", 3¼" and 4"

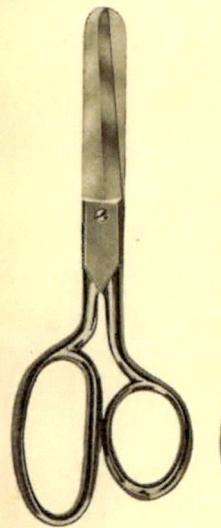

No. 1940. Bright
No. 1945. Nickel Plated
Sizes : 5", 5½" and 6"

No. 1960. Bright
No. 1965. Nickel Plated
Sizes : 4" to 6"

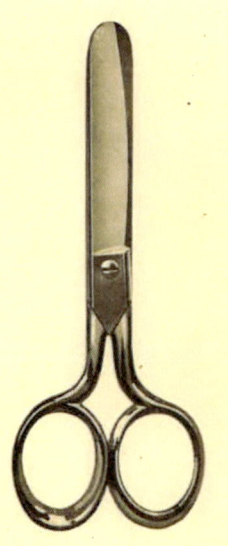

No. 1980. Bright
No. 1985. Nickel Plated
Sizes : 3" to 5"

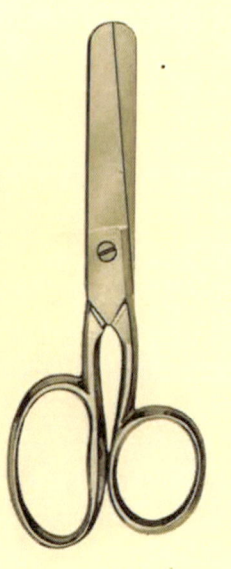

No. 710. Bright
No. 715. Nickel Plated
Sizes : 4½" to 6"

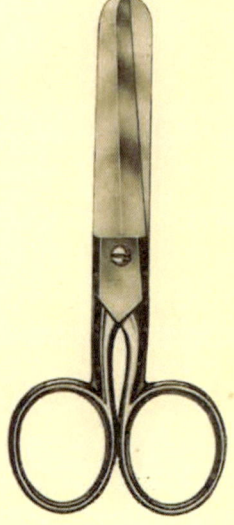

No. 1970. Bright
No. 1975. Nickel Plated
Sizes : 4" to 5"

SECTION D
PAGE 15

Taylor's Witness

Nail Scissors

Any pattern of straight nail scissor can be supplied with serrated blade, to prevent slipping when cutting, at an extra cost of 6/- per dozen.

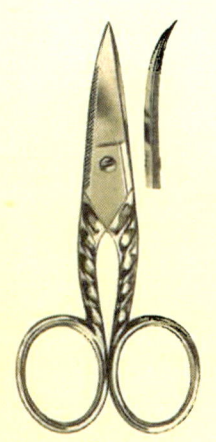

No. 2535. Nickel Plated
No. 2537. Nickel Plated Blades and Gilt Handles
Size : 3½″

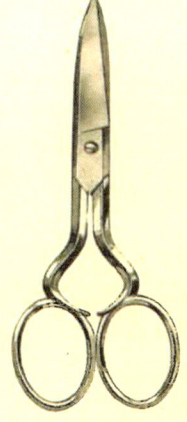

No. 2610. Bright
No. 2615. Nickel Plated
No. 2617. Nickel Plated Blades and Gilt Handles
No. 2618. Polished
Size : 3¾″

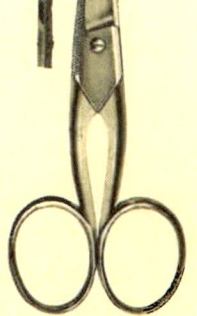

No. 2100. Bright
No. 2105. Nickel Plated
Sizes : 3″, 3½″, 4″

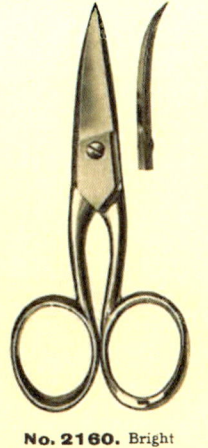

No. 2160. Bright
No. 2165. Nickel Plated
No. 2167. Nickel Plated Blades and Gilt Handles
No. 2168. Polished
Sizes : 3½″ and 4″

No. 2180. Bright
No. 2185. Nickel Plated
No. 2187. Nickel Plated Blades and Gilt Handles
Size : 3½″

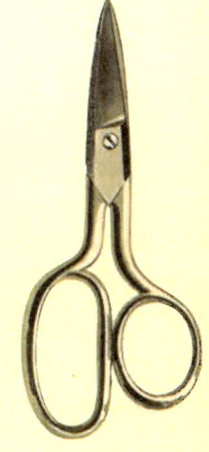

No. 2340. Bright
No. 2345. Nickel Plated
Size : 3¾″

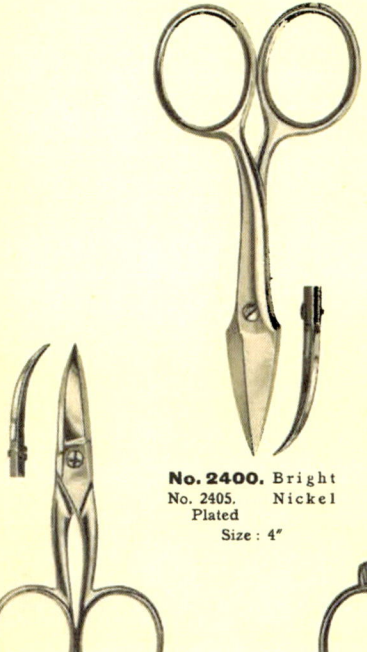

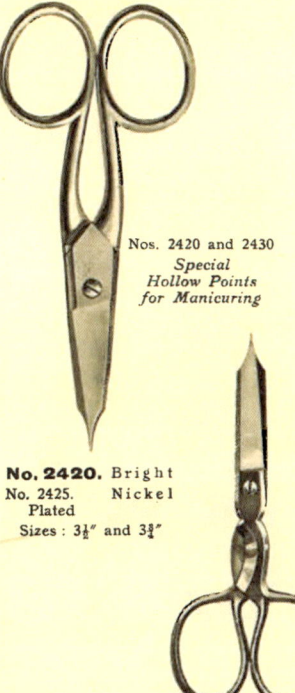

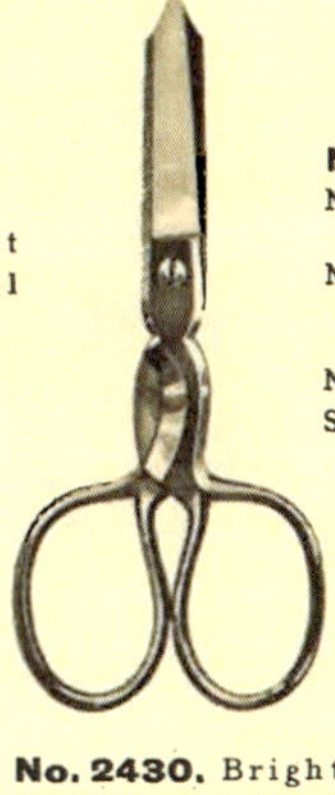

Nos. 2420 and 2430
Special Hollow Points for Manicuring

No. 2395. Nickel Plated
No. 2397. Nickel Plated Blades and Gilt Handles
Sizes : 2½″, 3″ and 3½″

No. 2400. Bright
No. 2405. Nickel Plated
Size : 4″

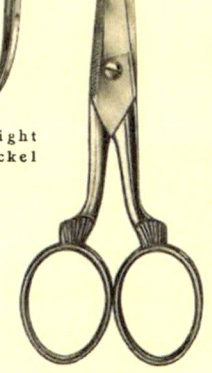

No. 2560. Bright
No. 2565. Nickel Plated
No. 2567. Nickel Plated Blades and Gilt Handles
Size : 3½″

No. 2420. Bright
No. 2425. Nickel Plated
Sizes : 3½″ and 3¾″

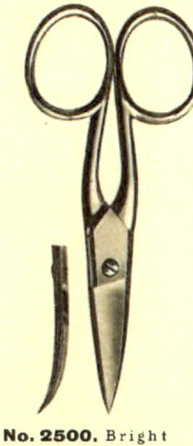

No. 2430. Bright
No. 2435. Nickel Plated
Sizes : 2¾″, 3½″, 4″

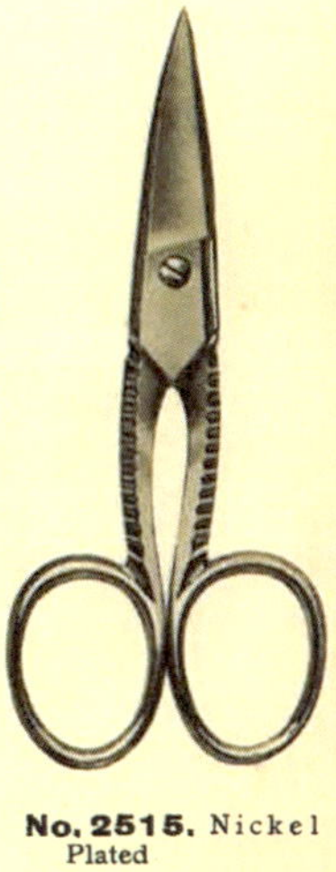

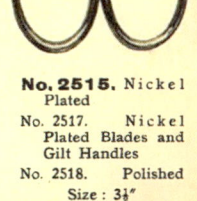

No. 2500. Bright
No. 2505. Nickel Plated
No. 2507. Nickel Plated Blades and Gilt Handles
No. 2508. Polished
Sizes : 2½″, 3″, 3½″, 4″

No. 2515. Nickel Plated
No. 2517. Nickel Plated Blades and Gilt Handles
No. 2518. Polished
Size : 3½″

Any of these patterns can be supplied with curved blades, if required. Add letter B to number when ordering

SECTION D
PAGE 16

Taylor's Witness Nail Scissors

IMPROVED FOLDING POCKET NAIL SCISSORS

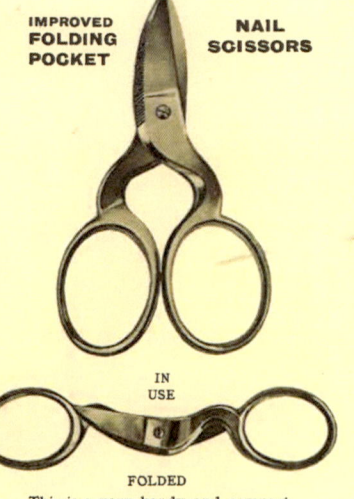

IN USE

FOLDED

This is a very handy and compact type of Folding Pocket Scissor. Perfectly flat when folded, with the points effectively protected.

No. 2705. Heavily Nickel Plated
Size : 3¾″ when folded
Supplied in either Paper or Leather Cases
No. 2700. Bright
No. 2705. Nickel Plated

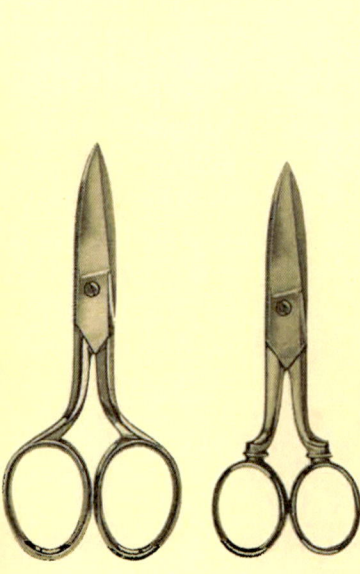

No. 2680. Bright
No. 2685. Nickel Plated
No. 2687. Nickel Plated Blades and Gilt Handles
No. 2688. Polished
Size : 3½″

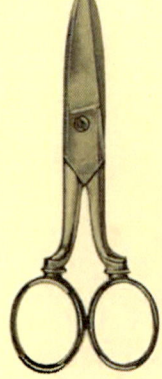

No. 2695. Nickel Plated
No. 2697. Nickel Plated Blades and Gilt Handles
Size : 3½″

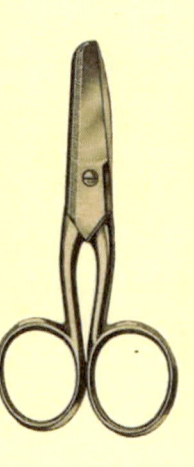

No. 2730. Bright
No. 2735. Nickel Plated
No. 2738. Polished
Size : 3½″

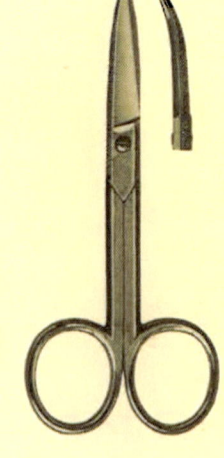

No. 2810. Bright
No. 2815. Nickel Plated
No. 2817. Nickel Plated Blades and Gilt Handles
Size : 4″

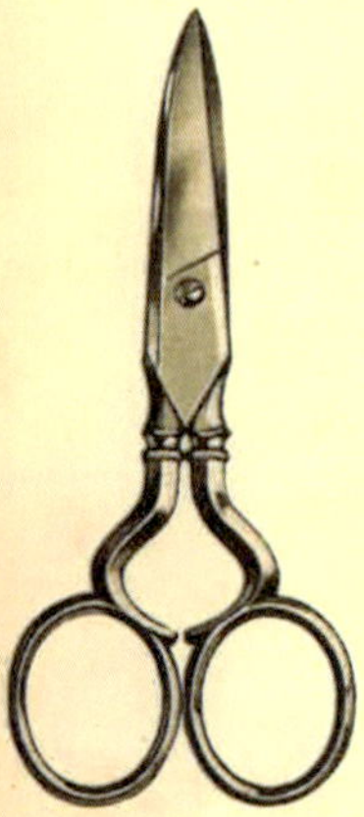

No. 2625. Nickel Plated
No. 2627. Nickel Plated Blades and Gilt Handles
Size : 3½″

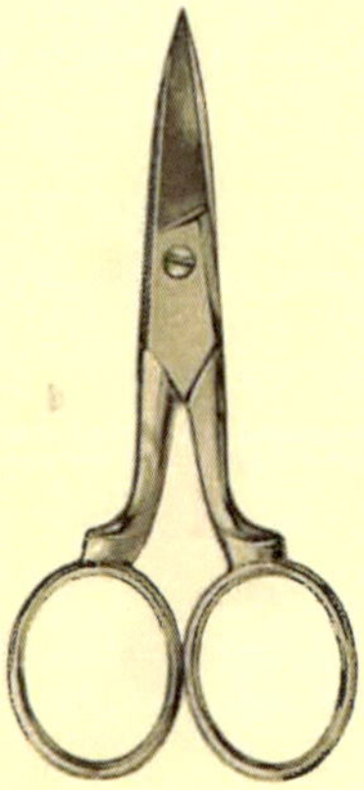

No. 2630. Bright
No. 2635. Nickel Plated
Size : 3½″

No. 2640. Bright
No. 2645. Nickel Plated
No. 2647. Nickel Plated Blades and Gilt Handles
No. 2648. Polished
Size : 3½″

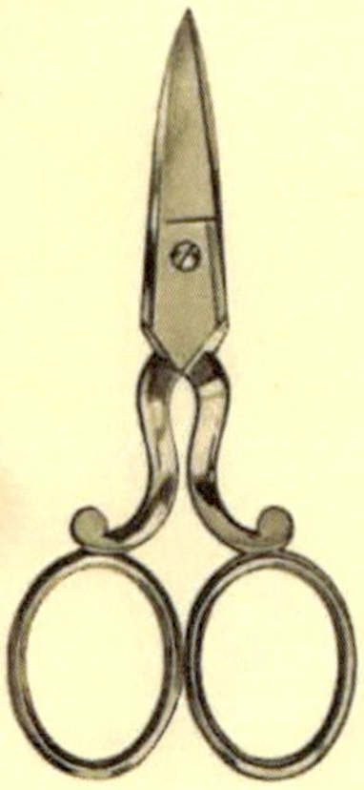

No. 2655. Nickel Plated
No. 2657. Nickel Plated Blades and Gilt Handles
Size : 3½″

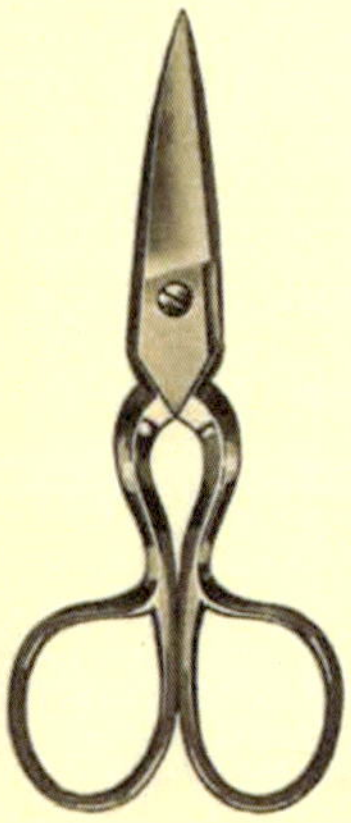

No. 2665. Nickel Plated
No. 2667. Nickel Plated Blades and Gilt Handles
No. 2668. Polished
Size : 3¾″

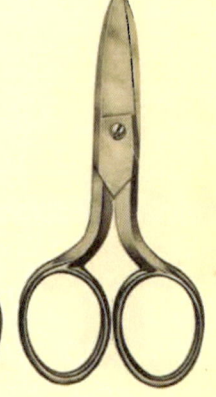

No. 2670. Bright
No. 2675. Nickel Plated
No. 2677. Nickel Plated Blades and Gilt Handles
No. 2678. Polished
Size : 3½″

SECTION D
PAGE 17

TAYLOR'S WITNESS

Nail and Manicure Scissors

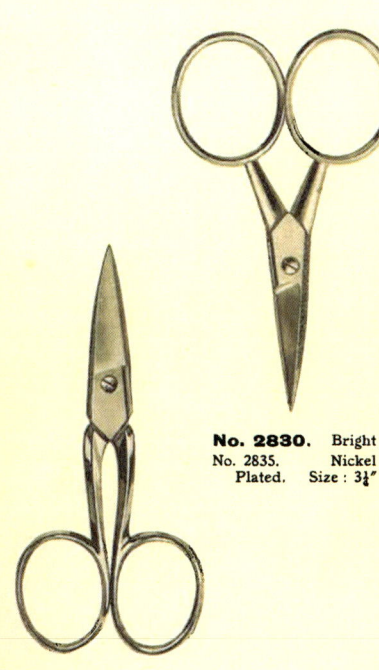

Nos. 2850, 2860 and 2870 are gentlemen's strong nail scissors with large handles

No. 2830. Bright
No. 2835. Nickel Plated. Size: 3¼″

No. 2850. Bright
No. 2855. Nickel Plated. Size: 3¾″

No. 2870. Bright
No. 2875. Nickel Plated. Size: 3¾″

No. 2825. Nickel Plated
No. 2827. Nickel Plated Blades and Gilt Handles
No. 2828. Polished
Size: 3⅜″

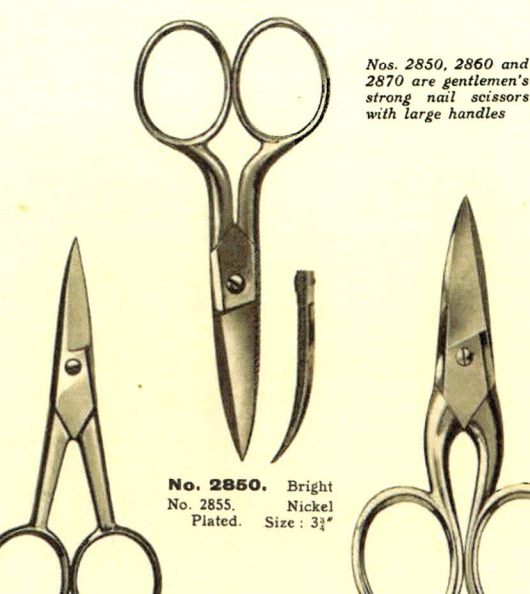

No. 2840. Bright
No. 2845. Nickel Plated. Size: 3½″

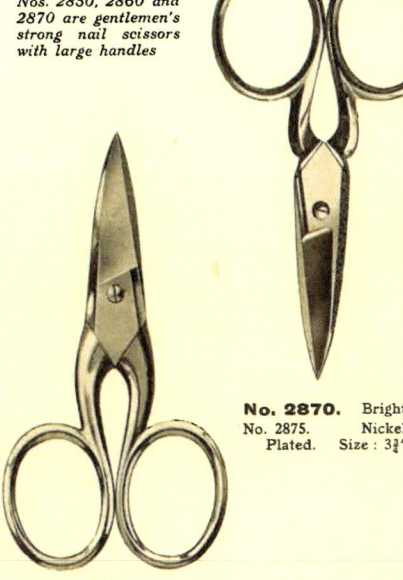

No. 2860. Bright
No. 2865. Nickel Plated. Size: 3½″

Manicure and Cuticle Scissors

WITH EXTRA FINE POINTS
For Manicure Cases see page 24

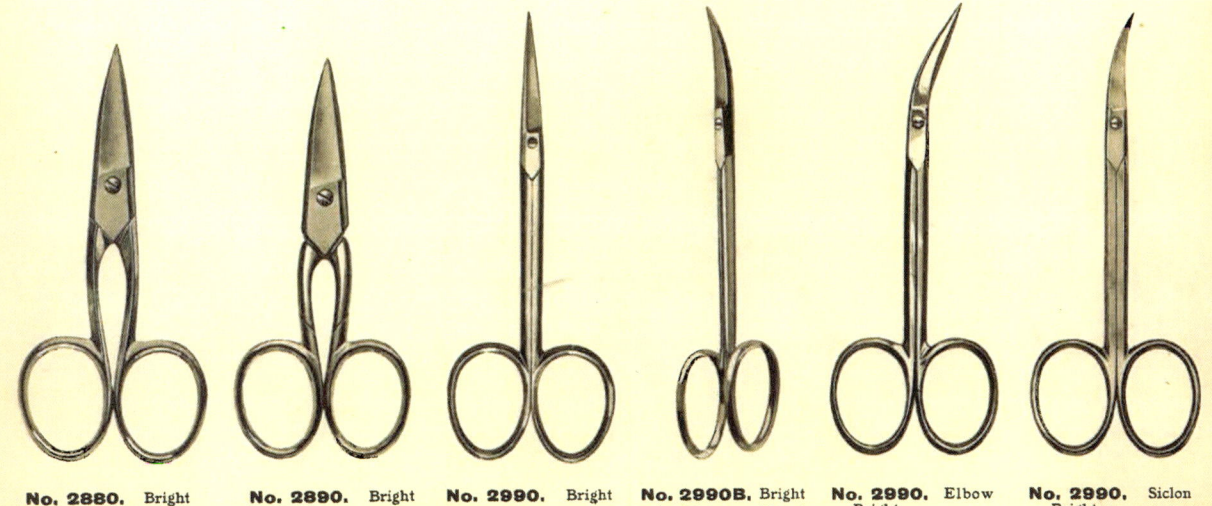

No. 2880. Bright
No. 2885. Nickel Plated
No. 2887. Nickel Plated Blades and Gilt Handles
No. 2888. Polished
Size: 3⅜″

No. 2890. Bright
No. 2895. Nickel Plated
No. 2897. Nickel Plated Blades and Gilt Handles
No. 2898. Polished
Size: 3⅜″

No. 2990. Bright
No. 2995. Nickel Plated
No. 2997. Nickel Plated Blades and Gilt Handles
No. 2998. Polished
No. 2999. Stainless
Sizes: 3″, 3½″ and 4″

No. 2990B. Bright
No. 2995B. Nickel Plated
No. 2997B. Nickel Plated Blades and Gilt Handles
No. 2998B. Polished
No. 2999B. Stainless
Sizes: 3″, 3½″ and 4″

No. 2990. Elbow Bright
No. 2995. Elbow Nickel Plated
No. 2997. Elbow Nickel Plated Blades and Gilt Handles
Sizes: 3½″ and 4″

No. 2990. Siclon Bright
No. 2995. Siclon Nickel Plated
No. 2997. Siclon Nickel Plated Blades and Gilt Handles
Sizes: 3½″ and 4″

SECTION D
PAGE 18

Taylor's Witness

Embroidery Scissors

WITH EXTRA FINE POINTS

"STORK"
EMBROIDERY SCISSORS
Forged Steel throughout
with fine points

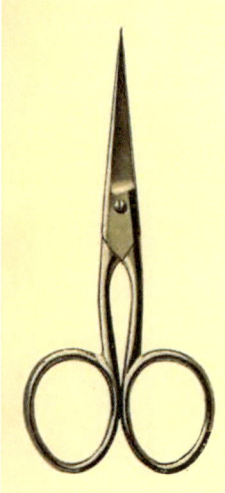

No. 3500. Bright
No. 3505. Nickel Plated
No. 3507. Nickel Plated Blades and Gilt Handles
No. 3508. Polished
Size : 3¾"

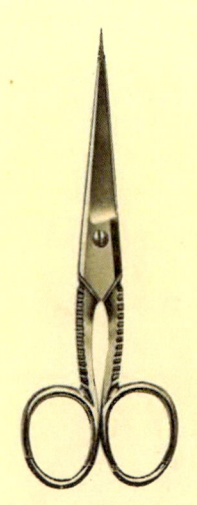

No. 3515. Nickel Plated
No. 3517. Nickel Plated Blades and Gilt Handles
No. 3518. Polished
Size : 3½"

No. 3000. Nickel Plated, with enamelled wings
No. 3005. Nickel Plated
No. 3007. Nickel Plated Blades, Gilt Handles and Bows
Size : 4"

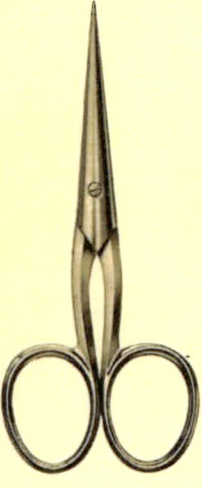

No. 3130. Bright
No. 3135. Nickel Plated
Size : 3½"

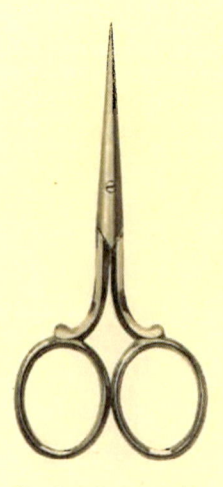

No. 3520. Bright
No. 3525. Nickel Plated
No. 3527. Nickel Plated Blades and Gilt Handles
Size : 3½"

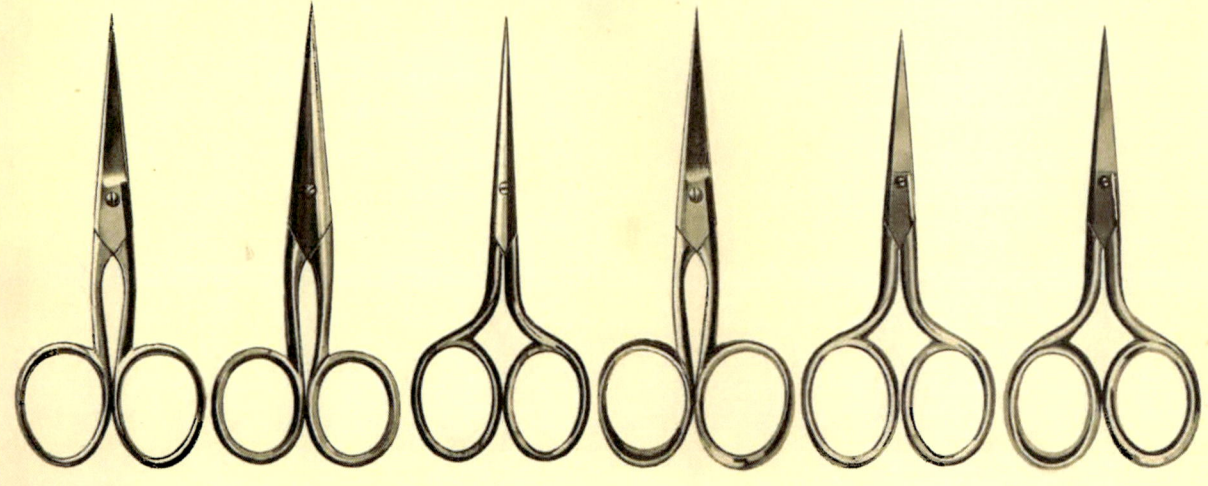

No. 3100. Bright
No. 3105. Nickel Plated
Size : 3½"

No. 3120. Bright
No. 3125. Nickel Plated
Size : 3½"

No. 3340. Bright
No. 3345. Nickel Plated
Size : 3½"

No. 3160. Bright
No. 3165. Nickel Plated
No. 3167. Nickel Plated Blades and Gilt Handles
No. 3168. Polished
Size : 3½"

No. 3170. Bright
No. 3175. Nickel Plated
No. 3177. Nickel Plated Blades and Gilt Handles
Size : 3", 3½" and 3¾"

No. 3180. Bright
No. 3185. Nickel Plated
No. 3187. Nickel Plated Blades and Gilt Handles
Size : 3½"

Taylor's Witness — Embroidery Scissors

WITH EXTRA FINE POINTS

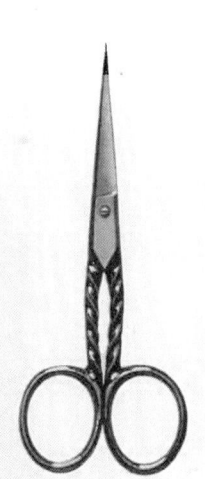

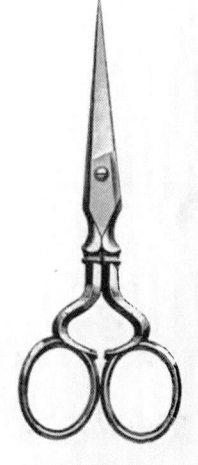

SECTION D
PAGE 19

No. 3535. Nickel Plated
No. 3537. Nickel Plated Blades and Gilt Handles
Size: 3½″

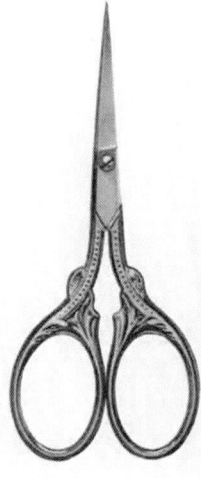

No. 3540. Nickel Plated with enamelled Shanks
No. 3545. Nickel Plated
No. 3547. Nickel Plated Blades and Gilt Handles
No. 3548. Polished
Size: 3½″

No. 3595. Nickel Plated
No. 3597. Nickel Plated Blades and Gilt Handles
No. 3598. Polished
Size: 3½″

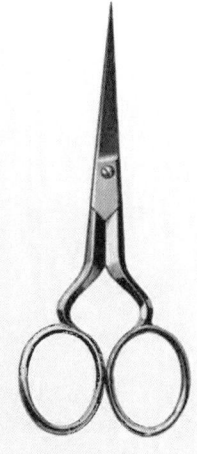

No. 3600. Bright
No. 3605. Nickel Plated
Size: 3½″

No. 3610. Bright
No. 3615. Nickel Plated
No. 3617. Nickel Plated Blades and Gilt Handles
No. 3618. Polished
Size: 3½″

No. 3625. Nickel Plated
No. 3627. Nickel Plated Blades and Gilt Handles
Size: 3½″

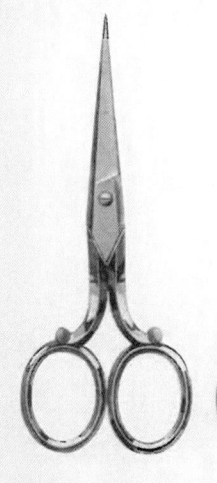

No. 3640. Bright
No. 3645. Nickel Plated
No. 3647. Nickel Plated Blades and Gilt Handles
No. 3648. Polished
Size: 3½″

No. 3655. Nickel Plated
No. 3657. Nickel Plated Blades and Gilt Handles
Size: 3½″

No. 3665. Nickel Plated
No. 3667. Nickel Plated Blades and Gilt Handles
No. 3668. Polished
Size: 3½″

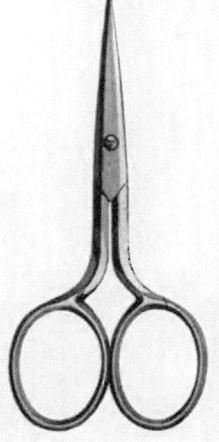

No. 3670. Bright
No. 3675. Nickel Plated
No. 3677. Nickel Plated Blades and Gilt Handles
No. 3678. Polished
Size: 3½″

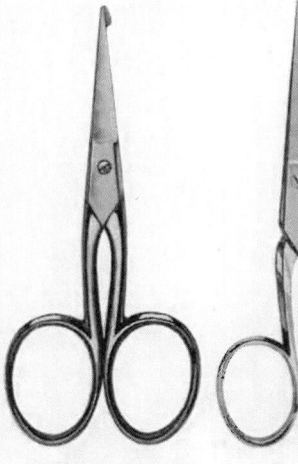

WITH LACE POINT
No. 3710. Bright
No. 3715. Nickel Plated
Size: 3½″

No. 3825. Nickel Plated
No. 3827. Nickel Plated Blades and Gilt Handles
No. 3828. Polished
Size: 3½″

SECTION D
PAGE 20

Taylor's Witness
Embroidery, Anglers and Button-hole Scissors

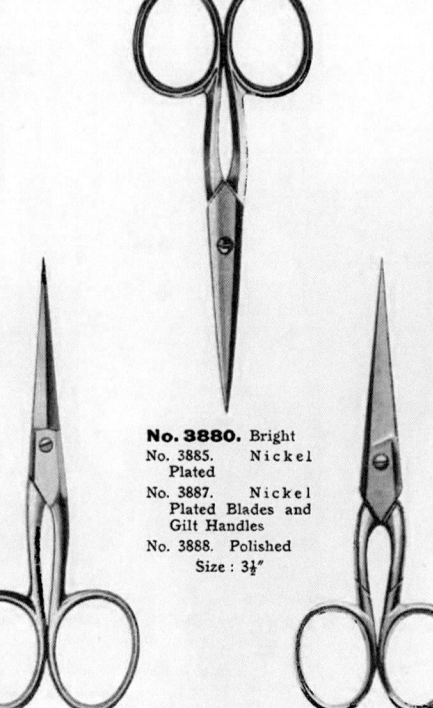

ANGLERS' POCKET SCISSORS

Nos. 3420 and 3430 are made with large thumb holes, expressly for the use of "Fly" fishermen.

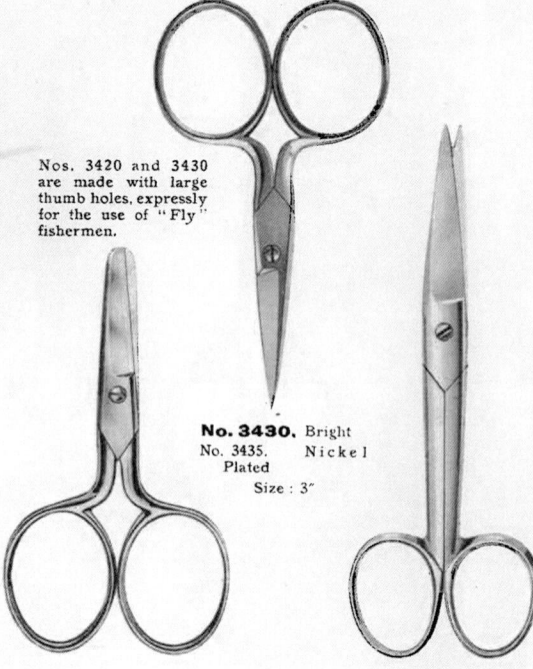

No. 3880. Bright
No. 3885.   Nickel Plated
No. 3887.   Nickel Plated Blades and Gilt Handles
No. 3888.   Polished
Size : 3½"

No. 3430. Bright
No. 3435.   Nickel Plated
Size : 3"

No. 3805. Nickel Plated
No. 3807.   Nickel Plated Blades and Gilt Handles
No. 3808.   Polished
Size : 3¼"

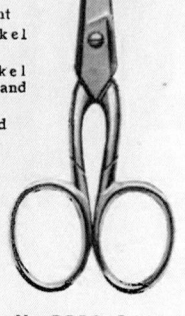

No. 3890. Bright
No. 3895.   Nickel Plated
No. 3897.   Nickel Plated Blades and Gilt Handles
No. 3898.   Polished
Size : 3½"

No. 3420. Bright
No. 3425.   Nickel Plated
Size : 3"

DISGORGER
No. 630. Bright
No. 635.   Nickel Plated
No. 639.   Stainless
Sizes : 4½" and 5"

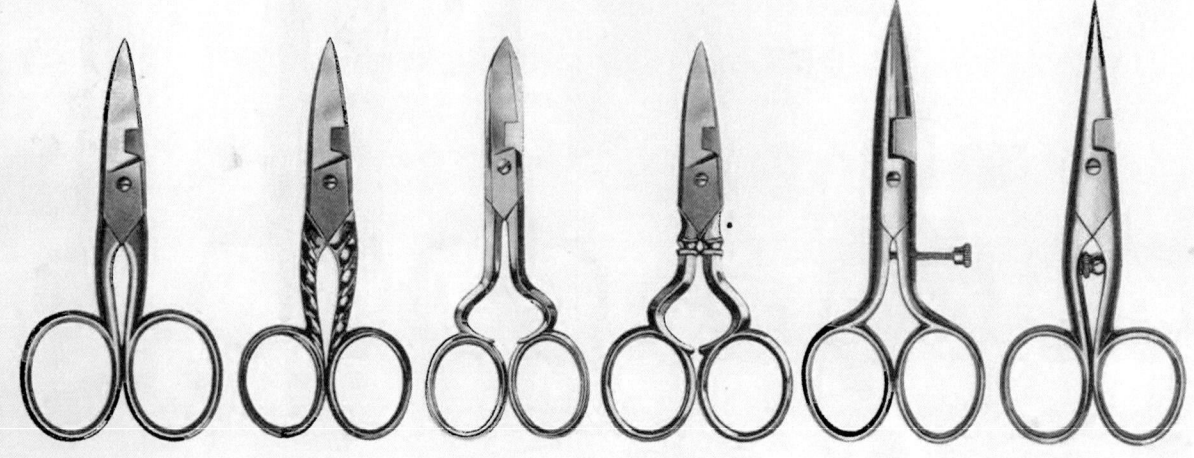

No. 4500. Bright
No. 4505.   Nickel Plated
No. 4507.   Nickel Plated Blades and Gilt Handles
No. 4508.   Polished
No. 4509.   Stainless
Size : 3¾"

No. 4535. Nickel Plated
No. 4537.   Nickel Plated Blades and Gilt Handles
Size : 3½"

No. 4610. Bright
No. 4615   Nickel Plated
No. 4617.   Nickel Plated Blades and Gilt Handles
No. 4618.   Polished
Size : 3½"

No. 4625. Nickel Plated
No. 4627.   Nickel Plated Blades and Gilt Handles
Size : 3½"

No. 4900. Bright
No. 4905.   Nickel Plated
No. 4910.   Bright (without screw)
No. 4915.   Nickel Plated (without screw)
Size : 4"

No. 4920. Bright
No. 4925.   Nickel Plated
No. 4930.   Bright (without screw)
No. 4935.   Nickel Plated (without screw)
Size : 4"

TAYLOR'S WITNESS

Ladies' Scissor Cases

SECTION D
PAGE 21

These cases can be fitted with any pattern scissors from pages 10 and 11. Prices range according to pattern.

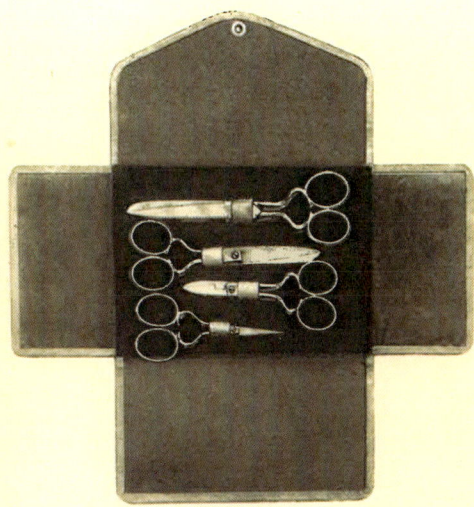

No. 500. 4 pairs
Made in Levant, Imitation Pigskin, Burmese, and Blue or Brown Moire Grain Leathers

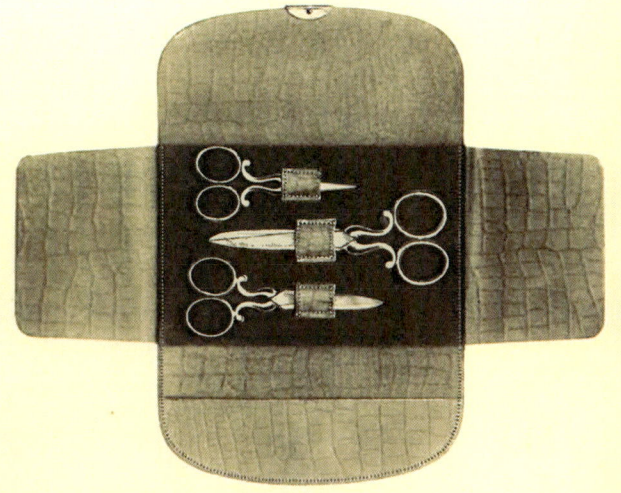

No. 510. 3 pairs
Made in Polished Crocodile, Grey Crocodile, and Imitation Pigskin Leathers

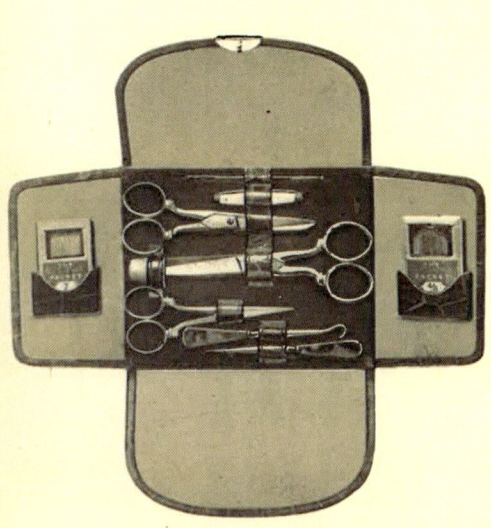

No. 505. Companion
Made in Polished Crocodile Leather

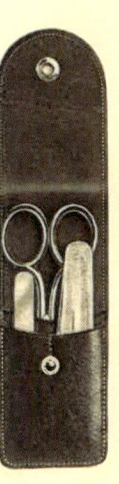

No. 520
Made in Black Morocco Leather

No. 515. 3 pairs
FLAP CASE
Made in Pigskin, Velvet Crocodile, Morocco Grain, and Brown or Blue Russian Leathers

No. 525.
SLIPPER
Made in Calf, Morocco, Hard Grain and Rexine Leathers

SECTION D
PAGE 22

Taylor's Witness — Ladies' Scissor Cases

These cases can be fitted with any pattern scissors from pages 10 and 11. Prices range according to pattern.

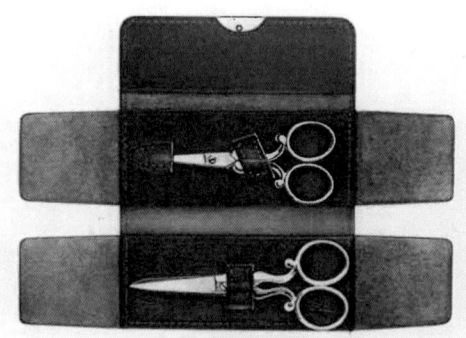

No. 530. 2 pairs
Made in Brown or Blue Russian and Batic Autumn Leathers

No. 535. 2 pairs
Made in Batic Autumn, and Brown or Blue Russian Leathers

No. 545. Made in Burmese, Levant, and Polished Crocodile Leathers

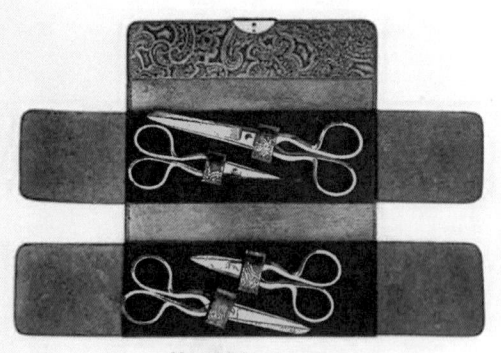

No. 550. 4 pairs
Made in Milanese, Burmese, Levant, Brown Russian and Morocco Grain Leathers

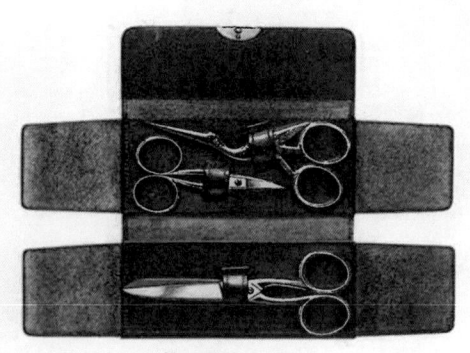

No. 540. 3 pairs
Made in Brown or Blue Russian and Batic Autumn Leathers

No. 555. Made in Polished Crocodile and Burmese Leathers

Taylor's Witness — Ladies' Scissor Cases

SECTION D
PAGE 23

These cases can be fitted with any pattern scissors from pages 10 and 11. Prices range according to pattern.

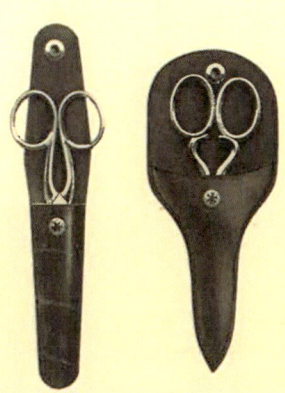

No. 557   No. 568
NAIL SCISSOR PURSES
Made in Velvet Hide and Crocodile Leathers

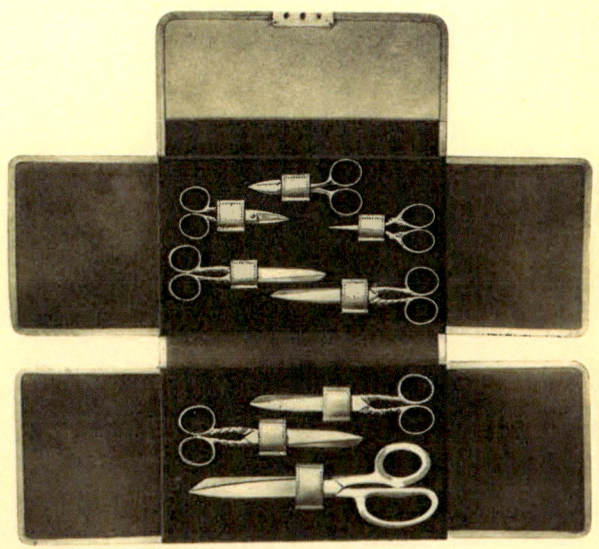

No. 560. 8 pairs
Made in Pigskin, Batic Autumn or Brown Russian Leathers

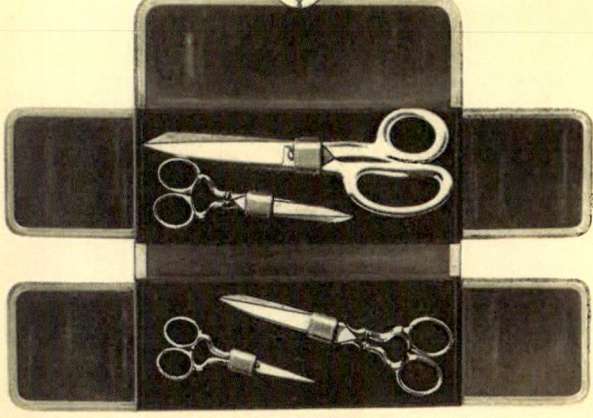

No. 565. 4 pairs
Made in Pigskin, Batic Autumn or Brown Russian Leathers

Sheaths can be supplied for all sizes of single scissors. For prices see separate price list

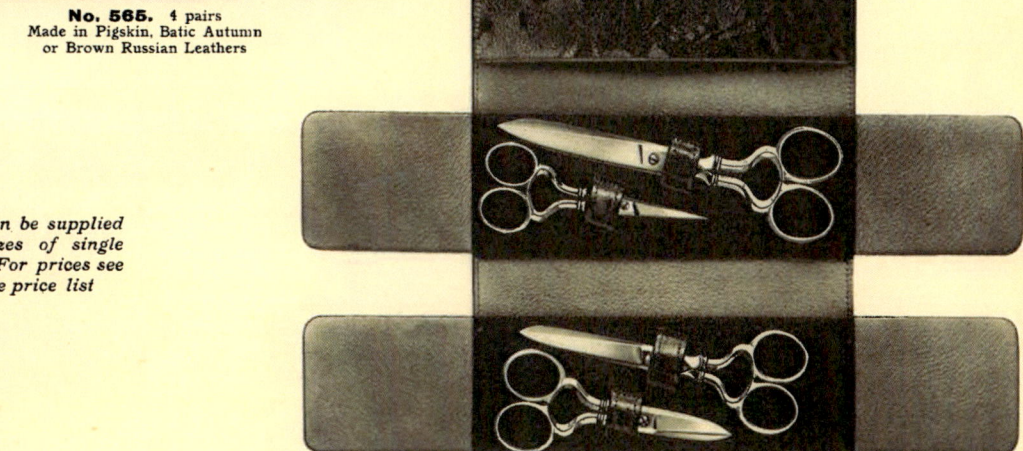

No. 570. 4 pairs
Made in Batic Autumn, Brown Russian or Pigskin Leathers

SECTION D
PAGE 24

Taylor's Witness — Manicure Cases

These cases can be fitted with any pattern scissors from pages 15, 16 and 17. Prices range according to pattern.

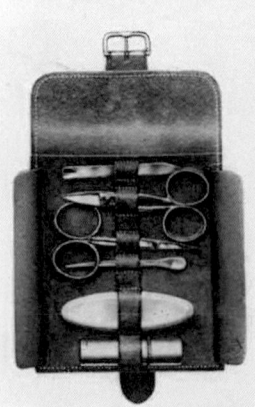

No. 575. Made in Velvet Hide, Russian and Polished Crocodile Leathers

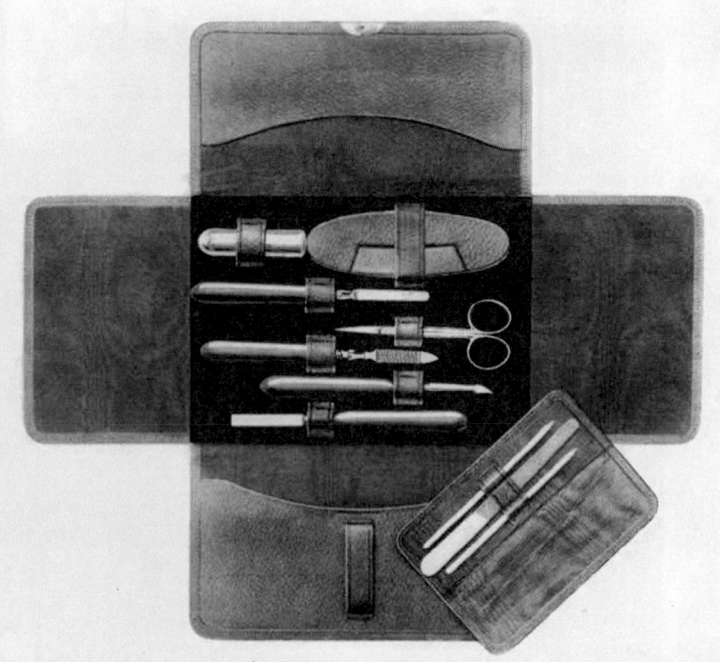

No. 580. Made in Puma, Russian and Polished Crocodile Leathers

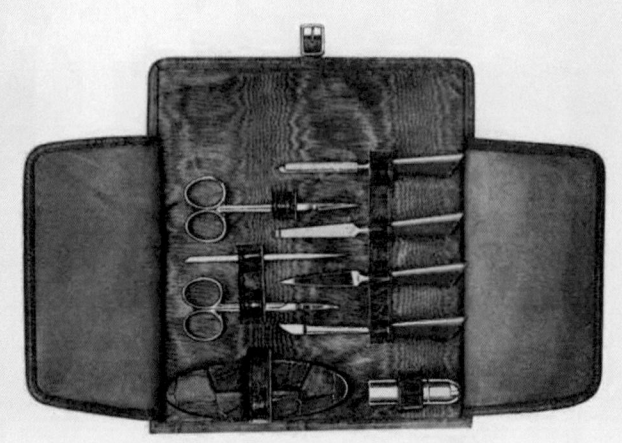

No. 585. Made in Brown or Blue Russian, Velvet Hide and Polished Crocodile Leathers

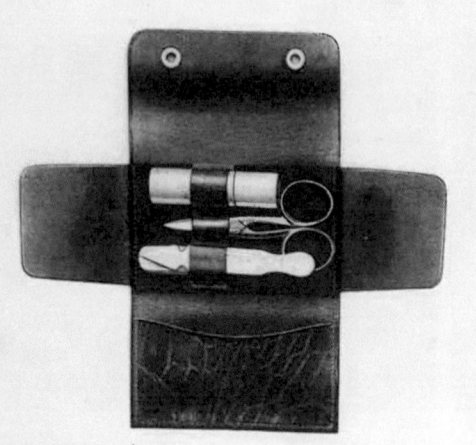

No. 590. Made in Polished Crocodile Leather

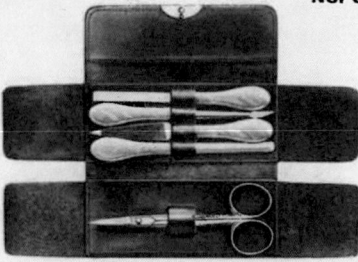

No. 595. Made in Brown or Blue Russian, Polished Crocodile and Batic Autumn Leathers

Taylor's Witness Manicure Cases

**SECTION D
PAGE 25**

No. 576
Made in Crocodile Grain Leather, Ebony or Bone Fittings

No. 577
Made in Crocodile Leather Calf, Ebony or Bone Fittings

No. 578
Made in Long Grain Leatherette, Ebony or Bone Fittings

No. 579
Made in Crocodile Grain Calf, Ebony or Bone Fittings

No. 581
Made in Crocodile Grain Calf, Ebony or Bone Fittings

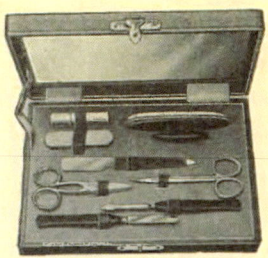

No. 582
Made in Morocco Leatherette, Ebony or Bone Fittings

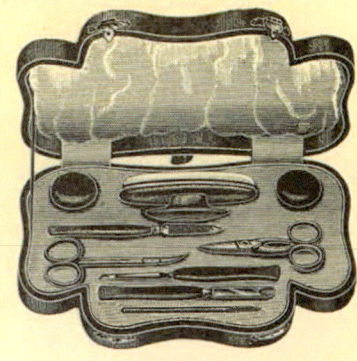

No. 583
Made in Long Grain Leather, Ebony or Bone Fittings

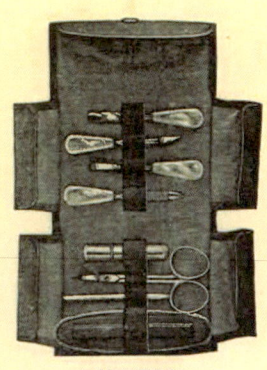

No. 584
Made in Velvet Calf, lined Moiré Silk. Ebony, Ivory, or Pearl Fittings

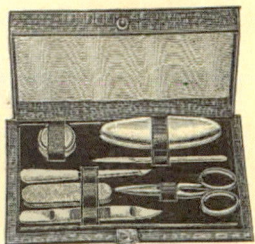

No. 586
Made in Crocodile Grain Leatherette, Ebony or Bone Fittings

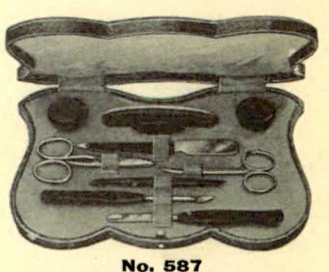

No. 587
Made in Polished Crocodile Leatherette, Ebony or Bone Fittings

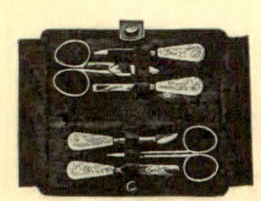

No. 588
Made in Long Grain Leather, Lined Moiré Silk. Ebony, Ivory or Pearl Fittings

No. 589
Made in Polished Crocodile Leatherette, Ebony or Bone Fittings

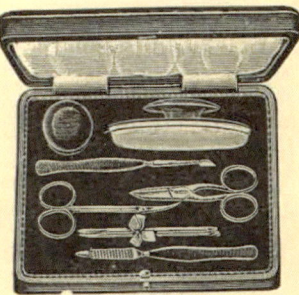

No. 591
Made in Morocco Grain Leather, Ebony or Bone Fittings

No. 592
Made in Morocco Grain Leatherette, Ebony or Bone Fittings

SECTION D
PAGE 26

Taylor's Witness Ladies' Companions

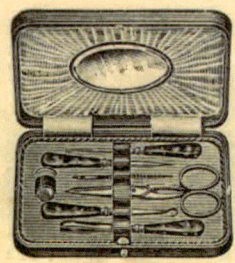

No. 501
Made in Grain Leather, lined
Apricot, Imitation Shell Fittings

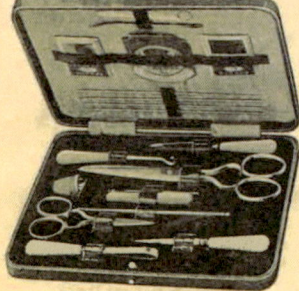

No. 506
Made in Long Grain Leather,
Bone or Pearl Fittings

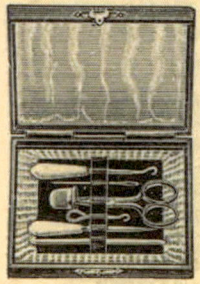

No. 511
Made in Long Grain Leatherette,
Bone or Pearl Fittings

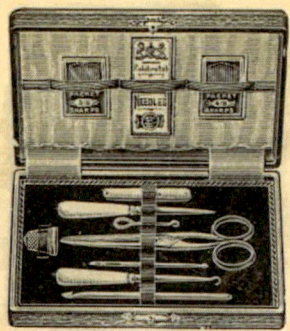

No. 502
Made in Long Grain Leatherette,
Bone or Pearl Fittings

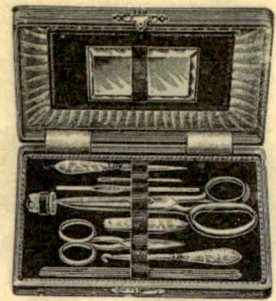

No. 507
Made in Seal Grain Leatherette,
Bone or Pearl Fittings

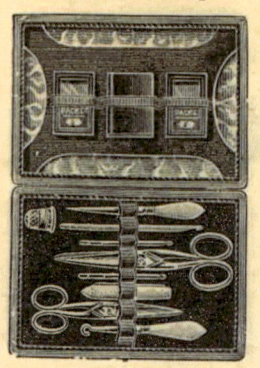

No. 512
Made in Long Grain Leatherette,
Bone or Pearl Fittings

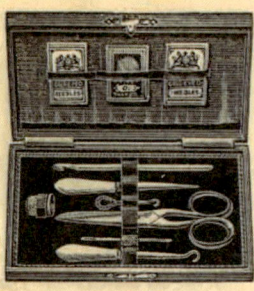

No. 503
Made in Long Grain Leatherette,
Bone or Pearl Fittings

No. 508
Made in Long Grain Leather,
Bone or Pearl Fittings

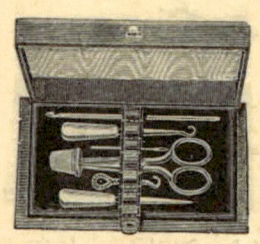

No. 513
Made in Crocodile Leatherette,
Bone or Pearl Fittings

No. 504
Made in Crocodile Grain
Leatherette, Bone or Pearl Fittings

No. 509
Made in Crushed Morocco
Leatherette, Bone or Pearl Fittings

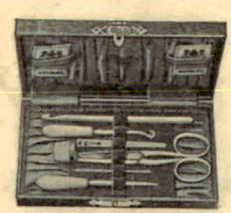

No. 514
Made in Long Grain Leatherette,
Bone or Pearl Fittings

Taylor's WITNESS
SHEFFIELD, ENGLAND.

RAZORS.
FOR EXCELLENCE OF MANUFACTURE.

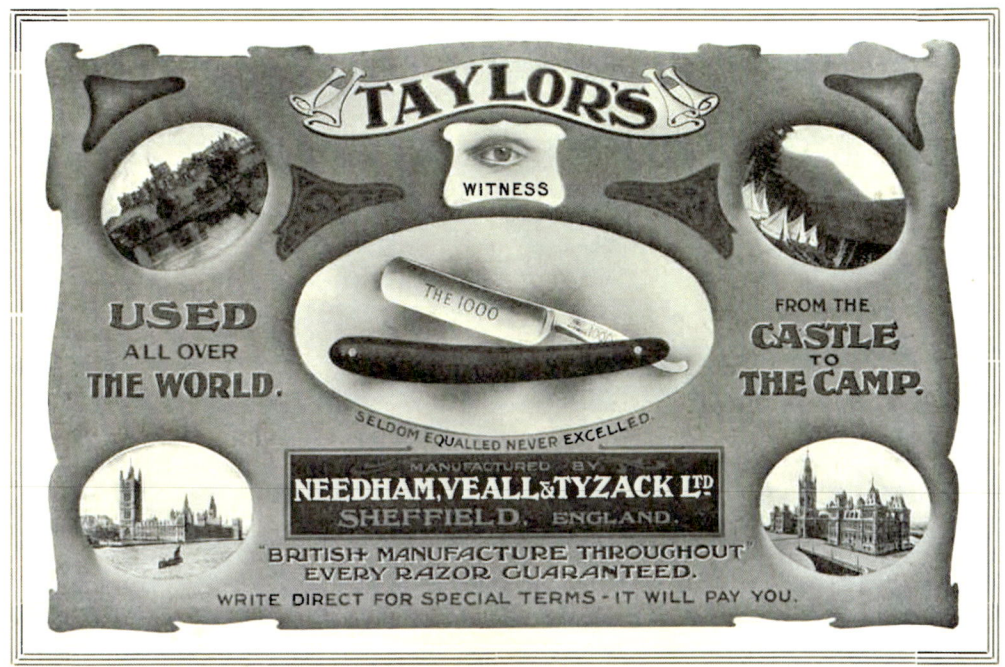

CHRISTCHURCH 1907. GRAHAMSTOWN 1899. MELBOURNE 1888. LONDON 1851. LONDON 1862. PARIS 1855. ANTWERP 1886. ADELAIDE 1887.

TAYLOR'S WITNESS

USED ALL OVER THE WORLD.

FROM THE CASTLE TO THE CAMP.

THE 1000

SELDOM EQUALLED NEVER EXCELLED.

MANUFACTURED BY
NEEDHAM, VEALL & TYZACK LTD
SHEFFIELD, ENGLAND.

"BRITISH MANUFACTURE THROUGHOUT"
EVERY RAZOR GUARANTEED.

WRITE DIRECT FOR SPECIAL TERMS - IT WILL PAY YOU.

HOLLOW-GRINDING.—There has been a renewal of the assertion that this important and highly skilled operation could not be performed in Sheffield or—not so satisfactorily as abroad. Such a statement is utterly wrong on both counts. Hollow-Grinding has been done in our Factories for nearly 50 years past, and of equal merit with the best done elsewhere.

Testimonials:—These continue to flow in from all quarters of the globe. Their testimony to the shaving qualities of the "Eyewitness" Razor, and, particularly the "One Thousand" (1000) is unexceptional and enthusiastic. As to the important point of ECONOMY, the Safety Razor is absolutely put to the blush. 35 years' wear for 5/6 makes the endless costly tale of Safety Razor blades look ill. Quality will tell, and No. 3017 on p. 7 provides any necessary "Safety" qualities.

All "EYEWITNESS" RAZORS are made of the very finest quality of Sheffield Steel, worked up by the most experienced Sheffield workmen and carefully hardened and tempered.

GUARANTEED PERFECT.

EXACT SIZE OF STONE
on which the "Eyewitness" Razors are ground.

SPECIAL ATTENTION IS GIVEN TO THE SETTING TO ENSURE EASY SHAVING.

The HOLLOW-GRINDING, down to an edge one 3000th part of an inch in thickness, is done by scientific Sheffield workmen. Every razor is guaranteed and sent out in perfect condition for immediate use.

TAYLOR'S WITNESS
SHEFFIELD, ENGLAND.

SECTION E
PAGE 2

"1000" Razor.

THE FINEST HOLLOW-GROUND RAZOR MADE.

FAC-SIMILE OF REGISTERED BOX.

Each Razor supplied wrapped in Tinfoil, in a Specially Designed and Decorated Tin Box.

SQUARE POINT.
$\frac{1}{2}$-IN. WIDE.
No. X 1000 $\frac{1}{2}$-in. Sq. Pt.

Made in $\frac{1}{2}''$, $\frac{5}{8}''$, $\frac{3}{4}''$, $\frac{7}{8}''$
EITHER ROUND OR SQUARE POINT.

Supplied also in Handsome Oak & Leather Cases containing 2, 3, 4 or 7 Razors.

The Best Strop for the "1000" Razor is the "1000" Strop.

To assure the Razor a fair chance of preserving its excessively fine and delicate shaving edge this Strop is recommended.

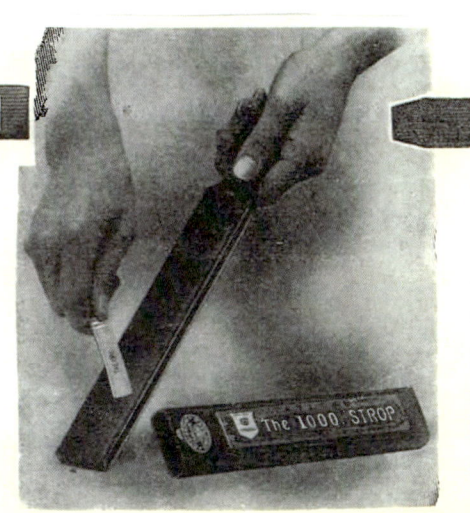

The "1000" Strop is made from selected material, specially adapted to provide the exact amount of friction needed without abrading the fine shaving edge and thus keeps it of the required silky smoothness.

SECTION E
PAGE 3

Taylor's WITNESS
SHEFFIELD, ENGLAND.

Razor Strops.

ON STROPS AND STROPPING.

HINTS ON STROPPING.

EVERY RAZOR is sent out PERFECT, and READY FOR IMMEDIATE USE.

The EDGE of a fine Razor being but $\frac{1}{3000}$ of an inch in thickness can so easily be ruined. The thumb should never be drawn across it.

Too heavy pressure must be avoided when stropping.

The strop must be a good

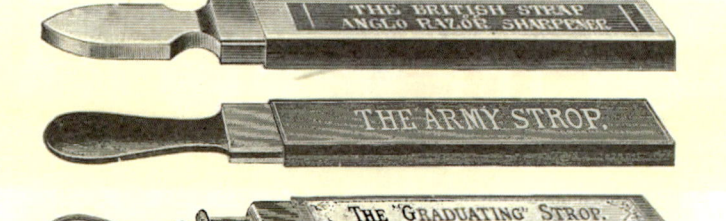

back down, at the end of the stroke without it touching the strop. Only a few strokes are necessary.

ALWAYS STROP AFTER USING THE RAZOR.

Taylor's "Eyewitness" Razor Paste will give the needful bite to the strop.

No. 1. Flat. — THE BRITISH STRAP ANGLO RAZOR SHARPENER

No. 2. Flat. — THE ARMY STROP.

No. 10. — The "Graduating" Strop.

No. 13. Cushion. — The "Flexible" Strop

No. 14. Cushion. — The Seal Skin Strop (for Hollow Ground Razors) REAL SEALSKIN

No. 16.

No. 52. Cushion.

No. 55.

No. 63. Cushion. — THE BELT STROP

No. 66. — The "Chieftain" Strop.

BELT STROPS.

BELT STROPS of the latest patterns at the best prices of the day.

SHAVING BRUSHES with Wood, Bone or Metal Handles in large assortment, and at prices to meet all requirements.

Taylor's Witness
Sheffield, England.

SECTION E
PAGE 4

Cases of H.G. Razors.

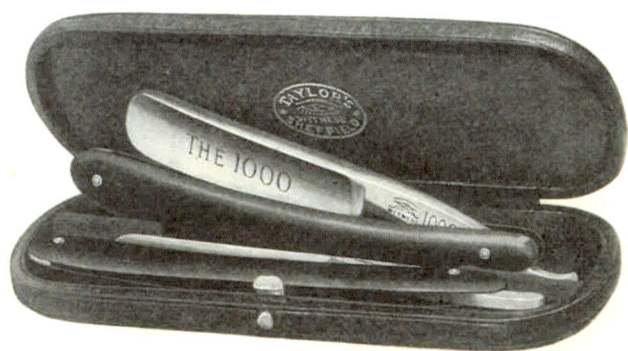

Morocco Case with One Pair of Razors.

The Cases illustrated give only a general idea how these are fitted.

A large and very varied assortment of Razors in Bag and Purse Etuis in modern and stylish patterns is at the disposal of our customers.

We shall be glad to submit a selection of these, on approval, in Leather and Wood. Customers may in this way insure the supply of new and up-to-date articles.

A FEW TESTIMONIALS.

"I am the possessor of three of the best Razors it is anybody's lot to have, No. '1000.'"
THORNBURY.

"Thirty-five years ago I bought a Taylor's 'Eyewitness' Razor for 5/6. I estimate I have used it 6000 times."
LANE COVE, N.S.W.

1922.
"I purchased one '1000' Razor in Cape Town in December, 1900, and have used this continuously ever since; never had it set."
O.F.S.

1922.
"I have one of your (2000) Razors purchased 1905, only stropped, never on a stone, and is in perfect condition still."
SOUTHSEA.

1921.
"21 years ago I purchased one of your Razors in Pietermaritzburg. This I have had in constant use ever since."

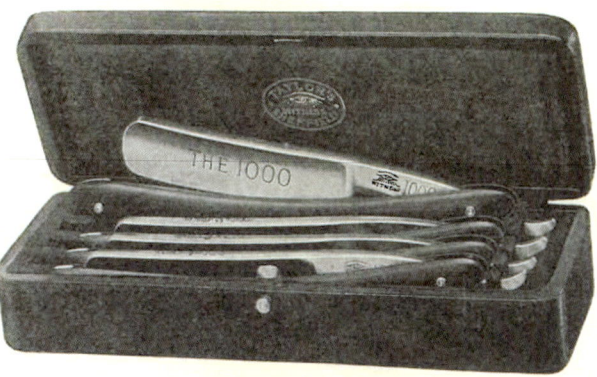

Morocco Case with Two Pairs of Razors Numbered 1—4

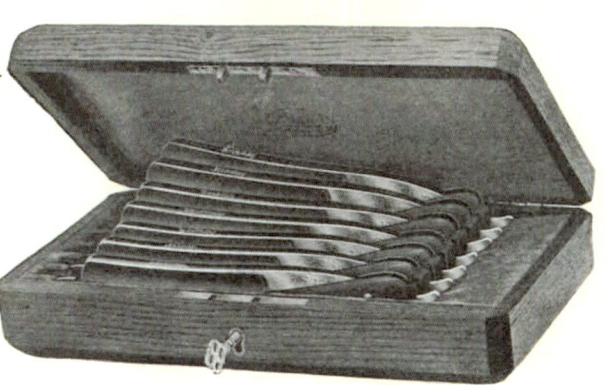

Oak Case with Seven Razors Lettered Days of Week.

It is an obvious advantage to possess more than a single Razor for shaving.

That all Razors occasionally need a "Rest" has been observed by all shavers.

The heavier the beard the more numerous should be the Razors to lengthen the "Rest."

Trouble and attention bestowed on Shaving Tackle is always repaid, hygienically and in added comfort and efficiency.

The right Strop (the "1000"), the right Soap, the right Water and a steady hand.

"London.
"The '1000' is the best Razor I have had in 40 years' experience."

"North Perth.
"About 15 years ago I bought one of your 'Eyewitness' Razors, two years later the handle broke, and six months the blade rested in my tool box occasionally cutting wood. Subsequently I put the blade into a handle and sharpened it. The result was satisfactory. It is the best Razor I have. The brand is the best I have used in over 30 years."

"Stamford Hill.
"A Case of Razors manufactured by your good selves in daily use for past 25 years. The material and workmanship must surpass anything in the Razor trade."

"Egyptian Exp. Force.
"I wish to thank you for your splendid Razor, 1000 'Eyewitness.' It is the finest I have come across for years. A man can appreciate a good razor out here. I strongly advise every lover of a clean shave to get the 1000 'Eyewitness.'"

SECTION E
PAGE 5

Taylor's Hollow Ground Razors.

WITNESS
SHEFFIELD, ENGLAND.

3001	3002	3003	3004	3005	3006
	5/8"	5/8"	1/2"	5/8"	1/2" 5/8"

The LETTERS prefixed to the numbers to denote the kind of Handle required are:—
A—Black; **F**—Ivory; **X**—Xylonite.

Taylor's Witness Hollow Ground Razors.

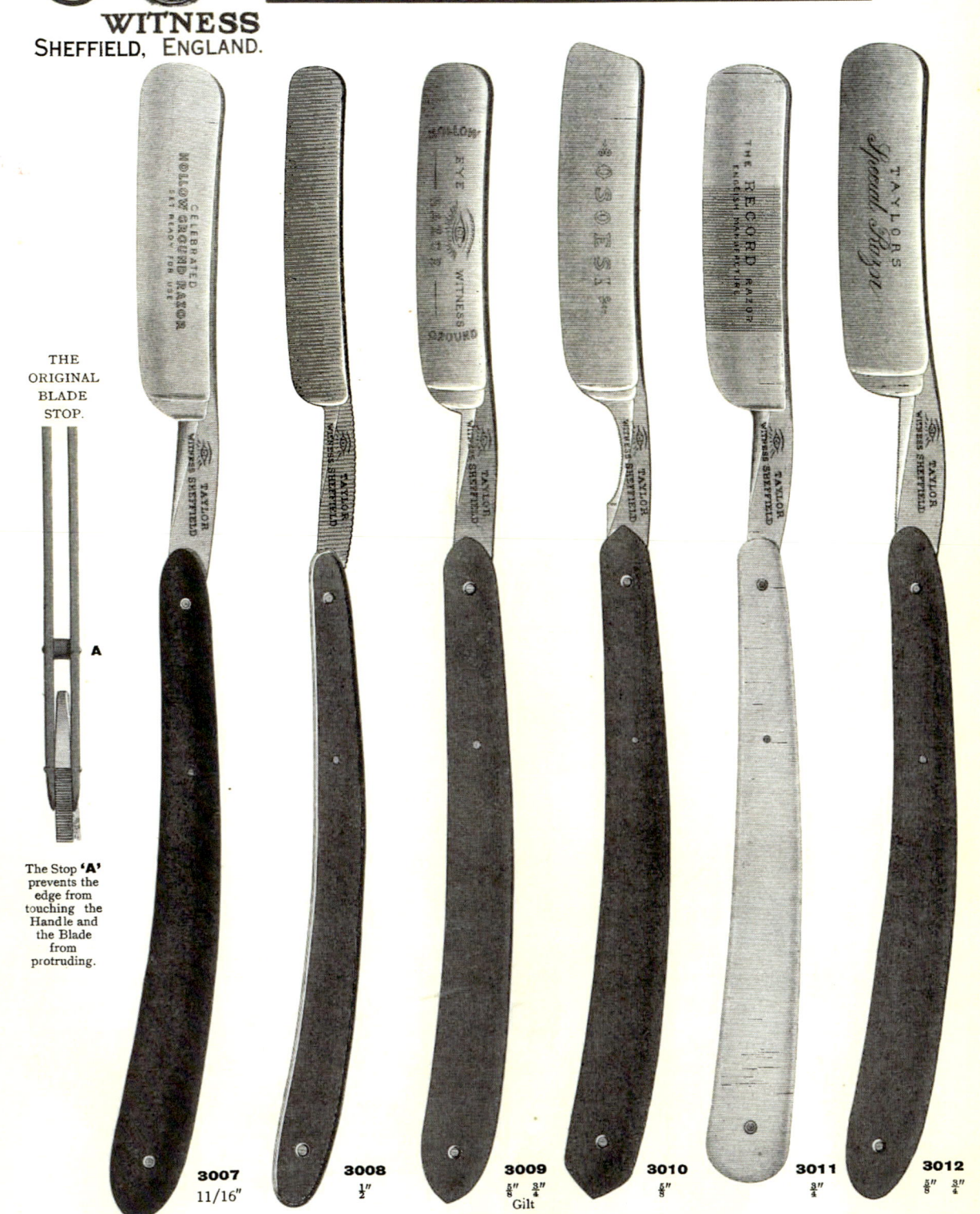

SHEFFIELD, ENGLAND.

SECTION E
PAGE 6

THE ORIGINAL BLADE STOP.

A

The Stop **'A'** prevents the edge from touching the Handle and the Blade from protruding.

3007	3008	3009	3010	3011	3012
11/16"	1/2"	5/8" 3/4" Gilt	5/8"	3/4"	5/8" 3/4"

All these Patterns have the Registered Blade Stop in the Handle which we first introduced.

The LETTERS prefixed to the numbers to denote the kind of Handle required are:—
A—Black; **F**—Ivory; **X**—Xylonite.

SECTION E
PAGE 7

Taylor's Witness Hollow Ground Razors.
SHEFFIELD, ENGLAND.

3013	3014	3015	3016	3017	3018
1/2" 5/8" 3/4" 7/8"	3/4"	1/2" 5/8" 3/4" 7/8"	1/2" 5/8" 3/4"	3/4" Safety Guard Razor. Guard Slides off for Cleaning.	1/2" 5/8" 3/4"

All these Patterns have the Registered Blade Stop in the Handle which we first introduced.
The LETTERS prefixed to the numbers to denote the kind of Handle required are:—
A—Black; **F**—Ivory; **X**—Xylonite.

Taylor's Witness Hollow Ground Razors.
Sheffield, England.

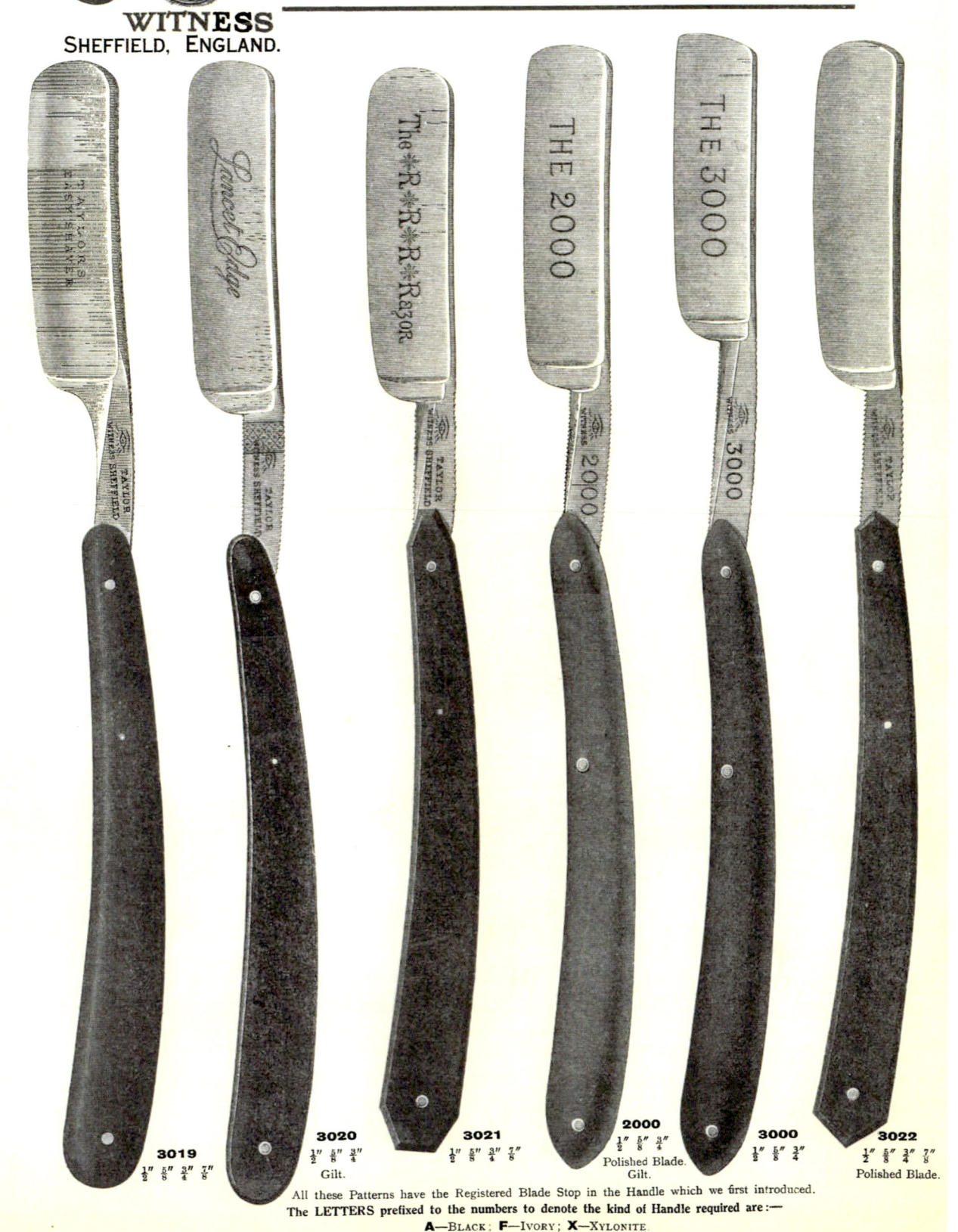

SECTION E — PAGE 8

3019	3020	3021	2000	3000	3022
1/2" 5/8" 3/4" 7/8"		1/2" 5/8" 3/4" 7/8"	1/2" 5/8" 3/4"	1/2" 5/8" 3/4"	1/2" 5/8" 3/4" 7/8"
	Gilt.		Polished Blade. Gilt.		Polished Blade.

All these Patterns have the Registered Blade Stop in the Handle which we first introduced.
The LETTERS prefixed to the numbers to denote the kind of Handle required are:—
A—Black; **F**—Ivory; **X**—Xylonite.

SECTION E
PAGE 9

Taylor's Witness
Sheffield, England.

Corn Knives and Razors.

The Illustrations are the Exact Size of articles shown.

No. M947

No. 948W

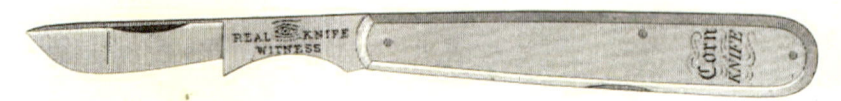

No. F952

No. F953

No. 3023

No. 3024

The LETTERS prefixed to the numbers to denote the kind of Handle required are:—

A—Black Horn or Vulcanite. **B**—White Bone. **F**—Ivory. **M**—Nickel. **W**—White Xylonite.